INTERNET BOOK PIRACY

THE FIGHT TO PROTECT AUTHORS, PUBLISHERS, AND OUR CULTURE

GINI GRAHAM SCOTT, PhD

ALLWORTH PRESS
NEW YORK

Allworth Press books may be purchased in bulk at special discounts for sales promotion, corporate gifts, fund-raising, or educational purposes. Special editions can also be created to specifications. For details, contact the Special Sales Department, Allworth Press, 307 West 36th Street, 11th Floor, New York, NY 10018 or info@skyhorsepublishing.com.

19 18 17 16 15   5 4 3 2 1

Published by Allworth Press, an imprint of Skyhorse Publishing, Inc.
307 West 36th Street, 11th Floor, New York, NY 10018.

Allworth Press® is a registered trademark of Skyhorse Publishing, Inc.®, a Delaware corporation.

www.allworth.com

Cover and interior design by Mary Belibasakis

Library of Congress Cataloging-in-Publication Data is available on file.

Print ISBN: 978-1-62153-485-3

Ebook ISBN: 978-1-62153-495-2

Printed in the United States of America.

About the Author

GINI GRAHAM SCOTT HAS PUBLISHED over fifty books with mainstream publishers, focusing on social trends, work and business relationships, and personal and professional development. Some of these books include *The New Middle Ages, Lies and Liars: How and Why Sociopaths Lie and How You Can Detect and Deal with Them, The Very Next New Thing, The Talk Show Revolution*, and *The Privacy Revolution.*

She has gained extensive media interest for previous books, including appearances on *Good Morning America, Oprah, Montel Williams, CNN*, and hundreds of radio interviews. She has frequently been quoted by the media and has set up websites to promote her most recent books, featured at www.ginigrahamscott.com and www.changemakerspublishingandwriting.com. As of this writing, she has about sixty thousand listings in Google Search Results.

She has become a regular Huffington Post blogger since December 2012 (www.huffingtonpost.com/gini-graham-scott) and has a Facebook page featuring her books and films at www.facebook.com/changemakerspublishing.

She has written, produced, and sometimes directed over sixty short videos, which are featured on her Changemakers Productions website at www.changemakersproductions.com and on YouTube at www.youtube.com/changemakersprod.

Her screenplays, mostly in the drama, crime, legal thriller, and sci-fi genres, include several that consider the social implications of science and technological breakthroughs and changes in society, including *The New Child, New Identity, Dead No More, Tax Revolt*, and *The Suicide Party.* Her first feature film, *Suicide Party Save Dave*, was released in 2015. A film by the same director, *Driver*, will be released in 2016.

She has a PhD in sociology from UC Berkeley and MAs in anthropology, pop culture and lifestyles, and organizational/consumer/audience behavior, and recreation and tourism from Cal State, East Bay. She is getting an MA in communications there in June 2017.

Table of Contents

Introduction

INTERNET BOOK PIRACY PROVIDES AN overview of the problem of piracy, which is threatening not only the livelihood of professional writers and the survival of many publishers, but also our culture, since many writers and publishers will stop writing and publishing because they can no longer afford to do so. Piracy has always been with us since the beginnings of writing, as one writer copied the writings of another. Just think of the monks copying manuscripts in the Middle Ages. Later, the development of the printing press made sharing the written word even easier. And in the last decade, the creation of ebooks has perpetrated copying and sharing material, as they can easily be duplicated and shared even when there are digital management locks since these can be broken, and printed books can be readily scanned. Thus piracy has become more rampant than ever, so that many millions of books have been stolen and made available as ebooks or PDFs for free or with payment to the pirates. The cost to individual writers and the book industry has been in the billions of dollars.

This book features twenty-three chapters, which describe:

- The extent and cost of the problem both in the US and globally

- The battles of the music and film industry against piracy

- The slow response of writers and publishers to the problem

- How some publishers have taken the pirates to court and won

- How to find out who the pirates are

- The new tools and weapons in the arsenal to fight pirates

- How the copyright law protects against infringement

- The procedures and penalties provided by copyright law

- What law enforcement is doing to stop the pirates

- How to get pirates to remove your book from their websites

- Ways to protect your material from infringement

- Strategies to use the pirates to monetize your material

- And more

A final section lists resources and major pirate sites, so writers can check if their own books have been illegally posted and report violations to writers, publishers, law enforcement, and the pirate monitoring and takedown services. It also includes various writer organizers, government agencies, and Internet sources to turn to for help.

It begins with a brief introduction to why I was inspired to write this book, followed by a section of interviews, also contained in the documentary series *The Battle Against Internet Piracy*, which is planned for release to the educational, library, and cable markets in 2016. These include the following:

- representative voices sharing the opinions of writers, self-publishers, and publishers who have been victimized by pirates;

- researchers and students involved in obtaining pirated materials although they don't call themselves pirates;

- a free-speech advocate discussing the competing claims of free speech and copyright protection;

- an intellectual property lawyer discussing the problems of protecting Internet piracy and finding alternate ways to use piracy to your own advantage;

- and a technology developer offering a platform to help writers and publishers offer their writing and make a profit.

These interviews represent a sampling of the range of experiences and opinions in today's struggle against the problem of piracy.

Discovering the Problem of Internet Book Piracy

I never thought much about the problem of Internet book piracy until it happened to me about two years ago in the winter of 2013. At the time, I was struggling with the many other problems confronting professional writers, making it harder than ever to make a living, turning more and more writers into a dying breed. One problem is that professional writers are being buried by millions of writers writing books and articles for free, so the value of their own writing goes down. Another problem is that the traditional publishers look to celebrities and well-known authorities with platforms, giving them the six-figure and million-dollar book deals, while the offers to other writers have dried up or provided much smaller advances or nothing upfront, since the publishers themselves are under seige with reduced sales and income. Some publishers have even turned to requiring authors to commit to buying a few thousand books. This high cost far outweighs any advance, if in fact there is one offered. And automated software is now writing simple books and articles, where readers can't tell the difference. In some research, readers even thought the machine-written content was created by the real writers, and the writing by real writers was created by the machines.

Now book pirates who upload pirated materials or run the piracy sites are earning millions from their work. Though a number of these sites have been shut down over the years by takedown notices and occasional lawsuits, some of the pirates are quick to put up another site under another name, while other pirates simply pick up the slack with new sites. Making the problem even more difficult is that many of these sites are in other countries, so an individual has little hope of enforcing any action. The efforts of law enforcement and lawyers can only go so far because of the high costs, delays, and the number of personnel required to enforce any criminal or civil action. So getting rid of the pirates has become something of a whack-a-mole operation, whereby one pirate goes down only for another to pop up.

Compounding the problem is that piracy has become so rampant. Around 50–70 percent of all ebooks are pirated, and around

40–70 percent of the population in various age groups and countries have engaged in obtaining pirated material—often knowingly, since piracy has become so widespread that it has gained a kind of popular acceptance. Sometimes individuals obtaining pirated material don't even realize it's pirated—they just think they have gotten a good deal because they got the book at a much lower price or are delighted to find it available for free.

Many pirates find ways to justify their actions by claiming that piracy really benefits writers, because they are becoming more well-known since they are reaching so many more readers, rather than languishing in obscurity. Or apologists argue that their actions are really affecting sales, because people pirating the books would normally not buy the book anyway, because they can't afford it or think it costs too much. Then, too, many students justify their actions on the grounds that they are forced to buy hugely overpriced books, sometimes because their professors have written them and they have to buy as a captive audience, so it is only fair for a group of students to join together by splitting the cost of one book that they share with one another.

Still other individuals claim that they are simply sharing books as part of a community, much like one might pass around a hard copy of a book or borrow a book from a library. These people fail to recognize how the Internet has created large "communities" of people who don't know each other, resulting in many thousands of people gaining access to a book for free. Plus, some argue that writers and publishers should simply adapt to the new technological modalities that have made ebooks the new model for publishing, and figure out new ways to make money from intellectual content—though these new ways are still uncertain—while piracy continues to grow.

Meanwhile, these all represent lost sales and income for the writers and publishers, who are struggling to survive and have taken the time and effort to write or publish the book in the first place. Plus, publishers have staff and office expenses to pay in order to produce the book. But as the income is lost to pirates, writers and publishers may find it unsustainable to keep writing or publishing books, resulting in the loss of these ideas and information, with many writers and publishers turning to other endeavors.

Becoming Aware of the Piracy Problem

I became aware of the piracy problem in early 2013, when I was doing a routine search to see where my name was showing up, since I was up to about 104,000 results on Google. Lo and behold, on the fourth page was the link announcing after my name: "download free. Electronic library. Finding books. 15+ items." When I went to the link, I discovered eighteen of my books. With one exception that indicated "link deleted by legal owner," all of them could be downloaded as PDFs. The website owner didn't even remove them after I wrote to their support email, stating in the strongest terms:

You do not have my permission or my publisher's permission to upload any of my books and offer them for free. Please be advised that I am making a copy of your pages, and this is to request that you immediately remove any of my books from your site. You are interfering with my ability to make a living as a writer, as well as with the other writers whose books you have copied on your site and are offering for free. I am also bringing this to the attention of members of ASJA (the American Society of Journalists and Authors) and other writers groups, as well as my attorney who will be in touch with you regarding the penalties for copyright infringement and other applicable offenses.

Even though I got an email back a few hours later saying "removed," in fact the titles weren't, since a friend sent me a PDF he downloaded from the site several hours after I got that message.

After that experience, I soon discovered the pervasiveness of this piracy problem, which is seriously undermining the sales of books and the ability of many writers to make a living. For example, a few major sites brag about the millions of books they have for download, often scanned and uploaded at no charge by a community of so-called bibliophiles who think information on the Internet should be free. And there are hundreds of these sites and millions of people downloading free books.

But at the time—and this is still the case—writers and publishers had done little to combat the problem, apart from sending out the occasional takedown notice and a 2012 lawsuit filed by John Wiley against about twenty thousand individuals who pirated some of its *Dummies* series books. However, as I learned back then, there are numerous ways to actively combat piracy, including filing lawsuits to go after the site owners, uploaders, and downloaders, and reporting the violations to government agencies that can go after the biggest pirates with criminal penalties. And now there are even more strategies, including using an anti-piracy service to send out notices of infringement and collect a small amount of funds for each infringement, like getting a parking ticket, in return for not taking the pirate to court. These services can also contact the web hosting service to take down their website, or notify advertisers to not advertise on known piracy sites.

Such efforts to fight back against the pirates are very much needed, because the damage to the industry and writers is enormous. For example, Attributor, a firm that specializes in monitoring online content, has claimed that book piracy costs the industry nearly $3 billion in sales, or over 10 percent of total revenue. In a 2010 study they counted 3.2 million in downloaded books, according to C. Max Magee in an article entitled "Confessions of a Book Pirate" (http://www.themillions.com/2010/01/confessions-of-a-book-pirate.html). And as of 2014, the costs are even greater, as will be described in this book.

Even a big raid in January 2012 on the popular cyberlocker Megaupload.com and its CEO Kim Dotcom—headed by US and Hong Kong authorities—didn't make much difference, since other pirates quickly pulled in their own Internet boats to take up the slack. As described in a March 2012 Attributor report, "The World After Megaupload," during the raid, the authorities seized and shut down nineteen related domains and reportedly froze $330 million in assets. Soon after, two other sites—FileSonic.com and Fileserve.com—stopped allowing the public to share hosted files. Together, these three sites were responsible for about 33 percent of all the pirated books available for free downloading.

But soon after that raid, two other sites grew in popularity—Putlocker and RapidShare—and in the first month after Megaupload went down, the number of available pirated books was up 13 percent. In its report, Attributor also identified the top twenty piracy spots, which included share-online.biz and ul.to, with 28 percent of the supply between them. There is even a website that lists the twenty best websites for downloading free ebooks (http://www.hongkiat.com/blog/20-best-websites-to-download-free-e-books), which might help the anti-piracy crusaders know where to look. While some of these free ebooks might actually be legal, a great many are pirated.

As of 2014 Megaupload founder Kim Dotcom was still at it. Not only had he managed to evade jail by fighting attempts by US prosecutors to extradite him on racketeering charges over his Megaupload site, but he has earned another 40 million New Zealand dollars (about $20 million US) after authorities froze over 40 million Zealand dollars at the time of his arrest. After that he started two new ventures, including file-sharing site Mega and music venture Baboom (http://metro. co.uk/2014/12/01/megauploads-kim-dotcom-avoids-jail-in-trial-for-internet-piracy-4968888). And the news about the Sony hack of data, films, and personal information of Sony personnel puts an even more frightening face on the menace of piracy to all intellectual property, not only books.

As I wrote back in 2013, the extent of the growing problem is evident in the very numbers reported on the piracy sites and, as will be discussed, now the problem is even worse. For example, bookos.org, which pirated eighteen of my books, proudly announced on its home page that it has 2,028,532 books available for download, and tuebl.com proclaims that it has thirty-five thousand books from nine thousand authors and 7.68 million downloads. The problem is further exacerbated because some of the pirates go to enormous lengths to try to skirt the law.

For example, according to the article "Book Piracy and Me" by Charles Sheehan-Miles, which is no longer online, TUEBL (The Ultimate Ebook Library) once operated out of Canada, using an IP-hiding service called CloudFare to hide its IP address and claims that it is operated as an Idaho-based ministry of the Kopimist Church, which is recognized by the Swedish government. It was and still may be led by Travis McCrea, who claims that "giving away other people's intellectual property is his religious vocation," and his website once claimed this to be a missionary project of the Kopimist Church of Idaho, and as such was a registered 501(c)3 organization, so any fees paid are considered a donation. Sheehan-Miles concluded his post: "So McCrea, TUEBL, and his Kopimist Church are raking in cash from advertising and tax-deductible donations in support of his activity of stealing from me and other authors."

Since then, he filed a complaint on March 29, 2013, with the IRS that TUEBL shouldn't have tax-exempt status if it is engaged in illegal activities or ones that violate important public policy.

But now it seems TUEBL has transformed itself yet again. It calls itself "the Ultimate Ebook Library," and describes itself as a site where authors can make money by giving digital versions of their books to readers, while readers can explore all sorts of books they may not have considered reading. Their idea is that "when a person loves an author, they become that author's biggest consumer. They see the author in person, they buy the physical copies of the book (frequently multiple, to give to friends and in different editions), and they support the author however they can (http://tuebl.ca/faq). But do readers really do that, or do they mostly just obtain free books? They also claim to be owned and operated by the EVIL LLC, which has a strange rant on its first page about the planet being occupied by the glorious Dominion, and EVIL LLC is seeking to fight against the growing threat of Exile usurpation (https://forums.wildstar-online.com/forums/index.php?/topic/71033-evil-llc-evil-a-limited-liability-company). It's hard to know if this is real or a parody, although it would seem to undermine TUEBL's credibility. In any case, TUEBL has a disclaimer that states that although they are a Canadian company, they have decided to comply with DMCA rules, so any author can send in a takedown notice and they will take down that book, although few writers have the time to commit to tracking down and sending takedown notices to all of the sites featuring free unauthorized copies of their book.

The costs of this piracy to individual writers can be devastating. For example, in a heartfelt post which is no longer online, "Piracy Sucks Donkey Balls . . . And Here's Why," Jennifer James (http://www.author-jenniferjames.com) states that pirates "help themselves to your art, the books you've spent thousands and thousands of hours busting ass on and give them away for free. Some are even enterprising enough to *charge* using PayPal and other checkout services for the stolen books!" In her case, one of her novels, *Love Kinection,* was pirated within hours of being live on Amazon, and since she didn't receive an advance from her publisher, she ended up earning only $117.76 for a book she spent months of work on. Later, she found LK and another of her books on another file-hosting site, where each book had been downloaded close to a thousand times each. So, as she describes it, "the pirates are robbing me blind" (https://www.goodreads.com/author_blog_posts/3954696-ebook-piracy-sucks-donkey-balls-and-here-s-why-with-math).

Thus, as I wrote then and feel is even more critical now, we need to take on the book pirates, much like the music and film industries have done. Waging their own piracy war eventually led to a new model for earning money from downloaded music and streaming films on services like iTunes and Netflix. In this case, the weapons include the criminal penalties that have undone companies like Megaupload and put their operators away for long jail terms. The theft of intangible intellectual property is real theft, much like breaking and entering a home and taking away money and objects of value, although in this case, the property taken is a book that an author has spent months nurturing until it is born.

But the FBI and other government agencies can only go after so many of the hundreds of pirates out there. So another big weapon is the lawsuit, which can be filed by publishers and authors with a number of pirated books, so taking legal action becomes cost effective and worthwhile. Or perhaps a class action suit might name several dozen of the pirate websites filed on behalf of the writers with stolen books on their site. Additionally, individuals can take assorted actions themselves, including sending cease and desist and takedown emails and collecting information that can help an attorney win a successful suit. And now the anti-piracy services can help by going after the pirates on behalf of writers, using the threat of further legal or criminal action to get some money from the pirates rather than face much more expensive actions against them.

So it is in this spirit of describing the problem of piracy, especially as it affects writers and publishers, and what to do about it, that I have written this book.

PART I

The Interviews

CHAPTER 1

Introduction to the Interviews

WHEN I FIRST BEGAN CONDUCTING the interviews with a mix of writers, publishers, lawyers, "pirates," and others involved in the piracy issue for the documentary *The Battle Against Internet Book Piracy*, I thought it was a straightforward matter of victims versus pirates, with some help for the victims from law enforcement and lawyers. The goal, I thought, was to help the victims of book piracy, myself included, find the sites where books were pirated, and then seek to get the books removed and possibly get some compensation for the infringement, or interest law enforcement in going after the biggest infringers.

But as I spoke to the interviewees, my own publishers, and others interested in this issue, it became far more complicated. For one thing, most writers and publishers had a kind of fatalistic "there's not much I can do" attitude. This was largely true, since about the most anyone could or did do was send out takedown notices to the infringers, and then if they didn't respond, to the website hosts and domain name servers, who did respond by removing the offending domain. However, often this was only a temporary solution, since the pirate would simply put up another site under another name, and it was back in business as usual. And making matters worse, further research on where one's books were pirated commonly revealed the book available through dozens if not hundreds of sites. So it was truly a "whack-a-mole" situation. Paying lawyers was too expensive for most writers and publishers, and law enforcement efforts against pirates were largely directed at the film, music, and software pirates, where the levels of piracy and the resources of the large companies that were victimized were much greater, and these companies were part of large industry organizations that helped in the battle. But by their very nature, writers and publishers were much smaller and less organized, so were more readily victimized with little consequence. At the same time, some of the "pirates" I spoke to didn't consider themselves pirates. This was because they were unaware that the material they received or shared freely was pirated by someone else, or they felt justified sharing it in the case of students because they thought the large companies were charging far too much for the required books often written by their professors and used in their classes. And then some interviews made an argument for free speech, changing the old model of selling books for something new, such as subscription services, or for finding ways to use what the pirates were doing to help promote one's own books or sell other material.

The following interviews reflect this range of viewpoints, and apart from my occasional commentary, I have chosen to let them speak in their own words. Then, the next section will discuss the even greater threat of piracy today, which is so vast that it threatens to undermine the very foundations of society. Such a threat is illustrated by the Sony hacking, which not only stole intellectual property but company data and personal records, much of which has been leaked to the media, as well as provided the fuel for the identity theft of everyone whose data is in the system. So the threat to books, along with films, music, software, and other intellectual property, is just the beginning.

These interviews help to illustrate the concerns and issues from the personal viewpoint of the major players in this struggle today. While these are single voices, their comments reflect similar experiences and viewpoints of others who are also victims, pirates, or others involved in this issue.

CHAPTER 2

An Interview with an Intellectual Property Lawyer

THE FOLLOWING INTERVIEW IS WITH Sandra Shepard, an intellectual property attorney based in San Rafael, California, who has been working in this field for about twenty years. She has been involved with licensing and working on Internet issues since 1988, and has sought to help her clients adapt to the way the technology has changed and has been used in different ways. As she describes it, she works with her clients as a strategist to help them monetize their intellectual property and avoid having their work pirated. She helps them take advantage of the situation when their work is pirated, and not become pirates themselves, such as by using the lines of a poem in the beginning of a chapter of their book, thinking it is just fair use when it is not. In her interview, she also explains the difficulties of applying the copyright laws today to protect copyright holders, since the laws were written at a time when there was real, physical property—but when intellectual property is stolen, it is copied and the copyright holder still has the original, no matter how many hundreds, thousands, or millions of copies are out there. As Shepard describes in her interview:

"Most people don't realize that half of the stuff they're doing on their website, they're pirates, too. I think when somebody finds that they have been pirated, unfortunately, sometimes it's a little bit too late for that, because a lot of people believe that they have copyright as soon as they write something. That's actually true because . . . as you doodle something or draw it or write it, it is the subject of copyright. However, you have to have filed a form with the copyright office, the Library of Congress, and then you have what's called statutory protection of whatever you filed. What that means is that as long as you've already filed that Form TX with the copyright office and then you find the piracy, then you have statutory protections, which means you don't have to prove it cost you any money. However, if you have not filed that Form TX, you have to actually prove that it cost you a certain amount, and that's usually a problem. It's very hard to do that.

"Also, many people don't know that they can't copy your work. I have a number of poets, for example, who are my clients, and they're forever finding their poem on a plate for sale on eBay, and it might have their name on it or it might say anonymous. Then, they will send out a letter that I have given them a template for. It is usually a very friendly letter that says, 'Perhaps you didn't know that you can't take my poem and sell it.' And usually people will stop.

"But if someone is instead a pirate where they really aren't going to stop, it's often hard to get them to stop, though most people may not know they can't take your book or poem or song or even a little piece of it and put it on a plate or include it on a website. So when you say, 'You can't do this,' perhaps they will stop or perhaps there are other things you can do.

"Usually (the infringed upon material) is on a website, and that website is not run by the person who is the pirate. So what you do is you contact the person who runs that site and you say, 'I own this poem. Here's the registration number, here's my information, here is where it's located,' give them the pin site, 'And you need to stop this because you are providing a forum for them to infringe my work.'"

But what if the infringer doesn't stop? Sometimes the organization they work for will take the responsibility and take it down, as an alternative to contacting the website host, such as when one professor used a book he downloaded for his class. As Shepard explains:

"Fairly recently, I had a client who wrote a book on music licensing, and a professor was actually using that book in part of his curriculum. And my client wasn't getting any money for it. The professor had just downloaded it and now it was on the college website to download for his class. He told my client that he wasn't going to take it down, and so my client contacted the college and said, 'Oh by the way, this book is up there. This belongs to us. We have filed the registered copyright. Here's the information.' And they took it down.

"So that's the strategy to use if the person who has pirated the material resists removing it. Usually the people that are providing the forum don't want to have something infringing on it. And they have the right to remove it. For example, when you post on a forum or website, those little click-through things that you never read but indicate 'I'll accept that' state the terms and conditions that usually include a phrase that you understand that posting something there is a privilege and not a right. What that means is that you don't have a *right* to post all your stuff here, and the service can take it off whenever they want. So usually the Googles, AOLs, or the colleges of the world will take your copyrighted material down, because they don't want to be the place where that infringing stuff is available."

Unfortunately, copyright law as it exists today can make it difficult to make a clear-cut case that piracy is theft. When someone takes your copyrighted material, since it is not tangible, physical property, it can give the pirate a ready out, such as saying they didn't know it was pirated material or claiming that by taking it, they weren't causing the owner any harm, because he or she still has the material. Or it opens the door to the many excuses that pirates and their defenders use to support them making this material to others, like claiming they are simply "sharing" something with friends or that they are helping to make an otherwise obscure owner more popular by sharing that work. Shepard explains this flaw in today's copyright law that can be used to the advantage of the pirates:

"One of the interesting things about intellectual property is that it is characterized as property, and there are three different kinds of property. There's personal property, which is like a pencil; there's real property, which is real estate; and there's intellectual property, which consists of trademarks, copyrights, or patents. This is property that you own because you came up with it out of your head. But the problem is that intellectual property law is based on personal property and realty law.

"For example, with personal property, you can readily tell if someone stole your pencil if you don't have it. With real property, you can readily tell if somebody is trespassing across your land, such as if you find broken grass or footprints there. But the problem with intellectual property is that it's very difficult to tell if somebody has taken or trespassed on your copyright, because you still have a copy of the physical book that has been scanned or the original digital file. An early example is all of the monks copying books, infringers all. But anybody who's copied anything without permission, that's the infringing item.

"And how can you tell when someone makes a copy? How would you know if somebody made a photo of a photo you took or made a copy of your book and gave it to somebody else. You can't really tell. It's not like your pencil, where you look at your desk and your pencil is not there; it's gone.

"So part of the problem with intellectual property is that it's very, very difficult to use those rules that the lawmakers created to cover intellectual property, since these laws are based on trespass and physical property ownership rules to apply to something where when you take it, it's still there. So again to take the pencil or real estate example, you can see something. But if somebody "takes" your story, you can't see a thing. Thus, the problem with the law is that it is crafted from law that's based on there being a discreet item, whereas, in actuality, intellectual property isn't a discreet item."

Still another problem, as Shepard points out, is that a competitor can use the intellectual property laws against you by, in effect, pirating your brand name or logo, and being the first to put in a claim for it. So besides stealing your creative work, pirates can steal your identity and reputation, and then use the power of the press and social media to present a very different picture of who you really are. And again the roots of the problem lie in the development of these laws to protect one's brand or image at a time when people knew each other personally or were part of a face-to-face community. As Shepard describes:

"Under trademark law, which is about branding, when you own a brand like a phrase or a logo, to get a trademark, you publish it in this Federal Register for six months. Then, people are allowed to say, 'Oh no, no, no. You should not own that,' but normally people don't read the Federal Register. But the law presumes that people are looking at it to see if somebody is infringing on their brand or trademark, or that people know what others are doing, such as back in the 1700s, when everybody knows everybody else. But the problem is that when someone files for a trademark and there is an opportunity for others to comment in the 'public comment' section, the average person won't see this. So you may not know that your biggest competitor has actually filed to use your logo or brand with the trademark office, because you don't check. So that's another part of the piracy problem, because the trademark law presumes that everyone who has a brand, phrase, or logo they love is checking for others using it, such as in the Federal Register, but we all know they are not. So this is another way someone could be a victim of piracy but not know it at the time.

"As a result, the following could happen to undermine your use of your own brand. Let's say that you've got a fantastic brand you are using, and you think you've got a great brand name, logo, or phrase, and your competitor decides that they want to file a trademark on that brand. So they file with the US Patent and Trademark Office, and they say that they own that. If you don't respond and tell them that, 'No, no. You can't do this. I own that brand or phrase,' then you will only own it in the spot that you have used it geographically, up until the time when they get it. After that they can own and use it in every other geographic region in the fifty states, except where you have used it in time before they have."

Thus, a competitor, someone with a grudge against you, or anyone who wants can effectively steal your brand, which is a form of identity theft and piracy. The same thing can happen if someone chooses to file for a copyright on your own material. Unless you are actively policing this, they can get a registration and then the ball is in your court to prove they don't really own it, which can be very time-consuming and expensive. As Shepard explains:

"Say you have written a book that you can copyright because it is your original material and say that you have not filed the Form TX with the copyright office to register the copyright. Then, if some-body steals that book and they file the Form TX and say they wrote it, as long as you can prove you wrote it by showing you have files that indicate you are first in time to create this with the exact phrases and the whole book before they do, they are never going to use that registration against you. But the Library of Congress, like the Patent and Trademark Office, has no responsibility to go out and prove that somebody else has already created or is using this mate-rial. So that's part of the problem. The copyright and trademark law presumes that you are policing your own intellectual property. It presumes that you are policing the copyright, brands, and logos of your own creations."

But most people don't, so they are at risk of pirates who jump the gun on their copyright or trademark registrations, besides being at risk of what is usually thought of as piracy—making copies of their books and sharing them. So that's why Shepard urges her writing clients to act quickly to protect their own material, as well as avoid infringing on the work of others. As she explains:

"That's why I will constantly tell my clients to get their material copyrighted or trademarked early on, especially authors that are poets or comedians, because if a comedian's got a really good joke, they should copyright just that joke.

"Also, I advise them how to avoid engaging in piracy themselves. For example, I tell them, 'You cannot put a phrase at the top of your chapter or anywhere else in your book, even if you say who it comes from, since that is infringement, although there might be a defense to it, such as "fair use."' This is different than plagiarism, which means that you're taking something and saying that it's yours, such as taking a book and saying that you wrote it. But if you use some-thing written by someone else, even if you use just a paragraph or put a quote around a sentence or two, and even if you attribute it, you have just infringed, though you might have an out through a defense to that infringement. For example, it could be 'fair use' if you meet five particular requirements, and if you don't meet these you are an infringer. For example, using something for educational purposes might be a defense. So when you say something is 'fair use' that means you have just said, 'I am an infringer, but I have a defense.' And often if you are making money on this material, you may not."

CHAPTER 3

Interviews with Writers and Self-Publishers

THE WRITERS I SPOKE WITH, many of them publishing their own books, echoed a similar refrain. They had discovered their books had been pirated, often by doing a search of their own name on the Internet to see what turned up, and then they discovered it had been uploaded somewhere or multiple places without their permission. They certainly weren't getting any money for it, though often the website was charging a subscription fee or featured ads. But after this discovery, they felt there was little they could do. They reported that their own income had been dropping, so now they were struggling financially, and they attributed much of this loss to the pirating of their books. But they felt helpless, and even if they were able to get the books removed from one place, they had already suffered the loss from books of their own that didn't sell since someone else could get it free. And then even after a book might be removed from one site, it could easily be uploaded again, by the website owner or by one of its subscribers or readers, and the book could be on so many other sites, the process of doing something, anything, seemed daunting, and the cost of trying to pursue the pirates legally was too high to even consider. The one upside was at least they had more readers, more people who knew their name, and perhaps maybe could buy some of their other books, if they had any.

It was a refrain I heard again and again from many writers I spoke to personally or encountered on writers' forums. In the face of piracy of their books as an electronic file on the Internet, what could they do other than face the loss, along with the many other losses writers now faced from lowered advances and royalties, fewer book deals, millions of other writers publishing their own books or writing for free, and other problems in a dying industry?

The interviews with a writer of books on magic and a writing team of a book on marketing one's music reflected these themes. The feeling of helplessness, frustration, and discouragement in these interviews was palpable, but the sad fact is there was little they could do individually to combat piracy. It can feel much like identity theft, except here ideas turned into words are stolen, not one's whole identity, though the victim can experience the same kinds of feelings of loss of something that has been close to them. And this feeling of loss goes beyond just losing money; there is a sense of being violated, of having property taken, as in any theft, and of helplessness and lost trust. They feel there is little they can do, and even a successful takedown notice won't remedy that sense of loss.

The experience is very different from when there is a pirate of a physical book that is copied and published under another name. For then, one can more readily go after the pirate, once discovered, and variously get the book removed from publication or get some compensation. But with electronic books on the Internet, it's not so easy or could prove impossible to stop or get any compensation.

Following are the two interviews that reflect these themes.

An Interview with a Writer and Self-Publisher of Books on Magic

One of the writers and self-publishers I interviewed was Roger Pierre. Roger has a small publishing company for his books on conjuring magic, based on using cards and coins, usually in a one-on-one close-up encounter with one or a small group of observers. He has been writing and self-publishing books since 1975, when he published a book on the magic of Francis Carlyle. Then, in 2010, he discovered on the Internet that the book had been pirated. As he describes it:

"I always check up on how the old copies of my books are doing, and about five years ago, while I was surfing the Internet, someone listed on Google said, 'Well, I like this book, but when's the CD coming out?' I was surprised, since as a publisher, I wondered what CD, since I had never planned to bring one out. So I started following the comments trail backwards, and I back trailed it to someone who was coming out with a CD that had a beautiful scan of my book in it.

"Luckily, because I had taken the precaution of getting a proper full copyright on the book and the man producing the CD was in the United States, we were able to negotiate something that was acceptable to both of us. He agreed to pay me an advance as a licensing fee and a royalty of future sales.

"But I think what often happens in this case, as with other older books, is there are a lot of magicians who have passed away and the family members don't really follow through properly to assert their own rights in the book, since this is part of the inheritance or estate. This is especially true for the older books that have come out of copyright or are close to coming out, unless the copyright is renewed. So there are many disreputable publishers of magic or of anything else out there that are searching these books out and taking advantage of the fact that there's nobody who's protecting the copyright. So you don't really know if they are making an honest mistake of thinking they can now publish the book, or they're trying to sneak something around on you or not."

As Roger pointed out, if he hadn't been able to negotiate a deal, the publisher could have been subjected to high statutory damages as well as actual damages. As Roger noted:

"You have up to a hundred and fifty thousand dollars in statutory damages in a copyright infringement case if you have registered your copyright, and are more likely to get that or more if you have a track record and can show high damages. Like in my case, my book sold out twice, so it would have been an easy case for me to show that if I had put out as many books as he had put out CDs, I might have made a certain amount of money and gotten my money back that way."

Then, too, the Internet had helped him both in tracking down the offender—who was US-based, so he was in a better position to enforce his rights and collect fees for the publisher's infringement—and in facilitating the piracy and the sale of the pirated work. As he explained:

"I think the Internet is a double-edged sword. First of all, it may be where they're taking your material. At the same time, it's the perfect place to go to find out about copyrighting. The government has a site with information on how and why to do it, along with the forms you need. And if you even go to Wiki, the online encyclopedia, the Wiki displays this information about copy in five sections and explains pretty well what to do, so you can do this by yourself. I didn't go to a lawyer when I copyrighted my book, since all the materials are available from the copyright office. But it's definitely important to do this when you publish or produce anything, since you shouldn't let this slip by. Whether you're doing a digital movie, a digital book, make sure you get copyright so you get some protection.

"Also, the Internet enables you to check on whether anyone is copying your work. When I do my own searches for myself, the search finds me and everything I've done. So, I think the best way to protect yourself from anyone taking your work is to check yourself out on a regular basis, even if it's only once every six months. Check yourself out to protect your work."

An Interview with the Authors of a Book on Music

Another interview with writers and self-publishers was with Seb Jarakian and Randy Schroeder, former partners in a music licensing company called Musync, which represents musicians, indie bands, and music labels. The company licenses their music to films, television, advertising, video games, and other users. Then, after they wrote a book called *Music Licensing Insider's Guide* to help musicians protect themselves, their own book was ripped off repeatedly through downloading, substantially curtailing sales.

Randy described the paradox:

"We felt a strong need to provide musicians with the ability to know and understand how to get their music in the hands of people that actually license their music. The problem currently is that musicians have very few ways to make money, such as through CD sales, where people license their music and make some money if they're good enough. But there's been so much piracy in that industry that what happens is that people lose much of this money they could legitimately make this way. So that's what our book focuses on—how to protect their material against piracy.

"So our book is available on Amazon and on iBooks and Apple. And then we have a CD version that contains directories of contacts in the industry. But the irony of the whole thing is that here we are helping musicians because of the piracy issues that have thwarted their ability to make money, and then we have people that are pirating our own book. So it's this crazy cycle that hopefully our book will prevent for musicians, while it is happening to ourselves."

So how did Randy and Seb discover and deal with their own piracy problem? Basically, they used the takedown notice approach used by other writers and publishers. This usually results in compliance, though in their case they ran into one pirate who was more elusive, so they did bring in an attorney to help them, which is less common. But in their case, their book was earning enough after five years of being on the market, so it was worth using an attorney to help scare the pirate into compliance and getting some compensation. Seb continues the story:

"When our book was pirated, we found out from a Google alert that it was hosted on a social sharing site and basically contacted the organization to pull down the book. A couple of them were fairly easy. They were actually companies based out of San Francisco so it was very easy to contact them to have them pull it down. One of them was a little more complicated. I believe it was a company in Europe and they were kind of giving us a little run around and actually gave us a notification saying that we have to abide by some kind of international law or something. I don't remember what it was. So basically, we had our attorney contact them and scare them to take the book down."

For most writers, the amount lost to piracy may be small, since the average self-published book sells only about 150 copies and usually the advance is the only money the writer sees from traditional publishers. Although collectively, the earnings of millions of writers combined is in the billions of dollars, though the actual amounts are hard to determine. But in some cases, for books with expectations of good sales, the earnings could be high. In these cases it is worth it to hire a lawyer to gain compensation or seek to destroy the piracy site so others don't become victims, too. As Randy explains:

"There's no real way of knowing how many books would be pirated, because once a book goes up on a piracy site, it's a new item. And a new item is the hot thing because it's usually at the top. And there are millions and millions of musicians that want this material. So it's highly likely that they could've taken thousands of books. And the book on Amazon is $9.95, so you can do the math, and see that it's not a small amount. At the same time, you're at a loss of what to do, other than contact the company that's hosting it to ask them to take down the book."

In turn, this loss of income can lead to many writers and other creative people dropping out of the industry—a concern of others in these industries and in society generally. Randy notes:

"One of the sad parts to me about the whole piracy issue is that it starts thwarting creativity. That's happening with musicians, with photographers, with any creative producers, because the things they create just become another commodity and they are not compensated for the value of their work. The result is that this situation keeps people from wanting to make the effort to protect their work and to be creative and put things out there. So there's a loss of that creativity to our culture."

So if writers individually can't do much about the problem, what might be done? One solution is the need for an attitude change. Since so many people have come to expect the ability to get things for free, education is needed to change that mind-set. Or maybe technology could help by placing limits on what people can see for free, requiring them to pay to gain access to the rest. As Seb describes it:

"I think everybody is really into getting things for free, and that is what has happened here. They don't think of the creator who is losing money; they just want to get something for free.

"I think one solution might be to restrict free access. For example, maybe there might be a future technology where if you download a digital book, only a certain amount of that book is available, and then when you pay for it, it unlocks the rest. But I'm sure many people will figure out ways to unlock the restriction, so they get the book for free anyways. So I think it's a tough one to try to control piracy that way.

"I think another approach is to provide more education about piracy, especially in countries that don't know that taking copy-righted work is piracy. So we have to educate people that they can't share copyrighted items. A lot of people steal a lot of things without understanding that what they are doing is stealing. For example, people think that once you own music, you can take that music, so if you're producing your own film, you can take that music and use it in your film, because you bought the CD. They think it's yours, that you have the rights to it. But you do not really have the rights to that music. So I think education is necessary to put that information out there to inform people, so they don't post things that do not belong to them.

"As for what should be done about book pirates, I think more education is definitely in order. But a big problem is how do you find a book pirate? Is it the person that's putting up or sharing these books on the sharing sites, or is it the companies that are hosting the material? I think the education should be to not share these materials, and we have to expose the people who are providing the sites to share these materials.

"At the same time, it is difficult to impose fines. For example, in the last ten to fifteen years, only a relatively small number of people have gotten fines for sharing CDs, and I wonder if the government will try to do something similar for sharing books. But the problem is really tough, because you have to both find the people who are involved in sharing what isn't theirs to share, and then you have to try to collect money from them. And this can be hard to do, especially if those sharing are from another country, and how do you get all the world governments involved? It's a complicated process to try to use enforcement to deal with the problem, so I think the main approach should be more education to explain that people don't have the right to share what they don't own and show how they are harming others, and just go from there."

CHAPTER 4

Interviews with Three Publishers

When I spoke with three publishers—Eve A. Ma, the publisher of Palomino Productions in El Cerrito, California; Jennifer Joseph, the publisher of Manic D Press in San Francisco; and Maria Danzilo, the Legal Director for Wiley in Hoboken, New Jersey—their comments echoed those of the writers in describing the losses they experienced. The big difference was that the damages were more extensive, especially as the publishers were larger, and had more books with wider distribution. Thus the potential losses due to piracy were that much greater. But except for Wiley, a much larger and well-financed publisher, the publishers, like the writers, felt they could do little. They were too small, had limited time and funds, and the pirates were too numerous and often were operating from other countries, making any response seem futile.

For these small publishers, piracy became a kind of cost of doing business, though Wiley did seek to achieve compensation. The company filed a lawsuit on behalf of one of its *Dummies* series books that was illegally uploaded and pirated, resulting in at least thirty-five thousand downloads. Eventually it did win, although in the larger scheme of things, that success is really limited in scope, since there are multiple offenders who weren't sued, and Wiley has hundreds of other books over which it didn't sue. So while it might have won in one suit, it is still a victim. It's like the Wild West, where a sheriff might shoot down one outlaw who has robbed a bank, but there are still dozens of other outlaws out there, waiting for the right opportunity to rob again, and even rob that same bank again and again.

An Interview with a Publisher of Scholarly Books

When I interviewed Eve Ma of Palomino Publishing, she emphasized the futility of doing anything and how others were benefiting financially at the expense of the victim of piracy, though she pointed out the one bright side of piracy—at least she would have more people reading her work. As Ma commented:

"To my knowledge, I have had only one book pirated and that was one of my scholarly books. It was about the Chinese in the United States during the Chinese revolution of 1911, and it was translated into Chinese by a publisher in China. It was printed and published there without my knowledge, and without, of course, since I didn't know about it, without paying me any money.

"The thought of hiring an international lawyer and starting a lawsuit in China or in an international court of law was a little daunting so I said, 'Well, at least a lot of people in China are reading it.'

"It's important if you're a writer, a filmmaker, a musician to get whatever money is due to the author. The author needs that money. If you take somebody else's work and make money off of it, you're really hurting the very thing that you like, and I think it's a real shame."

Like many other writers and publishers, Ma felt it would be fair to compensate the victims of piracy with the money they should have made were the material not pirated. But she felt the draconian punishments meted out through law enforcement or litigation were simply too high at hundreds of thousands in damages. She explained:

"There's always the question as to what should be done about book piracy or any other form of piracy of other people's creations. I do think that if you find somebody that's pirating something, they should be required to pay back any money they made to the person who created it. I think there should be some possibility of additional damages. But I don't believe in these huge two-billion-dollar mental stress damages or other excessive penalties. There should be some kind of additional damages, but reasonable ones."

An Interview with a Small Publisher of a Variety of Books

When I interviewed Jennifer Joseph, the publisher of the Manic D Press, she began by describing the broad mix of books she published since 1984, among them works of poetry, fiction, nonfiction, creative nonfiction, art books, children's books, and travel books. And then when she heard about a company that looked for pirated manuscripts and sent out takedown notices, she did a search and found many of her titles on multiple websites. But like many other writers and publishers, she felt it exhausting and futile to try to combat piracy on her own. Plus, it would take away the time she had to write and publish the books of her authors. As she explained:

"At our distributor's sales conference recently, they offered the publishers a chance to sign up for a yearlong contract with a company that would search for titles that are being pirated and would send takedown notices on your behalf. That sparked an interest for me. So I Googled some of our more popular titles and discovered they were pirated on multiple websites.

"But I didn't have much time to do anything, because it's really a game of whack-a-mole. As soon as you take down one site, something else pops up. Plus, it's really a full-time job chasing the digitization of your books around the Internet and trying to stop that. So it's a distraction.

"I think that most people are sending out takedown notices with varying degrees of success. Everybody agrees that it's a very time-consuming thing."

Joseph also expressed the popular sentiment among writers and other creators that people should be paid for their work if they are serious, professional writers. While many writers might offer their work for free, those doing it professionally need to get paid so they can survive. As Joseph noted:

"I think that everything can be free to a certain extent. However, if people are trying to keep a roof over their head and are doing the writing as work, it's not just a hobby, since everybody can be an author. They've reached a certain level where enough people agreed that their work is good. So they should be paid.

"Many writers and other people don't mind that pirates are making pirated copies of books, because they feel that this way, many readers will discover somebody's works. Say if an author has published three or five books, if these readers discover one book through an illegal download, maybe they'll seek out other titles by the same author and pay for those."

Another problem with piracy for the publisher, as Joseph pointed out, is that not only is it reducing the payment to the author, but behind the publication of the book are many other people who the publisher has to pay, including editors, artists, distributors, and sales people. But when books are pirated, the publisher may have to publish fewer books as a result of having less money to produce, distribute, and promote them. Plus, there is less money to pay for all the support people needed for each book. And, of course, if piracy siphons off enough income from a publisher, the publisher may not be able to afford to publish at all. As Joseph puts it:

"The situation in publishing is much like in the music industry. In music, many people think that music should be free and that well-known bands like Metallica should be giving away their music. But they think that without thinking that it costs money to have studio time, the instruments cost money, the engineers need to be paid.

"When it comes to publishing, it's the same thing. Many support people have to be paid. I always have to explain to my authors, yes, your name is on the book and your writing is in the book, but there are a thousand people in the background helping you find a readership—the guy packing the boxes at the warehouse, the guy unpacking the boxes at the bookstore, the guy delivering the boxes, the distributors who create the catalog, the sales people who pitch your books to the bookstores. There are so many people involved, and you have to remember them. And you have to be grateful that you've had this opportunity to have this huge amount of people behind you to get your work out into the world."

Some writers and publishers have talked about using digital rights management, or DRM, as an antidote to piracy, since it involves preventing a buyer from using that file on any other device. But this isn't a viable solution, as Joseph and many other publishers agree, because the

DRM can interfere with legitimate uses, such as a buyer getting a new computer or someone passing on without telling anyone else the password. Joseph explains the problem with DRM:

"One of the situations that a lot of technical people talk about is digital rights management, or so-called DRM, so that something can't be shared. It's like one book for one device. But then there are all these complications. If somebody passes on and they have this library of print books, they can't be inherited by a relative or anyone else handling the estate. That's because if somebody passes on and you don't have the password and username for their electronic device, their entire library is gone."

Thus, another technical solution to deal with the piracy problem is needed.

An Interview with a Representative for a Major Publisher

For large publishers, the problem of piracy is magnified, because they have many more books and therefore many more authors and support people depending on getting paid by them. Piracy undermines that ability. But unlike the individual writers and smaller publishers, they have the resources to take more aggressive action, like Wiley has done in suing one of the websites that pirated many of its books. Moreover, since they are much larger, they are in a better position to work closely with the government and law enforcement in crafting solutions to the problem, such as by creating stronger laws to prevent piracy in the first place.

These are some of the issues raised in my interview with Maria Danzilo, the Legal Director of Wiley, who sent a video to address the interview questions. In its over two hundred years of publishing, Wiley has published hundreds of thousands of books, including the works of over four hundred Nobel lawyers. As the Legal Director, Danzilo also manages Wiley's intellectual property protection program for its three core businesses: global education, global research, and professional development with an extensive and global digital business.

As Danzilo describes, piracy not only means that the creators of content won't get paid, but it may mean that these creative contributors stop contributing, resulting in a loss to society due to reduced innovation and creativity. And that's the reason that copyright law was created—to protect the creations of any creators, rewarding them so they will continue to create. As Danzilo explains:

"We are committed to continuing to combat online piracy. Our content is valuable to us, and we will continue to enforce and protect Wiley's intellectual property vigorously because in our business, it is important that creators are compensated.

"Piracy has an impact on the business, because it makes it impossible for anyone who contributes to the creative content to be paid for their work. If they're not paid, innovation and creativity will necessarily suffer.

"Online piracy causes significant damage to everyone in the chain of creativity by depriving creators of the fruits of their work. So the damage is to everyone in the value of chain of creativity, and as a result, our culture may suffer. What would the world be like without great books, music, other creative works, if economic incentives were taken away from creators?

"It's important to remember that copyright rights are derived from the US Constitution, and the Constitution provides that individuals and innovators, artists and creators, are rewarded for creating works through economic incentives. When those economic incentives are taken away, creativity and innovation will necessarily suffer."

So what is the solution when pirates still seek to benefit from the work of creators without compensating them? Like many writers, publishers, and other content creators today, Danzilo urges technological solutions along with government action to make the copyright laws even stronger to discourage piracy. As Danzilo points out:

"At Wiley, we believe that technological measures could be used to stop infringement before it occurs. These technological measures are not expensive and can be adopted more widely.

"We are aware that Congress is looking at potentially revising copyright law. We are working with Congress to participate in this revision process. We would like to see Congress establish stronger laws that include technological measures that will prevent piracy before it happens. The US government could be particularly helpful in vigorously supporting and providing tools to prevent access to the web of piracy sites and in starving piracy sites of ad revenue and other incomes sources, which they may use to sustain piracy."

Additionally, besides waiting for these technological fixes or for the government to act, Wiley has already taken some action itself by initiating a lawsuit against one of the pirate companies—an action that they subsequently won. While individual litigation might prove just a drop in the bucket, given the vast number of websites and millions of uploaders involved in the piracy of multiple books, this successful litigation might provide a model for other publishers or creators with sufficient resources to go after the pirates too. Not only might such a response result in the gain of justified compensation when they win, but the suit can show pirates the expensive costs of piracy, and thereby discourage them from doing it. As Danzilo describes:

"We brought a lawsuit in Germany where the courts were quite receptive to protecting intellectual property and we've been successful. A group of publishers brought that suit several years ago against a large site called RapidShare, and the highest court in Germany recently affirmed the decision in the lower courts. So Rapid-Share is now required to adopt the kind of technical measures to prevent piracy that I was speaking about."

And this success might well inspire other publishers and creators to take similar action, while sending a strong message to potential pirates about the consequences of getting caught.

CHAPTER 5

Interviews with Some Pirates (a.k.a. Researchers and Students)

WHEN I SOUGHT TO INTERVIEW pirates to learn how and why they do what they do, I initially found it hard to get anyone to come forward, even though statistics suggest that nearly 50 percent of the population acknowledges pirating something—from music and films to books and software—and those figures are around 70 percent for individuals from eighteen to twenty-nine. And then when I found two people who met the criteria for being a pirate—essentially downloading, streaming, or buying pirated material, neither wanted to claim the title of "pirate." Instead, both wanted to call what they did something else, such as being a "researcher" or a "student." Now certainly both individuals were, in fact, accurately describing one of the occupations they were engaged in. But then, under cover of these self-labels, they were actually engaging in piracy. For example, the "researcher" *was* actually researching various topics about which he was writing, while the "student" *was* actually enrolled in a college and taking classes. But the researcher commonly used pirated material he found useful for his subject, while the student teamed up with other students in a collective to split the costs of highly priced textbooks they needed for their classes.

In turn, they both described rationales to justify their decision to be pirates . . . er, researchers and students, who used pirated materials in the service of socially valued goals (i.e., the researcher writing an important paper or book; the student acquiring the book needed for MBA classes at a reasonable price).

Their responses, in turn, can be seen as a stand-in for the vast majority of individuals who engage in piracy for their own personal benefit of getting the information they need or entertainment they want at low cost. These individuals feel they are part of a community that shares information and defines away piracy as something else by considering it an ordinary, acceptable activity, whether it has formed online or is a group involved in some activity together. As such, they differ from the much smaller number of active pirates who are involved in running websites, making money for selling pirated materials, or uploading massive amounts of materials because they want to earn money doing so or gain recognition for their contribution to the pirate—whoops, sharing—community.

More specifically, here are the various issues and rationales for their actions as described in their interviews.

An Interview with a "Researcher"

My researcher interview was with Duncan, who described himself as an "independent researcher" who generally looked for material dealing with sports, health, personal development, and music. At one time, he got his information at the public library, and he compared accessing information online through blog sites or file sharing as essentially the same thing. It was free to look at this material at the library and one could take it out for free with just a card, so why should it be any different to get free information, where available, online?

The other comparison he made, much like others obtaining information through sharing files, was to sharing with others as part of a community. And those obtaining the information weren't the only part of this community; so were the writers who provided the information they shared. In fact, he considered the community to be helping the writer to reach more readers than he or she might otherwise. Or as Duncan explained:

"If you look at piracy from the old standpoint of the many generations in traditional publishing, I could see how piracy could be a problem. The publishers are thinking of the pirates as stealing something from them that is covered by a copyright. But if you embrace the new model based on a community that shares, then writers should be flattered because of the way the new model works. Because if somebody has read your material and is making comments about it online, you can reach a lot more readers that way. Then, those readers have a choice—whether to find your material through more traditional sources, like paying for it, or maybe borrowing the book from somebody or going to the library to get it. But whatever readers do, you as a writer are reaching far more readers through this sharing by others and you're participating in a community. And that's the whole point of this new online sharing model. You're building a community this way."

It's a community that doesn't view this "sharing" of files as piracy, since they are like people lending something they own to others and getting loans from others in return. So they don't think what they are doing is or should be considered illegal, and therefore should not be penalized heavily. Conversely, writers and publishers might view them as sharing something they don't own, so they are really giving or obtaining stolen property. Or as Duncan explained the online community view:

"This community of people who do file sharing don't consider themselves as pirating or engaging in an illegal activity. They see it as sharing, like being part of an online lending community. So when you ask questions like, "Is this illegal?" or, "Is this piracy?" those terms don't register with people that are sharing, because in their belief system, they are engaging in lending to each other as part of a community.

"Accordingly, given their view that they are engaging in justifiable actions, they think the penalties for any actions of piracy should be much lower."

So how did this process of sharing work in the community? Duncan went on to explain:

"When you download, you're downloading from one online source directly onto your computer or whatever device you're using. By contrast, file sharing is peer-to-peer, so basically somebody uploads a piece of material, whether it's music, writing, or a film. And then this file-sharing program, which uses a BitTorrent platform, doesn't just download from one person. Rather, it picks seven or eight people who have that file, and it downloads simultaneously a section from all of them at the same time. The reason for this simultaneous download of parts from different users is that it's quicker to get a file from a computer as compared to having to wait for the download time for a file from just one source. And the process occurs automatically when you go to share a file; there are no terms of use that come up or statements that you have to accept these terms when you share files; it's just assumed that you're sharing when you do so.

"This is basically how it happens. Let's say somebody gets a book on Amazon, which they pay for. Then, they download it onto their computer and read it. After that, they think the book is great; they're very excited about it, so they want to share it with others. Since the file is located on their own computer, a lot of times, they don't even have to upload it; they just have to participate in a file-sharing program that looks through their computer's hard drive. Once the program finds the file by its name, it can upload this material, and often people don't even know their material is being uploaded. It's being shared.

"Then, after you upload something, others in the online community may be excited to share this material with their peer group, their friends. They'll tell them, 'Hey, look what I just read. This would really be great if you read it, too. I'm sharing it with you.'"

Still another rationale for considering this kind of file sharing perfectly legal is that Amazon offers its own incentive for sharing to encourage book purchases. Plus, the experience of sharing a book online is much like sharing a book one has either bought in a bookstore or obtained from a library, according to Duncan. As he explains:

"There is another thing online that you can do on Amazon. When I buy a book there, I can still share that with my friends, just like a library. Amazon usually gives buyers about a two-week time frame, where others can download the book that a buyer purchased and read it for free.

"The experience is the same as going to a library. Whether someone goes to the library and checks out a book in person or buys it online and shares a book with me, or if I file share a book I have bought or borrowed from a library, it's the same experience to me. The book is from one, singular source—the library or store, whether online or on a street. It's only when you look at this act of sharing from the writers' or publishers' perspective that you think of it as one copy going to a bunch of people. But from the perspective of those in the community, it's just one document. So if one has possession of the document, then one can share it with others.

"This is the way it is in the new model, whereby people in general are sharing as part of a community. For instance, in the old model, if I had a book and I was in a community, it would be fine for me to pass that book through a network of friends in that community. The new model simply applies this old model to our new technologies, so in today's mode somebody who has a piece of material online is like that person sharing a book. So now people are sharing that material through different vehicles for their peer group to participate in and read online, instead of passing around a physical book."

This is a completely opposite perspective from those held by the authors and publishers who see the material that is shared as separate from the physical book or online container for that material. This is what they want to protect from multiple copying, which they see as theft, not sharing, because they are losing money from these acts of sharing. But from the perspective of the online community members, this action of sharing shouldn't be subject to high criminal penalties. Since most people who are sharing don't think they are doing anything illegal, the more appropriate response from writers, publishers, and the government would be to educate them that what they are doing is wrong, and perhaps send repeated reminders to wean them off bad habits. Or perhaps reduce their online bandwidth to lessen their ability to share. As Duncan commented:

"Penalties with $150,000 or more for sharing are excessive. For example, in a criminal proceeding, the fine can be $250,000 for each offense; $150,000 for a willful infringement in a civil case. I think these penalties are too high, because the government is criminalizing something that doesn't need to be criminalized. I think that when you do that, you'll maybe catch one or two people and try to make them pay an exorbitant amount of money that they can't afford.

"But that approach is not going to change the habits of people that are file sharing at all. I think education is probably the best strategy to use. A lot of people, or even the majority of people, don't even know they're doing something illegal. It's just a habit that they've gotten into because they feel file sharing is a convenient way of getting material.

"Instead, a way to educate people is to send them a notice from their Internet service provider saying, 'Hey, what you're doing is illegal.' It's a reminder notice. Then, if that doesn't work, send them several reminders and then maybe limit their bandwidth in the case of the big offenders who are doing a lot of file sharing. Sending these notices would be a great way of not just penalizing somebody; instead you're weaning somebody off their habits. And it's really important to do so, because when people have a habit, it's an automatic response. They don't mean to do anything illegal. It's just that they spend so much time online. They date online, they find cooking recipes online, they read material online, they get their news online, because they're part of this online community. So a lot of times they don't realize that they're doing anything illegal.

"For instance, in my personal life, if I was to receive a notice saying, 'Hey, we just want to let you know that what you're doing is something the courts have deemed an illegal activity. Is there any way we could help you break your habit in doing this? Please let us know or we're going to take these actions,' it's a completely different and better approach than threatening me from the outset. This kind of notice enlists my participation. However, if you send me a notice saying, 'Cease and desist or we're going to fine you $150,000,' you're coming from a completely different place."

By contrast, using threats of legal action or criminalizing the act of sharing would only result in confusion or resistance, because of the different perspective of those who believed they were part of a sharing community, although there was general agreement that—claiming someone else's work as one's own—was definitely wrong. As Duncan noted:

"Any time you bring in legal jargon and try to apply it to a mass audience, nobody knows what that means. You have to use terminology that the average person is going to recognize, acknowledge, and accept. You also have to consider your motive in getting out a message about why sharing is wrong. Is your motive to criminalize or is it to educate? When you use legal jargon, you make it sound very serious and people are going to go to jail, you're criminalizing somebody. But when you put your message in terms where you want to educate somebody, you're coming from a completely different place, and you'll get a completely different, more cooperative response.

"However, in the case of plagiarism, the situation is different. Taking somebody else's material in its exact form or even translating it and putting your name on it and then publishing it in China, India, or some other country is plagiarism. And that's plagiarism across the board. Whether you're old school or new school, in any community, that's straight-out plagiarism, which should be penalized and should be criminalized. I would be more concerned about that than somebody who is sharing my work online and may actually be doing me a favor by giving me a wider audience, so I don't think there's much difficulty in arguing with that premise that plagiarism is wrong."

This argument that those sharing the material are helping authors is one that resonates widely with this online sharing community, and a key way that they define what they are doing as not piracy. They even use examples of what Google is doing—making more information widely available—to support their position, though writers and publishers have actively opposed Google's efforts. Some have even taken Google to court to stop this widespread distribution of free books or to make sure that a system is in place to compensate the writers for each download. Duncan explains this community position:

"Even companies like Google are making large amounts of documents freely available to people. There's one project that Google participates in called the Gutenberg Project, which is putting a very large number of books online for free.

"So I think it's really important for every writer, regardless of their medium, to turn the mirror on themselves and ask: Why are you writing this? If it's for the message, then somebody who's pirating your material will be an asset to you and not a deterrent, because they are spreading your message.

"So that's how you flip the switch and stop looking at people as pirates and start looking at them as soldiers who are distributing your work for you because really, that's what file sharing is about. Many people will still go to whatever source where they can get the physical book. They will still go to Amazon; they will still go to Barnes and Noble; they will still get their books through bookstores. But how did they hear about it? In a great many cases, they heard about it through a friend, an online blog, or through their own online channels. So in that respect, online sharing is actually helping the writer get the message out to many more people."

In short, Duncan's interview reflects the popular opinion among many modern-day pirates who consider themselves researchers or online file-sharing community members. They believe they are not pirates and are not engaging in anything illegal. They need some education to convince them of the other perspective—held by the writers, publishers, and law enforcement—that they are in fact engaging in piracy that is undermining the ability of writers and publishers to make money and survive in today's economy. So should the new model be embraced as one that writers, publishers, and others should accept and adapt to, as the price of social change making old models obsolete? Or are their arguments really an apology for supporting their participation in illegal activities that could lead many writers to abandon their profession and many publishers to go out of business, no longer able to compete against the free sharing of their material? The debate goes on, though from the perspective of writers and publishers, it is only fueling the continuation of the theft of their material, by providing a justification for that theft.

An Interview with a Student Sharing Books with Other Students

Another rationale that some pirates use is that the cost of certain books is much too high, and if they are part of an audience that has to buy these books, such as students in a class where the professor requires them to read the books, they are justified in sharing them. So they aren't pirates doing anything illegal; they are students taking action against an unfair system. That's the opinion shared by A. Otto Thay, the owner of a consulting firm called Envisioneering, which helps companies to visualize information. In the course of doing this consulting, he discovered many revealing things in the company database that the CEOs didn't even know about, so he wrote a book to be marketed to students to help them better understand what was going on in different companies. That led him to talk to both students and professors, who told him about the common practice of professors only using their own books in their classes and arranging with other professors to use each other's books, so they can sell their books to a captive audience. And those books are overpriced, so students are justified in creating their own network to buy one book and share it among themselves. As Thay explained:

"In other words, these professors have a system where they only buy books from other professors, and the reason they can do so is because these professors have a captive audience. The students can't go anywhere else for these books, so they are able to overcharge these students. That's why graduate books often cost about three to five hundred dollars a copy, which is ridiculous.

"And so some of the students I spoke to at grad schools told me they have a way of getting around this. They have an underground system where one of them makes copies of the books, so they provide it free for all the students.

"The situation is different for professional book writers, since their books are the main source of their income. So yes, book piracy is a problem for writers, like myself too, although I do consulting and other things.

"But with professors, it's the outrageous prices that they are charging for their books that's the problem. They don't need to make money off of their books, because they're already making thousands of dollars in their salary. So it's unjustified for college universities to charge these high prices, and only fair for students to create this underground system to get around their system.

"I can see where ordinary writers and publishers would have a problem with readers sharing their books, because it does drive them out of business. But the situation is different for the textbook publishers, since they're getting a big percentage of the five hundred dollars per copy for these overpriced books, versus the twenty dollars per copy for the average book written by a professional writer. Unfortunately, a lot of students don't know about this underground system, so they end up paying full price for the books, so these books are still being sold and those publishers will still be profitable, while the small publishers with the writers of ordinary books are having problems due to readers sharing their books. And in that case, readers should buy their books and pay the full price.

"By contrast, the students are justified in sharing these books among themselves because of the outrageous prices that the professors are charging for their books, whereas there's no justification for pirating a regular book which sells for around twenty dollars or even less. So I can understand going from five hundred dollars to a dollar or a few dollars for the cost to buy a book, though I don't think it's right to go from twenty dollars to five dollars or whatever it costs to buy pirated copies of these regular books.

"In the case of your average writer or regular writers who are also professors, this is their main source of income, so they are basically losing their livelihood when their books are pirated, so it's important to control and prevent piracy or go after the offenders. But where students are finding a way to gain access to these overpriced books they are forced to buy by their professors, then I think sharing these books, so everyone pays much less or nothing, is fine. That shouldn't be considered piracy or theft."

In short, as these interviews illustrate, for the average person engaged in what writers, publishers, and law enforcement consider piracy, they considered their actions to either not be piracy, since they are sharing information with peers, or to be justified because they are facing an unjust system where books are grossly overpriced and they are forced to buy them. These kinds of justifications might apply to the 50–70 percent of the population of different age groups engaging in piracy to some extent. This is in contrast to the much smaller group of active pirates who are engaging in it as a business through running online websites or copying and reselling pirated books at a reduced price, such as at local flea markets.

A comparison might be to the sale of drugs, which has been criminalized for decades and has only recently, at the end of 2014, been decriminalized under Federal Law by the Obama administration. The vast majority of the users are like the researchers and students, involved in obtaining the drugs for their own personal use, while a whole criminal enterprise is much like the pirates in operating the production, distribution, and sale of the product. The big difference, of course, is that in the case of pirating of books by the small-scale users, there are writer and publisher victims, whereas the users of drugs for recreational or medical purposes generally don't see themselves as victims, unless they should get bad drugs or get addicted from drug overuse and abuse.

In any case, the vast number of researcher-student "pirates" illustrates the difficulties of dealing with the problem, where they are defining themselves as not engaged in piracy or are justified in their actions. Perhaps consider the problem a little like the situation that existed in Prohibition, where the popular use of alcohol was so great that ultimately, Prohibition was ended. At the same time, while it existed, Prohibition triggered the genesis of organized crime, and even after it ended, the criminal organizations it spawned generally continued; they just turned to other activities, such as prostitution, gambling, and drugs. Similarly, the popularity of file sharing and getting overpriced books at a discount has created a vast network of pirate sites today. These sites are making huge sums of money through advertising, subscriptions, or lower-priced but illegal downloads, where the writers and publishers don't get paid.

CHAPTER 6

The Free Speech, Technology, and Piracy Controversy

ANOTHER BIG ISSUE RAISED BY piracy is that of free speech and the degree to which current concepts of piracy might be outdated. Some believe that those against piracy should yield when there is a conflict between free speech rights and claims of piracy that challenge that right. A related issue is the development of new technologies that create new ways of distributing books and other creative materials that may undermine current definitions of piracy.

My interview with Parker Higgins, a free-speech advocate working with the Electronic Frontiers Foundation, helped to examine these issues and suggest new ways of looking at the piracy–free speech conflict in light of the new technologies.

A key problem, as Higgins points out, is the way that the copyright holders have sought new agreements or laws that might not only protect the rights holders, but restrict legitimate speech or communications. As Higgins explains:

"At the Electronic Frontiers Foundation, we've been working on issues like piracy in unauthorized downloading for over a decade now. Whether we're talking about books, movies, or music, what we've seen over and over is in an effort to reduce unauthorized downloading, the rights holders have pushed for new voluntary agreements or laws that end up restricting other kinds of legitimate speech or communications.

"One of the ways that these efforts to reduce piracy end up affecting legitimate speech is by affecting what sorts of technologies people are allowed to use or develop. One example we've seen for a long time is in the development of peer-to-peer, or P2P, technologies, which by themselves have many legitimate uses. People who want to distribute something cheaply or people who want to make sure that everyone has the latest version of something are among the many reasons to use P2P technologies.

"BitTorrent is a popular example. BitTorrent is a technology and protocol, a lot like email is a protocol, and there are different ways of implementing it. When you're downloading a file, it goes faster for everybody when you download parts of that file from different users who already have parts of the file, because as more people are downloading something, you get a bigger swarm providing these parts. And that's the opposite of the way a centralized server works in that the more people who are trying to get access to something, the slower it goes.

"So there are a lot of people who like that quality when they are legitimately transferring a large file they own. At the same time, people who are trying to distribute free content like that they don't have to pay for all the bandwidth and it's faster if more people use it. So those legitimate users are affected negatively when companies go after BitTorrent as technology because it has been used for piracy.

"The big question is how do you distinguish between legitimate speech and infringement? It's the hard question that underlies this whole debate. And the answer is that there's no technical way to make this distinction, especially when you have to account for uses such as if I bought a DVD or the hardcover version of a book, but now I'm going to be traveling and I don't have the hard copy, so I want to download a copy. A lot of people would view that kind of downloading of something I already bought as somehow less infringing than if you download the most recent best seller because you want to read it.

"But there's no way to distinguish those different uses technically. And so, what we've seen in practice, both with books and previously with music and movies, is that companies go after all the uses of a new technology and let it get sorted out afterwards."

Higgins used the Google Books lawsuit as an illustration of this conflict between the new ways to distribute and consume books—made possible by the new digital technologies—and the old ways of thinking about the buying and sharing of physical books. One problem has been that there is not yet an agreed-upon way to distribute books that satisfies those who want to read books and the authors and publishers who want their books distributed in such a way that they get paid. As Higgins describes it:

"One of the interesting things about the Google Books lawsuit is that it reveals a different understanding between some of the parties involved. What triggered this suit is that Google was digitizing books in the same way that it scans websites. Some of these books are copyrighted works in much the same way that some websites are copyrighted. In both cases, the idea is that we can scan it in order to index it and thereby point people to the right place. Then, maybe they'll actually buy the book, or maybe they'll go and get it from the library.

"But that's not the model that many publishers and authors use when they're thinking about books. While some did agree with Google, many considered that books should be treated like the physical book. It's closed until you buy it or get it from the library, and you don't have full access to what's inside until you buy it or borrow it at the library. Even if you want to just look something up, it's considered bad form to just go into the bookstore and read the part that you're interested in.

"Now, given the new technologies, I think we're going to see a lot more of those changes of models, so that people have a different view on how they want to interact with books. And I think that's what's going to drive the changes in the way people consume books. For example, right now there's no way to subscribe to get the latest paperback in the mail, and maybe the new model for distribution would be something like that, if people would really like to become subscribers. Or maybe the new distribution model for books will be something else entirely. We don't know the best way now, so we need to see people try out these different things to see really what sticks."

Yet, while we may not know the exact new model going forward, Higgins expressed a view shared by a growing number today: Most individuals will want to do what is the fastest and most convenient, while paying a reasonable and fair price for doing so, while using the new technologies. Then, if this happens, the problem of piracy will go away, or at least become very much reduced, since people will be willing to do what's fair. As Higgins noted:

"Whenever you're talking about unauthorized downloading, it's important to keep in mind that some people won't buy something, whether it's cheap and convenient or really hard to download. But those people are not the people to worry about, since they are only a small percentage of the people involved in piracy. There's a much larger percentage of people who will choose the most convenient way to get the best product, and they don't mind paying a fair price for that. So, I think given how hard it is to separate out what we consider good downloading from bad downloading, the real opportunity lies in making legitimate purchases easier, more convenient, and higher quality.

"So instead of trying to decide how to make computers know which users or which downloads are infringing, it would be much better to make it really, really easy for consumers to buy the books they want, and let's make those books as good as anything they can find on the internet. This way, when it's easy, when the price is competitive, and when the quality of the book is good, the problem of piracy will evaporate."

This is the same approach that has worked well for music and movies, Higgins suggests. He believes that some entrepreneur will be the one to come up with the new approach that works, since established companies have too much invested in the way the system works now. As Higgins describes it, this approach makes perfect sense, and it is necessary to do something to embrace change, given the new technologies, since the current models aren't working. As Higgins notes:

"That's what we have seen works well with, for example, with music and movies – (a simple subscription or low-cost purchase model that makes it inexpensive and cheap to pay). There's probably no greater impact on reducing movie downloading than the widespread availability of Netflix. What works about Netflix and makes it take a big bite out of unauthorized downloading is that it has a lot of what viewers want, though still not as much as what it could, and it's available when you want it and it's inexpensive.

"Likewise, you might imagine those same qualities with a little modification applied to the book market. Maybe this new approach will be something like a library, but whoever is going to create the next model for what works for books will create a major transformation in the marketplace. I think we'll see a lot of things not work or only partially work, before we realize that something has definitely worked.

"So that need to experiment with different approaches makes it difficult to imagine that somebody who has a lot invested in the way that things currently work is going to take that risk. You never know, it could happen, but I think we're likely to see the new system come from somebody who is a smaller player. For example, maybe a group of independent authors or self-published authors might figure out something and only realize after it's already been running that it is successful and that it has obviated the problem of unauthorized downloading."

At the same time, still other models might work for other authors, since there is no one-size-fits-all model for everyone. For example, for most authors, the piracy is less of a problem than remaining unknown; piracy might be one more way to help let people know about them and their book, and then they could leverage that into a paying book deal. Or some authors might use ebooks for free download as something of a loss leader, and then turn interest in them into getting speaking engagements or doing book tours to sell hardcover books. So different things may work for different authors as a way to make money. As Higgins comments:

"For the vast majority of authors, nearly more than 90 percent, you haven't heard of them, and I haven't heard of them. The biggest threat they face is that no one will know about their book. They may have experienced a couple of downloads that weren't authorized, but for them, obscurity is a much greater threat than piracy.

"Thus, for such authors, sharing free ebooks may work well. For example, a former EFF employee and now an EFF fellow is the author Cory Doctorow, who makes ebooks available on his website, and then sells hardcover editions. He does book tours where he sells those hardcovers and signs them. And he also gets speaking engagements.

"So not exactly the same precise combination is going to work for everybody, but the same precise combination has never worked for everybody. We'll always have authors who do different things to make money, and for Doctorow, since he makes ebooks available for free download on his website, piracy is not a problem.

"While very few authors have been able to completely eliminate the problem of Internet piracy like this, looking at his model might be an instructive way to go for some authors.

"Thus, in thinking about what comes next, what ends up displacing both unauthorized downloading and the book market today, we need to recognize that the new model will be a lot of different things. There's no reason why the monolith of publishing has to be replaced by a monolith of digital publishing distribution.

"And so we're going to see a lot of different things that work in the future. So the model for book distribution may not look like what we have today, but it will work and it will end up with people getting paid."

Thus, new technologies have brought about the free speech versus piracy conundrum, which could well be resolved by new models providing different approaches to distribution for writers and publishers. So instead of fighting against piracy, there could be new techniques that lead to both sharing and writers and publishers getting paid, as well as spreading information about their books. We won't know exactly which new models will work for a while. But the interview with Higgins has pointed out the need to look for these new models. Some suggestions are provided in the final set of interviews with Sandra Shepard, the intellectual property lawyer, and with Alex Semeny, who has developed an online platform where authors can share their work and get paid whenever anyone downloads what they have written.

CHAPTER 7

Alternate Ways to Monetize Your Writing

GIVEN THE VAST NUMBER OF pirates and the difficulty of combatting the piracy of one's material once a file is copied and shared, it can be difficult to fight back. While takedown notices may stop some pirates, as might lawsuits and criminal charges, that may not be enough to stop additional pirates who pop up like weeds that keep coming back.

Another approach is to find ways to use the pirates to help monetize your writing that leads to other material you have written that is only available for purchase—or use them to help publicize your work to a paying audience. That's the approach of Sandra Shepard, an intellectual property lawyer and strategist based in San Rafael, who commonly finds that after people discover their material has been stolen online, they are eager to sue. Their first questions are: "How can I sue these people?" "How much can I get?" and "How do I get them to pay?"

But her approach is quite different in that she encourages people to use the pirates to gain more attention for other work they can sell. As she explains:

"What I mostly will say to them is that you're looking at piracy from the wrong direction. You really need to try to use the pirates. How can you use them? Well, what you need to do is to think about your digital book as a way to get people to your website."

The goal of this approach is to use a link to your website in this pirated material as a marketing tool to get people to purchase additional material from you, whether you are writing fiction or nonfiction. Shepard explains:

"From a fiction standpoint, say you're writing a book that's based in Hawaii. You might put some links in the manuscript that lead people to your website where they can see the area that you're talking about. And perhaps there are posters by a photographer along with a message that says: 'Hey, if somebody buys these, I'll give you a percentage of them.' Or perhaps your website might lead them to a place where they can buy published books or other materials."

Or if one has a nonfiction book, there could be related products available, as Shepard describes:

"Here's how you might monetize a nonfiction book. Let's say that it's a book on art forgery, and you are going to tell people how to know if something is a real Michelangelo sculpture. So then you say in your writing that a Michelangelo will always have this sort of scratching and other distinctive qualities, but then you say that 'if you want to see what I'm talking about, click on this link and it will take you to my website and I'll show you the difference between a forgery and a non-forgery.'

"Then to monetize that you can do one of two things. Number one, you charge them a little bit to see the video, say thirty cents. Or you surround the images with advertisements that people can click through if they're interested in those things. So there might be an advertisement for an art auction, an advertisement for paint cleaner. In other words, you offer them whatever you have, and your deal with them is that if somebody clicks through from your website, they will pay you a little bit."

Her rationale is that it is virtually impossible to stop the pirates, so you should do what you can to use them for promotional and sales purposes—a kind of "If you can't beat them, join them" approach. Or as she puts it:

"My view as a strategist is that it is very difficult to get the pirates to stop, so why not work with the pirates? Use your book as a loss leader to a certain extent. Obviously make the money where you can make money. However, you can also monetize what the pirates are doing by using them to bring people to your website."

Another way to monetize what the pirates are doing is by mentioning a product after you set up an affiliate link, so that any clicks on that link in a pirated copy of your book bring you income. As Shepard explains:

"Say you're talking about shopping carts, because you're teaching people how to put a website up with a shopping cart. You could put a link to the cart and say: 'Hey, here's a fantastic shopping cart.' Then, if they click on that link in your book, you get a percentage from the shopping cart people. Or set up a link to any products you like. So the whole point here is that it's great if you make some money on the sales of the book. But if pirates take a hundred thousand copies, that's great, too, because you are making money when people click on the links in your book and buy something as a result."

Still another way to monetize a pirated book, Shepard suggests, is to include a link to your website and an incentive to get people to go there, such as by inviting people to go to your website to learn more. Then, once they are there, you can get their email address or other information, say by having them fill out a form. As Shepard points out:

"You want to get people to go to your website to see more, because the most important thing is to gather people's information. If somebody downloads your book, whether they buy it or because they're a pirate, you don't get any of that information.

"Say I download your book from Amazon. You have no idea that I've done that. So you need to capture me, but how do you do this? For that, you need me to go to your website and maybe do an opt-in or something like that to get more information they want. One way to do that is to place at the end of your chapter or in a smaller version of your book a phrase like: 'If you want more information on this, go to my website.' Then, you capture that person there by saying, 'If you want the rest of this information, just give me your email address.' Or you give them a chapter in return for their email address."

The strategy is to give out some information, causing the recipient to want more, but the only way he or she can access it is by providing some personal information or paying for the additional material, or both. As Shepard puts it:

"In other words, the only way you can get whatever this thing is or to get more of it is for you to register on the author's website.

"It's the same kind of approach used on many TV shows. Often a show will try to get people to go to their website, because they want to monetize them. It could be any TV show. Whatever it is, a little announcement comes up on the bottom of the screen that says something like, 'Want to find out more about this? Go to www.cbs.com/underthedome' or 'thebridge' or whatever the name of the show is.

"You can come up with creative ways to get them to sign in at your site. For example, the new *Hawaii Five-0* did a show where they had four different endings. They invited people to go to their website and vote for who they wanted to die. Then, they could win something. And the next week, at the TV show, they showed the ending with the most votes, although they had all the endings on their website. Thus, in this way they were trying to drive people to that website using their *Hawaii Five-0*–related swag and questionnaires to answer in return for an entry.

"So in both cases, the filmmakers are capturing those people with an appeal to do something, such as join their cause, and that's what authors need to do.

"For example, musicians do this all the time with their own music, though you can't take a quote or tiny piece of music you haven't written. But if you wrote that music, you could put a little piece of it out there, like on iTunes, though when you click on iTunes, you only get a minute, or even a few seconds. Likewise, you can put out a short piece to everyone, such as on your Facebook page or YouTube account.

"Then, when a person likes something of yours, you say in an email, 'If you like this and want the rest of it, go to my website.' Then, on your website, they pay you 99 cents and you send them the mp3, CD, DVD, or whatever.

"So again, you are sending a little tiny piece of whatever you are producing creatively as loss leader. Then, you monetize what you would otherwise be selling on the backend."

This approach is very different from the "go after the pirates to defeat them" approach that is common. But in Shepard's view, that approach hasn't worked because it's like the whack-a-mole effort, with an elusive target that keeps coming back again and again. As she explains:

"You would think a lawyer would say, 'Sue the bastards!' to get rid of the pirates or be compensated for their damages. But the whole point of this alternate approach is that going after the pirates is like scooping a bucket out of the ocean. I think that a lot of lawyers and people seem to think that a creative work is like a pie, in that if somebody takes a little piece of the pie, then I don't have that piece of pie anymore. But with copyrighted and digital work, pirating that work is like taking a bucket out of the ocean. But when someone does that, can you even tell? No, you can't. It's not like taking some physical property, because when you take that it's gone. So that's the problem. A pirate can take a copyrighted work online, but it's still there and it's so hard to stop the pirates from doing this. So the next question is how do you monetize it? How can you profit from your creative work other than this way?"

While directing pirates to a website to buy other material might be one approach to monetizing piracy, another is providing an alternate platform where writers can gain compensation, such as a Netflix- or Hulu-type service for books. Still another approach to compensating writers for work that would otherwise be pirated is some kind of application that provides a small payment anytime a particular work is shared. An example of this is the AtContent system described by its co-founder and CEO Alex Semeny:

"AtContent helps bloggers and writers protect their content from plagiarism and piracy outside of their own sites and blogs, so they get compensation for it.

"For example, say you are a writer or blogger, and you have your own blog. There is a problem when a lot of people steal your content, but you know nothing about this audience outside of your blog or website who is reading your content. So you don't know who is in the audience and therefore you don't have any way to control this content or date who's reading it and when. Also you lose the opportunity to build a partnership with these other bloggers who are copying and spread your material, because you don't know who they are.

"So what AtContent does is we allow bloggers to install our special plug-in on their blog and synchronize with our platform. After that, any other person can still illegally post their post to any other site, but with our content duplication, it is like embedding YouTube videos on any other site. And the author of this content then has the ability from another site to update, track, or write about this content on other sites. Plus the author can see the complete statistics and analytics about the audiences on all of these sites.

"So this system is a way of bringing a whole new audience to the author of the content, and it gives him or her total control on this content outside of his or her own site. And he could even use this to contact those reading his material elsewhere, and let them know that he has other available content that they can purchase."

Plus, the AtContent team is developing still other ways that the original content creator can be paid for his work, which are still in the development/testing phase. For example, one approach is to provide a way to pay the author of content for every thousand views. As Semeny explains:

"One way this might work is if the author of an ebook publishes his or her chapter as an article by using Adcontent technology with plagiarism and piracy protection. Then, with this app in place, the other person can legally post the original author's chapter to another blog, and if this chapter gets over one thousand views there, then the person who posted this chapter will pay the author of the ebook for each one thousand views of the material posted. In this way, the person posting the material will have an incentive to make money for him or herself by posting it, and at the same time the author will get paid."

In sum, these different approaches to monetizing pirated content are ways to deal with the seemingly impossible and time-consuming task of stopping the pirates. While some pirates may be put out of operation by the crackdown efforts through law enforcement of litigation, others take their place, and many pirates subjected to restrictions and penalties will find some way to come back again. But through these various strategies of monetization, instead of being victims of piracy, affected individuals can find ways to monetize by getting the pirates to buy other material. This can be material handled through referrals to the author's websites or other content for sale. In addition, low-cost alternatives can make it easier for pirates to simply purchase something legitimately, or authors can create a legal platform for compensation from the poster, who is generally posting this material to make money from the author's work. So it becomes a win-win for the pirates and the author, who is no longer a victim.

PART II

The Problem of
Internet Piracy

CHAPTER 8

A Rebuttal to Book Piracy Advocates and Apologists

Given the arguments previously cited by the researchers and online community members featured in Chapter 5, I wanted to start this discussion of the problem of piracy for writers and publishers (as well as filmmakers and musicians) with this rebuttal to the piracy advocates. For under the cover of claims about how they are actually benefiting writers and publishers, they are taking their work, without any payment to or permission from the writer or publisher whose work has been taken. As noted in Chapters 6 and 7, some individuals have found ways to gain some benefits from piracy, such as by using it to publicize their work and gain more income by directing readers of their purloined work to their website or source of other books for sale. Or they have found work-arounds such as featuring their work on platforms where readers are charged a small amount for each download or streaming of their book.

But whatever they choose to do to freely give away, distribute, or sell their work should be their choice, since they have written or otherwise created the work in the first place. The choice of what to do shouldn't be up to others who pirate their work. The harms to writers and publishers can be very real, despite the claims of benefits to them made by pirates and online sharing communities that pirate their work without the creator's permission. This is true regardless of what they may choose to call themselves, such as researchers and students, and regardless of the arguments they may give about the many benefits to writers and publishers.

Writers and publishers, just like those in the music and film industry, know the harm the pirates are causing. Individuals as well as companies have lost millions of dollars because their work has been pirated, and some individuals are barely surviving because their income from books, records, and indie films has been severely reduced by the thieves who have made their work available for free or for a small payment that doesn't go to them but to the pirates.

Such pirates can wear many hats, from the owners of websites with pirated material to the uploaders and downloaders of copyright-protected work. But whatever their hat, they are violating copyrights and taking away income that belongs to the copyright owners. It is not just a civil violation, but a crime of theft—stealing from the copyright owner, and when multiple files are involved, generally valued at $500 or more, depending on the state, this is grand theft which is a felony (http://en.wikipedia.org/wiki/Grand_theft).

Today the criminals are rarely caught and the crime is barely prosecuted, because intellectual piracy is so rampant, and the police and federal agents have other priorities in violent crime. Also, few civil suits have been filed so far, because of the time and energy involved in going after the pirates. But now there are new efforts to pursue the pirates through both criminal prosecutions and civil litigation, such as a 2010 lawsuit by Wiley and five other publishers against RapidShare, based in Germany, for pirating its books. The lawsuit requires them to monitor its site to ensure that copyrighted material is not being uploaded and prevent unauthorized access to the material by users, or be subject to substantial fines for non-compliance (http://www.wiley.com/WileyCDA/PressRelease/pressReleaseId-69777.html). And Wiley obtained one default judgment against one BitTorrent sharer for its *Word Press for Dummies* book for $7,000 for copyright violation and counterfeiting (http://www.teleread.com/copy-right/john-wiley-sons-wins-default-judgment-in-peer-to-peer-lawsuit), though for the most part, most civil litigation and criminal prosecutions have largely been targeting the pirates of films, music, and software, and the sellers of counterfeit goods.

Though these efforts against the book pirates are still limited, such efforts against intellectual piracy are much needed, because the pirates are doing serious harm to the victims. Some of the other strategies to combat piracy—such as finding other platforms for selling books at a lower price to make pirated books less attractive or using pirated books to direct traffic to one's website to sell other books—might work for some. But they ignore the critical requirement that authors and publishers need to have a choice on how they want to sell or distribute their books, and piracy takes away that option.

It's the distinction between someone choosing to give their property to someone, which is a gift, and someone taking their property without permission, which is theft. Certainly, the pirates have their defenders, primarily other pirates who are hosting, uploading, or downloading copyrighted material without permission. In effect, the uploaders and downloaders are like the receivers of stolen property, who are claiming they have committed no offense by using this stolen property themselves or claiming that they were entitled to take this property, because it is in a file that can be easily duplicated and shared, unlike a physical object. Another argument is that he or she was just making this material available for the common good. Or maybe the pirate cites the familiar refrain that "information wants to be free."

But it doesn't matter how many *mea culpas* or excuses the pirates and their advocates give, including saying that the popularity of pirated books means that writers and publishers should recognize the new model and adapt to it. It is like arguing that just because criminal gangs have gained power in much of Mexico or that ISIS now has taken over certain cities in Iraq, Afghanistan, or Syria, residents should bow to the new overlords who are making the rules. But generally writers and publishers don't want to submit to the pirates; they want to maintain or regain the power to control their work, so unless they give their permission, the pirates have illegally taken their work and infringed on their copyright—a position that law enforcement takes, too, as it seeks to fight back against the pirates, generally by targeting the most active pirates who are doing the most business, and thereby costing writers and publishers the most money.

So now, it's time to counter these common arguments and excuses. Following are the major arguments and rebuttals.

It's not stealing, because people who download free copies of the book wouldn't have bought it anyway.

But that isn't true. There is an inverse relationship between piracy and book sales, meaning that the more a book is pirated, the more the sales go down. For example, in a March 20, 2013, article, "Book Piracy and Me," which is no longer available online, Charles Sheehan-Miles writes, "In each case when a new title has been released *sales dropped* significantly, after the books made it only to the main book pirating sites such as Mobilism, TUEBL and Mobile9." In a March 14, 2013, discussion no longer online, "Online Book Piracy: The Myths and the Facts," A. Giovanni points out the commonly recognized truth reported in multiple studies: "Numerous surveys have come to the same conclusion: piracy causes a drop in actual sales and deprives the authors and publishers of income" (http://voices.yahoo.com/online-bookpiracy-12048507.html).

I have noted this sales drop myself in my declining royalty statements for a number of books, including *A Survival Guide to Working with Humans* and *30 Days to a More Powerful Memory*, both published by AMACOM and widely pirated. On one site, scribd.com, which also has legal content, the books were repeatedly uploaded by multiple users with thousands of downloads. It is unlikely that many of these readers would have bought the book if they weren't offered the chance to get it for free. Certainly, individuals have the option of not buying the book or of borrowing it from a library or a friend. They just don't have my permission to steal it by getting a free pirated copy of my book.

There would be no need for piracy if people could easily buy the book at a low cost.

That's not true either, now that most books are available on Kindle, Smashwords, and various ebook platforms and are priced at around $2.99 to $3.99 for most new books, and some are available for as little as $.99 or nothing, since new books are available for a few months for free through Amazon Prime and authors can elect to post their books there in return for a promotional push. Ebooks represented over a quarter of all book sales in 2013 (http://www.digitalbookworld.com/2014/ebook-growth-slows-to-single-digits-in-u-s-in-2013), up to about 30 percent in 2014 (http://www.forbes.com/sites/jeffbercovici/2014/02/10/amazon-vs-book-publishers-by-the-numbers), and about 50 percent of all Americans own an ebook or tablet (http://www.pewinternet.org/2014/01/16/e-reading-rises-as-device-ownership-jumps). Those who want to read low-cost books can easily do so—and those who don't yet have an e-reader or tablet can buy one for as little as $60 for an Amazon Kindle reader.

Authors should actually thank the pirates for helping to publicize their books.

Absolutely not true either. In some cases, writers have chosen to give away all or sections of their books to publicize them—such as Cory Doctorow, a Canadian sci-fi writer and journalist who has offered many of his books for free through a Creative Commons download (http://en.wikipedia.org/wiki/Cory_Doctorow)—but that's by their own choice. So if writers want to share their book, they can upload the book themselves. But no one else has the right to make that decision for them. While these free offers have gained some writers publicity, particularly when the idea of giving away a book for free was relatively new, generally the publicity value of free pirated books is nil, as Charles Sheehan-Miles notes in his article "Book Piracy and Me," which is no longer online. I found this to be true myself. Despite many thousands of downloads, I never got a single call or email from an author, journalist, or broadcaster about any of my books they had seen on a pirated site. Moreover, as A. Giovanni notes in his article "Online Book Piracy: The Myths and the Facts," which is no longer online, "Publishers establish their own marketing system . . . When books are stolen and resold or given away by thieves, the author and publisher are robbed of their strategy."

Information should be free and sharing is natural on the Internet.

Yes, certainly, a lot of information is given out for free, including material in the public domain and assorted books, papers, and documents that individuals, institutions, and companies contribute to the mix. Also, Wikipedia and other sites that compile these materials are certainly doing a public service. However, if the information is the property of an author or publisher who chooses not to share it freely, then that isn't offered for free. It's the difference between someone who chooses to give away no longer wanted property by putting it in front of their house for anyone to take, and someone who decides to have a garage sale. In the first case, you are free to take what you want; in the second case, anything you take is stealing. Moreover, it shouldn't be the responsibility of writers and publishers to spend their time tracking down their stolen property from hundreds of sites where it might be posted; anyone posting copyrighted material should have to ask for their permission to post it.

If I buy a book, I should be able to share it with others; so why can't I upload it on a file-sharing site?

Here the big difference comes from sharing a physical object versus posting a file of a book that can be duplicated or downloaded hundreds or thousands of times. In the first case, a single object is passed around by friends, family members, or from a library. But sharing a file is akin to becoming a publisher of that book yourself and then giving it to others for free, or in some cases, getting money from those who download it, such as subscribers paying a premium for a multiple-download service. But this is publishing without permission and without paying any money to the original publisher, or to the author who has assigned the copyright to that publisher for the term of publication.

Everyone's doing it and you can't stop it.

As one writer commented in an email to me: "This has been a long ongoing battle for over ten years . . . but I fear there is little anybody can do about Internet piracy. It will always exist in some form. If you look hard enough, you can find pretty much anything . . . and books of all kinds. The huge corporations have not been able to stop it as a whole. There have been some arrests, some sites closed down. But there are always more cropping up with better security. Unless the Internet is policed . . . this is the way it's always going to be, unfortunately."

Still another writer, Dan Graziano, commented in an article "Digital piracy cannot be stopped" (http://bgr.com/2012/08/06/online-piracy-authorities-struggle): "Each day more and more users are turning to peer-to-peer file-sharing websites . . . and online pirates always seem to be one step ahead of the authorities."

However, just because thousands if not millions of people are doing it, that doesn't make stealing anything right. When people text on their phone while driving or cheat on their income tax, the authorities don't look the other way, just because something has become common practice. And if you own a home or a car, you don't leave your door unlocked, because the burglars are likely to get in anyway once they target your house or car. So individuals and the authorities do what they can to keep the criminals from committing their crimes, even though filing lawsuits, making arrests, getting convictions, and sending offenders to prison won't stop the crimes entirely.

In sum, despite the various arguments supporting piracy, it is a crime and a violation of copyright under civil law. Though little has been done to stem the piracy tide, the various efforts to stop it through criminal penalties and civil litigation will at least help to reduce the actions of the pirates to some degree, though an even more active effort is needed to go after the book pirates. Such an approach helped the music and film industry reduce the problem and ultimately develop low-cost alternatives, such as iTunes, Hulu, and Netflix, which have provided a legitimate way to get online content. Now writers and book publishing companies might do the same by ignoring the excuses and apologists for piracy, because these crimes and civil wrongs are costing writers and publishers billions of dollars in lost income. It is time to say *stop the pirates* and ignore those who would give excuses or apologies that encourage piracy to continue.

CHAPTER 9

The Damage of Internet Piracy by the Numbers

DESPITE THE CLAIMS OF THE "researchers," "students," and other piracy explainers, defenders, and supporters, piracy has resulted in major damages. In fact, the fallout from the Sony hacking upheaval shows just how damaging a piracy attack can be; a hack to steal books, music, films, software, or anything else can readily turn into the theft of other information, such as internal memos, employee data, and financial records. So this is all the more reason why the battle against Internet piracy can reach far beyond just protecting individual works by writers and publishers from theft.

While most pirating theft takes the form of uploading copyrighted material onto websites without permission, it could easily take the form of hacking this material from targeted computers, such as those of publishers or high-profile writers. Then the hackers could go even further to look for personal and financial information. We are now in the age of cyberwarfare, as shown by the hacker attack that has been attributed to North Korea. Two days after that, North Korea's own Internet system went down, whether in direct retaliation from US hackers on the instructions of US intelligence operatives, or maybe they just went down. At this writing it's hard to know—only that the Sony hack and the downing of the Internet in North Korea shows what is possible, whether to gain an advantage in war or in commerce. Writers and publishers can just as easily become the targets should piracy shift from illegal downloading, uploading, and website postings to directly finding files to pirate on the computers of anyone connected to the Internet in any way.

But that's a potential threat for the future. Here's a look at the damages of piracy by the numbers. The numbers vary based on how the data is sliced and diced by different sources and for different time periods, but they present a frightening picture of the extent of damage to individuals and companies and to the economy as a whole. While most of this damage is to film, music, and software companies—who have taken the most aggressive stance in fighting back themselves or with the help of law enforcement—the numbers portray the devastation wreaked in the publishing industry, too.

For example, in the article "Piracy's Ripple Effect on the Global Economy," Wayne Scholes, CEO of Red Touch Media based in Utah, outlines the way piracy spread from the music industry to affect all content creators.[1] As he points out, approximately 2.4 million US employees, including technicians, editors, producers, and camera operators, make up the entertainment industry, which contributes approximately $80 billion each year to the US economy. But that number is "nowhere close to what it should be," since it is estimated that 750,000 jobs have been lost due to online piracy.

Such piracy has become rampant, with free online file-sharing services stepping in to fill the consumer demand for digital content since it became a mass market about fifteen years ago. And so now about 70 percent of online users don't see illegal downloading as a form of theft. Rather, online "theft" has become so pervasive, especially of music and films, that many consumers have come to expect getting free content online. In fact, according to Scholes, "95 percent of online music downloads are illegal, and the average mobile phone, iPod, or tablet contains $800 worth of pirated content."[2]

The devastation to the music industry, beginning with the introduction of Napster in 1999, started the piracy incursion, like pirates getting a foothold on a spit of land and then spreading outward from there to undermine the economy of one country after another. As Scholes notes, before Napster, global music sales were over $38 billion. But even after Napster was shut down, music revenues continued to drop over the next decade, until 2012 when they went up 3 percent due to iTunes and Amazon providing a way to buy legal content for a small sum that provided a more convenient alternative to stealing it. Even so, the music industry's sales are less than half what they were in 1999, since they are about $16.5 billion a year.[3]

Likewise, the cost to the film and software industry is in the multibillions, facilitated by the development of file-sharing services like Bit-Torrent, which permitted users to share larger files. For instance, in 2010, pirates downloaded over 17 million copies of James Cameron's film *Avatar*, and even though some content distribution services like Netflix, iTunes, Amazon, and Epix have created a way to access films and videos legally, piracy has continued to make up a large percentage of the content online, costing the US economy about $250 billion a year. And this is not only the cost to the companies owning the content, but to the hundreds of thousands of people who lose their jobs.

In another study called "Sizing the Piracy Universe" conducted by NetNames, a British brand protection firm for NBCUniversal in 2013, it was found that in January 2013, 432 million users infringed on copyrighted material, an increase of 10 percent from 2011.[4] The study also found that 76 percent of the infringing users—327 million of them—came from North America, Europe, and Asia-Pacific, where approximately one quarter of the Internet users in those areas—over 300 million people—infringed on copyright materials at least once.[5] Another startling finding was that about one-fourth of the total bandwidth used by all Internet users—9567 petabytes—was for infringing content.[6] Or expressed another way, almost a quarter—23.76 percent—of all Internet traffic, apart from pornography, was infringing copy.[7]

Still other findings by NetNames have shown the trend for peer-to-peer distribution systems to increase, while direct-download cyberlockers have declined. As Richard Verrier reports in a January 2012 *Los Angeles Times* article, "Online Piracy of Entertainment Content Keeps Soaring," the Megaupload direct-download cyberlocker (the one famously run by Kim Dotcom who is still fighting the government) was closed due to the actions of international law enforcement. The result was that many other major direct-download cyberlocks closed or changed the way they operated to avoid a similar takedown. So the number of visitors declined by 8 percent to 149 million from November

2011 to January 2013, while the number of pages they viewed dropped 41 percent to 2.3 billion. But at the same time, the page views on the BitTorrent websites using a peer-to-peer distribution system increased, suggesting that they were taking up the slack as users switched from downloading to file sharing. As Verrier notes, in January 2013, these BitTorrent websites had 7.4 billion page views, up 31 percent from November 2011, while the video streaming sites increased 34 percent to 4.2 billion page views in the same period.

While government officials—such as Sen. Orrin Hatch of Utah, co-chairman of the International Anti-Piracy Caucus—have agreed that online piracy has been weakening the economy, piracy has become so common in the entertainment field that some legitimate video-streaming websites are studying what the pirates are doing to better compete with them. For example, Netflix monitors the file-sharing platforms to see what is most popular to decide what to buy, since according to CEO Reed Hastings, some illegal file-sharing "creates the demand for content that is available on legal download platforms."[8]

While the publishing industry hasn't been as hard hit financially as the music, film, and software industries, simply because publishing income is much less, the level of piracy for books, especially for best sellers, is huge, contributing to large income losses for both publishers and writers. For instance, a study of book piracy on Kindle conducted by PiracyTakeDown (www.piracytakedown.com), as reported by Shota on May 13, 2014, 63 percent of the top thirty bestsellers were pirated by being distributed over cyberlockers or torrent.[9] And here are some more recent numbers from a Global Post article from April 2014:[10]

- According to one of the biggest studies conducted by Musicmetric in 2012, the United States and Australia have the most pirates. The US had the highest number of downloads per country— more than 96.8 million downloads in just six months—while Australia had the highest number downloads per capita.

- The US economy has been losing $12.5 billion in revenues and other economic measures each year due to online piracy in the music industry, based on estimates by the Institute for Policy Innovation.[11] This number would be even greater if the other heavily impacted industries were included in the study—most notably the film, software, and publishing industries.

- Over 146 million visits occurred each day at forty-three of the world's digital piracy sites, such as RapidShare.com, in 2011, according to a report commissioned by the US Chamber of Commerce.

- In the decade since the peer-to-peer file-sharing site Napster was created in 1999, music sales in the US dropped 47 percent to only $7.7 billion, according to the Recording Industry Association of America. In 1913, the most pirated musician was Bruno Mars, who experienced nearly 5.8 million downloads of his music, according to Musicmetric.

- The computer software industry has been especially hard hit. About 42 percent of the software used worldwide was pirated in 2010, resulting in the illegal downloading of about $59 billion in software, according to a major Business Software Alliance study.

- Some of the most popular films were also the most heavily downloaded. For example, the *Game of Thrones* season four premiere was downloaded illegally more than one million times, according to the piracy tracking website Torrent Freak. The most downloads occurred in Australia, followed by the United States and the United Kingdom. In 2013, the most illegally downloaded movie was *The Hobbit: An Unexpected Journey*, which was downloaded over eight million times, followed by *Django Unchained* and *Fast and Furious 6*, also according to a TorrentFreak report.

- Another big consumer of pirated materials is Spain. According to an April 2014 study by La Coalición, a Spanish industry lobby group, 50 percent of the Internet users in Spain illegally obtained digital content, and 84 percent of the content consumed in Spain was illegal. The pirates were especially partial to films, followed by music, books, and video games.

Finally, here are some numbers for ebook piracy developed by the web hosting blog "Who Is Hosting This?"[12]

- The ebook pirate sites library.nu and iFile.it had an annual revenue of $10 million, until they were closed down in 2012.

- Ebooks represent about 22.5 percent of books sold to consumers today, and 76 percent of the digital content for academic use is available for free from pirate sites.[13] About 25 percent of all ebooks in the US are copied or downloaded for free, while 75 percent are bought and paid for. About 31 percent of ebook owners got their ebook for free, compared to the 69 percent who purchased all of their ebooks.

In sum, as these numbers show, piracy is a major problem in all of the fields offering digital creative content. Even if something doesn't start out in a digital format, such as a hardcover or paperback book, it can be readily scanned and become a part of the digital universe. In turn, there are serious economic costs involved for individual writers and publishers and for the many jobs lost in these industries, due to the loss of income sustained by the companies, resulting in reduced operations. While individually, some writers may claim they have gained from their work being made available for free—such as blogger, journalist, and sci-fi author Cory Doctorow, and Paulo Coelho, author of *The Alchemist*, who was selling one thousand copies a year before he personally released a pirated Russian version that resulted in sales exploding to ten million a year—on balance, as these numbers show, piracy is a serious economic threat.

No wonder even President Obama has expressed support for efforts to go after piracy. Obama nominated a new "piracy czar" in August 2014, Danny Marti, a copyright and trademark attorney in Washington, DC, to the Intellectual Property Enforcement Coordinator post, established in 2008 to coordinate the administration's policy on intellectual property and piracy. Obama ultimately backed off from supporting the Stop Online Piracy Act of 2012, supported by the Hollywood studios and the MPAA to help shut down foreign websites and file-sharing sites that facilitate piracy, primarily of music and movies. He withdrew support because of the blowback from web companies and Internet freedom activists who felt the bill could restrict the web by destroying the fundamental openness of the Internet and prevent future Internet companies, like Facebook and eBay, from getting on the ground.[14] A key reason for choosing him has been to show the administration's support for a position that derives from the creation of the office in 2008 to fight piracy, a position considered increasingly important to support "the millions of workers who comprise the country's $1 trillion copyright economy."[15]

This battle against piracy has become a major struggle of our times. A vast number of pirates are making available trillions of dollars of copyrighted material worldwide for free, undermining the incomes of millions of creative content developers and thousands of companies offering creative materials. At the same time, the forces seeking to prevent piracy are up against millions of users who are downloading, sharing, or purchasing pirated copyrighted materials and feel there is nothing wrong with doing so. For example, reflecting similar numbers in other countries, 70 percent of online users in Denmark indicated that they believe there is nothing wrong with piracy, according to a Rockwood Foundation Research Unit study.[16]

Thus the numbers illustrating the problem, as well as those who don't think it's a problem, are clear. The following chapters will describe in more detail the extent and impact of piracy around the world and in the United States, and discuss what might be done about it as a society, as well as what individuals can do when their own work has been pirated.

CHAPTER 10

The Worldwide Epidemic of Book Piracy

BOOK PIRACY IS AN EPIDEMIC affecting writers and publishers in countries around the world. That's why law enforcement efforts are involving agencies worldwide, as in the Kim Dotcom Megaupload case, in which the FBI recruited the assistance of the New Zealand police to arrest the key operators in order to shut down the operation. Likewise, the people uploading and downloading pirated files are located around the world. So it doesn't matter where a locker, storage facility, server, or provider service is located. The offenders, like the victims, are located everywhere, and now, as awareness of the problem is growing, law enforcement agencies are mobilizing globally to fight the problem. So are governments in many countries, because they recognize the threat to their own economies, as the pirates syphon out income from creators and companies selling their work.

While law enforcement and civil litigation has generally only been able to target the biggest offenders, other regulations and policy changes may have more effect, such as sending takedown notices to the web-hosts, so they don't get shut down for aiding and abetting the pirates, and companies not advertising on identified piracy sites. It may also be possible for Google and other search engines to block access to these domains on their servers, so people can't find these pirate sites unless they have a correct IP address and use another server that doesn't block the domain.

Although piracy and "information should be free" advocates decry the growing Internet piracy crackdown by law enforcement and litigation, these efforts are needed to counteract the growing piracy explosion that could destroy the very industries now losing billions in earnings for individuals and companies worldwide. The problem is much like game poaching because of the high profits the poachers and their buyers can make, such as in killing elephants for their tusks. For a time the poachers and buyers can literally make a killing; but then the population of animals victimized by poaching declines, so they become an endangered species. Though that can initially make the proceeds from poaching even greater, because of the reduced supply, if poaching continues, the species can die out completely. This kills off not only the game, but the income from poaching that species.

So it is with the worldwide piracy of books, as well as music, films, and other intellectual property. At some point, the writers of pirated books may stop writing because they are not earning enough to sustain them, or publishers will no longer offer them contracts because their books aren't selling well enough to justify it. And many companies will go under, since they can't survive the lower earnings, resulting in even fewer books from mainstream publishers. It's a matter of simple economics and survival. As the pirates become more pervasive and powerful in making pirated books available, and more and more people worldwide upload and download pirated files, writers and publishers are doomed to earn less and less, and may choose to write or publish less and less.

Worldwide Piracy by the Numbers

This danger of piracy worldwide—indicating the need for an organized, global counterattack by law enforcement—is evident in recent articles and stats on worldwide book piracy.

For example, in an article about piracy in Russia from an author who discovered his book was being translated by a rogue translator, Peter Mountford describes how pirated books reportedly comprise up to 90 percent of Russian ebook downloads. As he explains: "According to Rospechat, the state agency that regulates mass media, Russians have access to more than 100,000 pirated titles and just 60,000 legitimate titles, with illegal downloads costing legitimate vendors several billion rubles a year."[17]

Or take what is happening in Africa. While Ebola and other contagious diseases there have been getting massive press coverage and have helped to illustrate the connectedness of all countries in today's global world, the extent of book piracy in Africa is largely unknown, but similarly pervasive.

For example, here's an article about book piracy in the schools of Uganda, where several schools have even connived with book pirates to provide books for less than half the price for the legitimate publisher. As described in an article in the *Observer*, "Schools Accused of Abetting Book Piracy" by Moses Talemwa, some schools collaborating with the pirates tell the parents there is a list of books needed that can only be acquired at a special price at the school. Then, the pirates buy a genuine copy of the book, scan it into a computer, reprint it, and sell it, mostly to the schools at a lower price than the genuine article. And often there is little difference between the real and pirated book, though sometimes the pirated copies have unclear print, missing pages, or upside-down pages. But even so, many parents are unbothered by the difference, claiming they would rather buy the cheaper, often-pirated copy, as long as it has the same information.[18] The result is that the publishers could be losing 90 percent of their proceeds from book publishing, so they have started to fight back. One way is with the help of the East African Educational Publishers (EAEP), which has joined with some of the bigger publishers to print flyers for the bookshops and schools to describe the program. Also, the police, working with the Uganda Intellectual Rights Organization, launched a campaign in which the wares and printers of several pirates were seized. In addition, the publishers signed a memorandum of understanding for the Uganda Revenue Authority to not clear pirates who print their books outside of the country, such as Kenya. And they are appealing to the schools and parents to buy genuine books to support the publishing industry. And that's just one problem with printed books.

In Somalia, the piracy problem is made even worse because of the country's lack of copyright control and professional publishing houses. As a result, as described in the News Blaze story "Somalia: Book Piracy

Kills Author Creativity" by Mohamed Abdullahi Abubakar, "if you publish a book in Somalia, within a short period of time, you see your book
copied and republished hugely without your permission."[19]

In Zimbabwe, the piracy problem is exacerbated because of a large
community of street vendors selling books, especially textbooks. In
turn, parents and students are drawn to buying these much cheaper
books. It operates by an anonymous supplier who owns the copying
and binding machines and sells a high volume of photocopied books at
a much lower price than the original. Plus, many books are published
abroad. And then, keeping costs down even more, often these books
are sold through an open-air market, and many are sold on the side-
walks. Though some vendors justify their business on the grounds they
are educating the nation and contributing to the literacy of the country,
authors find they are not receiving royalties on these book sales, and the
publishers are, of course, losing the income they would normally get for
these books to the pirates.[20]

The devastation wrought to the local authors and book publishers is
described in stark terms by Vincent Gono in the *Sunday News* article
"Piracy Hits Local Book Industry." As he writes:

"The proliferation of pirate activities in the country is heavily
threatening the book industry with massive reproduction of both
fiction and nonfiction books with reckless abandon.

"The illegally reproduced books are later sold on the streets while
authors and publishers wallow in poverty as they get nothing for
their intellect . . .

"As a result, the authors were becoming increasingly reluctant to
write while publishing companies were also collapsing. Bookshops
are also not spared the agony as they are facing stiff competition
from the illegal but booming street business.

"Rampant book piracy has led to the closure of publishing houses
such as Longman and College Press as well as bookshops throwing
hundreds of workers onto the streets where they are exposed to the
vagaries of the harsh economy.

"In the absence of action from stakeholders and law enforcement
agents, the book industry would continue to suffer and buckle
under the weight of piracy and in the process the country would be

losing various revenue avenues and could soon become an importer of books."[21]

In fact in Zimbabwe, as in Uganda, the schools were actively contributing to the piracy problem. In Zimbabwe it was even conducted within the schools, in that some schools were encouraging the violation of copyright laws by purchasing their own large photocopying machines for reproducing academic books as well as allowing students to copy these books.[22]

In Nigeria, book piracy has resulted in domestic publishing houses losing $125 million each year, according to the chairman of a Nigerian publishing company. The result, according to the president of the Nigerian Publishers Association (NPA), Ngwobia Okereke, is that book piracy is the major problem threatening the book industry in Nigeria. He urged the government to increase the enforcement of copyright laws, such as by using special algorithms to detect illegal downloads, security printing devices, and moral suasion to convince people not to engage in piracy.[23] One of the major sources of piracy, as in many other countries, is the schools who obtain their books from a pirate rather than the publishing company, as one author's rep found. When he approached some schools to supply them the books, he learned they had gotten the same book from someone else. Then, he filed a report with the anti-copyright commission that someone had pirated the book.[24]

In Kenya, the threat of piracy to the Kenya book industry was a major topic of discussion at the annual Nairobi International Bookfair, organized by the Kenya Publishers Association (KPA) in September 2014. The business of the publishers was down, in part by the high cost of books and the value-added tax under the VAT Act, which added a 16 percent tax to school study materials. But mostly the concern was about the devastating effects of piracy on the industry, resulting in billions of dollars annually—an estimated $2 billion in 2011 and expected to increase even more due to the increasing use of digital technology.[25]

Still other countries reporting the devastation of piracy and the difficulties of combatting it include Poland, the UAE, Korea, Hong Kong, the Philippines, and Peru. Here are some highlights from these reports:

- According to a study for the broadband industry group Syngal, the Polish economy loses up to PLN 700 million a year due to illegal downloads of video content, which is twice the Ministry of Culture's annual budget. The study further found that 20 percent of all Poles and 30 percent of Internet users used websites allowing them illegal access to video content. About 400–500 million illegal film streams were accessed each year, as well as 650–750 million episodes of TV programs and 150–180 million sporting events. Why so much? Because users liked the wide range of free content, so they did so, even though 77 percent of the users said they realized their activities were illegal.[26]

- According to a report by the Korean Film Council (KOFIC), the costs of online film piracy are estimated to be $3.3 billion or KW3.75 trillion won, a year. During the period from February to April 2013, an average of 2,322 films illegally circulated each month on ninety-three online storage and sharing sites.[27]

- In Hong Kong, the comic book industry and its writers are struggling against apps and websites that offer their material, usually scanned, from the original for free rather than buying the more expensive individual copies. As an article in the *South China Morning Post* describes: "The stream of free content has been devastating for local comic publishers, particularly those reprinting Japanese manga." For example, as reported by the director of the Hong Kong Comics and Animation Federation, at the height of the popularity of comics in the 1990s, a single issue might sell over two hundred thousand copies. But now even the more popular comics don't sell more than twenty thousand copies—a huge drop, and a new comic might sell less than one thousand copies.[28]

- In Lima, Peru, much of the pirated book market consists of sales on the street and in bookstores that sell mostly pirated books. For example, one street in downtown Lima, Jiron Quilca, is one of the major hubs of pirated books, where they are sold by dozens of shops, though sometimes they are sold along with used books and even some legitimate copies. They are also sold by street vendors, on highway stands, inside markets, and on the city's most popular beaches. The books are produced on old presses in illegal workshops throughout the city's low-income areas, and unlike digital files, which are easily reproduced and uploaded, sometimes they suffer from being printed on cheap paper with cheap binding, and sometimes the text is even crooked or whole chapters are missing. The extent of this vast enterprise is shown by the fact that Peru's pirated book publishers employ more workers than do legal publishers, and it is estimated that they cause the industry $52 million in losses each year. And so far the authorities have made little headway. For example, after hearing about the extensive piracy, Peru's intellectual-property protection agency INDECOPI sought to fight the book pirates and get illegal copies off the streets. But even after raids on informal booksellers by officials, the shopkeepers were able to resupply their popular pirated books within days.[29]

- In Indonesia the problem was much the same, with piracy especially appealing to students because of the high cost of college books and the need to get pirated books to support their studies. So even though the pirated books could easily be indicated by the slightly blurry text and black and white pictures, any raids on the bookstores to confiscate pirated books proved generally useless. It didn't matter if they confiscated the pirated books and fined the booksellers, such as one seller who lost books worth about 500,000 Rp after a raid on behalf of the Jakarta Chapter of the Association of Indonesian Publishers (IKAPI and had to pay a fine of 2.5 million RP after two days in jail). The pirates simply provided the booksellers with more books. As the chairman of the IKAPI, Hikmat Kurnia, put it: "Raiding book stalls is expensive, and the police cannot initiate the measure because piracy is only considered a crime if someone reports it to the police."[30]

There is even a website devoted to keeping track of these global piracy stats: Havocscope, a website dedicated to global black market information. For example:

- In the UK, over a three-month period ending in January 2013, almost 400 million digital files were pirated by Internet users. These pirated ebooks make up 29 percent of all book downloads in the UK. In 2011, publishers issued 115,000 legal notices to websites offering free pirated copies of books, an increase of 130 percent from the number of notices sent out in 2010.[31] And the worst book pirates are the students, according to an online data-monitoring company, NetNames. When the company looked at the availability of fifty popular textbooks in different fields of study in the UK, they found that 76 percent of the titles were available to download for free from one ebook sharing site. Of these, the science and engineering books were the most pirated, mainly because of the high costs of these books, though piracy of films and music is far greater.

- In Spain, electronic book piracy caused the book industry to lose up to $467 million in income—nearly 12 percent of its total revenue, according to the Federation of Publishers' Associates and the ISBN Agency of Spain.

- In Russia, as of 2012, over one hundred thousand ebooks were available on book piracy websites, compared to sixty thousand available on legitimate websites, according to Russia's Press and Communications Agency. The problem is especially severe there, since as much as 90 percent of the ebook market in Russia is made up of pirated books.

- In Pakistan, the government loses up to $221 million in tax revenue due to pirating of intellectual property in the country.

- An estimated 20 percent of all ebooks downloaded onto e-readers were believed to have been pirated in 2011—a percentage that has certainly increased since then.

- In Peru, more pirated copies of books were sold than legitimate books, and the pirated books publishing industry employs more people than does the legal book industry.

- In Chile, from 2011 to 2013 authorities seized over 362,000 pirated books, mostly children's books and literature books, valued at $1.5 million from stores across the country. Increasingly, textbooks are being pirated due to the much lower costs. For example, the main textbook used in health programs in universities throughout Chile is *Atlas of Human Anatomy*, but at $200 a pop for a legitimate textbook, the $35 cost for the pirated books makes for a hard-to-resist bargain. In fact, the trade in pirated books is so great there that smugglers from Peru brings in books strapped to their bodies like drug mules.[32]

- In Germany, the book industry has reported that 60 percent of all ebooks downloaded were pirated in 2011. At the time, the ebook market was only a tiny percentage of the market—but now ebook readership has zoomed worldwide, so ebook piracy is even more of a problem (http://www.havocscope.com/tag/book-piracy).

And one of the worst of the countries for piracy is Australia. For example, according to statistics released by TorrentFreak and reported in the article "Australia Extends Global Internet Piracy Lead," published on Delimiter, "Australia has dramatically extended its lead over other countries when it comes to the levels of Australians pirating popular US television shows." As one example, the series finale of the AMC show *Breaking Bad* was downloaded more than five hundred thousand times in twelve hours after the first copy appeared online, and based on a sample of over ten thousand people who shared the site, Australians represented 18 percent of the total, with the US (14.5 percent) and UK (9.3 percent) second and third, and India (5.7 percent) and Canada (5.1 percent) fourth and fifth. In another TorrentFreak study, Australians were the most prolific pirates of the popular show *Game of Thrones*.[33] In fact, there almost seems to be a perverse pride among Australians in having the title of most pirates, or as one Australian news site put it: "Let's face it Australia. We're a nation of pirates. Figures show that we are among the worst in the world when it comes to illegally downloading TV shows and movies."[34] In fact, a further analysis showed that the city of Melbourne had the greatest percentage of pirates, followed by Athens and then Sydney.[35]

However, a key factor influencing piracy in Australia is the higher taxes there, compared to the United States, for digital products such as movies, music, software, and games. Overall, they are 50 percent higher in Australia than other countries, leading Australians to feel they are getting ripped off. Many seek to circumvent geo-blocks leading to higher prices being selectively charged in different countries, as well as use file-sharing websites like TorrentFreak for illegal downloading, such as downloading 1.5 million copies of *Game of Thrones* in twelve hours after the finale of its latest season.[36]

In short, the piracy problem worldwide is pervasive and growing, and it threatens to not only destroy the writers and publishers who are victimized, but take away tax funds from the governments that would otherwise collect taxes on the sale of books, were they not pirated. Individually, writers and publishers can do little in the face of the growing pirate menace besides sending out takedown notices, which are often ignored or the book is soon replaced or access is activated again. That's why, in response, law enforcement agencies around the world are increasingly organizing to take action, while a growing number of companies have initiated litigation against the biggest offenders. Now, since there are more and more pirates, such efforts are increasingly needed to take down the biggest offenders and keep the piracy scourge from spreading even more.

The Worldwide Efforts to Stop Piracy

Unfortunately, not only do the statistics show the extent of piracy in undermining the publishing industry and writers—as well as sapping billions from the music and film industries and the economy as a whole—but the efforts to combat it seem to have little effect. Despite some notable arrests, fines, and website takedowns, there exists the widespread practice and acceptance of piracy. Pirates continue to pop up again or others take their place, and the problem continues. But with that caveat, here are examples of how different countries have sought to combat book and other forms of piracy:

- The Philippines has started to crack down on piracy both for books sold in the schools and to consumers. A key reason for the crackdown is that US publishers have been restricted from marketing their textbooks and print books there because of the sanctions imposed by the United States Trade Representatives 301 Report, which has created trade barriers due to extensive abuses of intellectual property laws there, including the piracy of copyrighted books. As a result, for the first time in twenty years, due to the anti-piracy measures of the Intellectual Property Office and National Book Development Board, the US has removed the Philippines from its 301 list. Yet, even so, the Philippines has a big hurdle to completely stopping piracy because of the general acceptance and the practice of organized crime in photocopying and scanning complete textbooks and selling them directly to schools, colleges, and universities. While these institutions are aware that they may be buying some pirated books, it is hard to tell the difference.[37]

- The UAE has similarly sought to cut down on book piracy in the schools. It did so through the Abu Dhabi Department of Economic Development (DED), which instituted the first-ever campaign against book piracy in the region in the schools by conducting inspections to see if pirated books were being used there. The result was the discovery and seizing of pirated books that violated the UAE copyright law. In support of the campaign, the Deputy CEO of the Arabian Anti-Piracy Alliance (AAA), Ola Khudair, had this to say: "The degraded quality of the pirated books severely affects the students' ability to maintain the text books for an average life period during the term, as well puts unwanted burden on the parents to repeatedly buy the books. The Publishers put in a lot of efforts to develop content of text books and pirates steal these text books without any return to the Publishers for investing into the development of the text books."[38]

- In July 2014, the Australian government developed a plan to crack down on Australians engaging in online piracy, which has been costing right holders around $1.4 billion a year,[39] by increasing the liability of Internet service providers for copyright infringement and introducing an anti-piracy Internet filter, although such measures have proven ineffective against piracy in other countries and simply made it more expensive for consumers to obtain copyrighted material.[40] And then in October, the Australian Parliament passed legislation for mandatory data retention whereby telecommunications companies would be forced to retain customer data that could be used by rights holders to "hunt down Australians who are alleged to have downloaded copyright infringing TV shows, films, or movies," which could be used both by law enforcement agencies for investigating crimes and civil investors looking into online copyright infringement. Under this legislation, the rights holders could seek court injunctions ordering ISPs to block overseas websites hosting pirated material.[41] The copyright owners would pay their own costs for identifying the infringers and advising the Internet service providers, while the providers would pay the costs of matching the IP addresses in the infringement notices, sending out notices to subscribers, and mitigating the offense through the necessary technical measures.[42] In December 2014, still more changes were proposed by Australian Attorney-General George Brandis and Communications Minister Malcolm Turnbull to block Australians from accessing overseas websites hosting pirated movies and shows.[43] Yet, even these penalties weren't enough for the companies that own the rights to movies and TV shows, since they wanted even tougher laws and punitive penalties, including restricting any Internet users caught downloading illegal content to slower download speeds.[44]

In the meantime, some film companies in Australia, as in other countries, have been coming up with their own strategies to discourage piracy, such as releasing movies more quickly and more cheaply to discourage pirating. This is a strategy that Village Roadshow decided after it discovered it had made a big mistake in delaying the release of *The Lego Movie*, which was made in Australia, until after it was released in the United States in order to coincide with the local school holidays. But this window allowed time for the pirates to readily download it.[45] So they felt lower prices and a faster release would provide an incentive for consumers to get their material legally. In fact, as argued by former chairman of the Australian Competition and Consumer Commission Allen Fels—and an expert panel member chosen by the government for its cost-benefit analysis of the National Broadband Network, Henry Ergas—the government efforts to target illegal downloading would increase the price that copyright holders can charge, thereby "making legitimate consumers worse off, which in turn increases the incentive for piracy, offsetting the effects of stricter enforcement." Plus, this government crackdown on pirates would discourage companies from investing in more innovative ways to distribute their content, such as by investing in online video-on-demand services.[46]

In turn, some consumer advocates, such as Alan Kirkland, the CEO of Choice, Australia's leading consumer advocacy organization, have argued that the solution to stopping piracy is not to engage in expensive schemes to block websites. Instead, the providers should make it easier for Australians who want to pay for quality content to do so. As Kirkland argues, the big Hollywood studios and big companies like Foxtel, a major distributor of films in Australia, are trying to get laws that protect their outdated business models by aggressively going after the pirates at the expense of Australian consumers by keeping the price high. Though it is possible for TV content to be delivered instantly over the Internet, this option is "not available, or not available at a fair price" for consumers. As Kirkland writes:

"The government is consulting on laws to try to stop online piracy, but its proposals don't actually address the reasons people download content without paying. The laws being considered involve introducing an industry-run internet filter—where ISPs will be required to block some sites. In addition, they'll make internet service providers responsible for policing alleged illegal downloading occurring on their services.

"These laws will create costs for all users of internet services, whether they download illegally or not. To implement a filter system, ISPs will need to increase expenditure on infrastructure to support the policy. Policing downloads and serving users with "warning notices" also has costs . . ..

"More importantly, international experience with these kinds of laws shows that they don't work to stop piracy . . . . Artists and creators deserve to be paid for their hard work. I do not support piracy at all. But if we want to stop piracy, we need to address the real causes of piracy by giving Australians more options for watching television or listening to music."[47]

In Canada, an anti-piracy firm has started targeting Canadians who download pirated materials. The suits have been launched by Canipre, based in Montreal, the only anti-piracy enforcement firm in Canada. After monitoring the Canadian users downloading pirated materials for several months, it has obtained over one million evidence files, and one of its clients, Voltage Pictures, the producer of hundreds of films including *The Hurt Locker*, has taken its case to the Federal Court in Toronto. The company has sought customer information for over one thousand IP addresses from TekSavvy, an Ontario-based Internet provider whose users have the IP addresses flagged by Canipre. Should Tek-Savvy be forced to hand over its customer information, this will help to fuel the battle against the Internet pirates, and according to its managing director Barry Logan, Canipre has a "long list of clients waiting to go to court." However, unlike the US, where between 200,000 and 250,000 people have been sued over piracy in a two-year period from 2011–2013 with a potential of $150,000 in damages, the compensation in Canada is much less. Canada has a limit of $5,000 under Bill C-11 for non-commercial copyright infringement, which applies to the average individual who downloads films or other protected material for their own personal use, since Parliament has not wanted the courts to be used for such litigation. But now that could change, given the huge culture of piracy—about 370,000 BitTorrent transactions in a month for Canipre's clients alone, many of which are used for duplicating copyrighted material. Canipre's approach is to conduct what it calls an "aggressive takedown campaign," where it searches for its clients' content on websites where pirated content is known to be available. Then, it sends out a massive series of takedown requests—one thousand to two thousand at a time. Besides seeking to sue people, this approach is designed to provide an educational message to "change the sense of entitlement that people have regarding Internet-based theft of property. On strategy is the "file saturation" method, where the company uploads a harmless file to sharing websites that is similar to the file the individual is looking for, except it is completely useless, with a goal of making it harder and more time consuming to download copyrighted material illegally.[48]

In the UK, a new police unit under the direction of the City of London Police has been set up to tackle online piracy, along with other forms of intellectual property crime, such as counterfeit goods. One of the first of its kind in the world, the unit was set up by the Intellectual Property Office with £2.5 million in funding. The hope is to combat the increasing threat of online intellectual property crime to the UK's creative industries, which are worth over £36 billion a year and employ over 1.5 million people. And the potential for loss is huge, since about seven million people visit sites with illegal content in the UK per month. Globally it is projected that piracy will account for about $240 billion by 2015, and about 250,000 jobs could be at risk according to the 2010 TERA Report from the Creative Coalition. Or as the Commissioner of the City of London Police, Adrian Leppard, put it, the reason for setting up the unit is that "Intellectual property crime is costing the UK economy hundreds of millions of pounds each year, with organised crime gangs causing significant damage to industries that produce legitimate, high quality, physical goods and online and digital content in an increasingly competitive climate."[49]

Besides the government setting up a police unit, a private effort by the entertainment industry and UK Internet service providers has also been launched to combat Internet piracy. Under this approach, the major British ISPs will send "educational" letters to people suspected of illegal downloading to let them know how films, software, music, and books can be downloaded through more official channels. Starting in 2013, these major providers, including BT, Sky, TalkTalk, and Virgin Media, will send out a series of four alerts, using increasingly harsh language. The approach is similar to what is used in both the United States and New Zealand, except there is no further action after the fourth letter. In New Zealand, there is a three-strikes law, whereby the illegal downloader can be subjected to fines of up to £7,600, and in the United States, a six-strike campaign involved its five biggest ISPs issuing warning notices to suspected illegal downloaders, and after the sixth warning, the individual's Internet access could be restricted.

However, this Creative Content UK approach—which was developed after nearly four years of discussions between the government, ISPs, and the BPI and Motion Picture Association representing the music and film industries—has left the entertainment industry unhappy, since they initially wanted the ISPs to keep a database of suspected illegal downloaders and warn them they might possibly be prosecuted or have their Internet connection slowed down or cut off entirely. But the new rules just provide a warning. As a government spokeswoman for Creative Content UK put it, the rules were designed for "persuading the persuadable" to stop downloading on the grounds that many people might not be aware that what they are doing is illegal. The idea is to make people aware of the negative impact of illegal downloading and promote the use of legal digital content.[50]

However, in the UK, if the letters don't work, the rights holder might still ask for a rapid implementation of the Digital Economy Act, leading to stricter enforcement of penalties. At the same time, the government was considering other measures for targeting Internet piracy, such as blocking the large file-sharing websites like Pirate Bay through the ISPs, and removing pirated content from search engine results.[51] Still, for now, the UK campaign may be a way of learning how seriously illegal downloaders take threats, and if they fail to respond to them, then more stringent actions against them may be on the way.[52]

In Nigeria, the strategy against pirates has included making arrests in response to reports of piracy. For example, the Nigeria Copyrights Commission (NCC) arrested the owner of a bookshop in Minna, Niger, after the Meybiks Nigeria Publishers reported that its book *Basic Civic Education for Senior Secondary School*—approved for use by the Niger State Government in the schools—was pirated. In making the arrest, they acted under the law in Nigeria, Section 38 under the Copyrights Act, which permits the authorities to "arrest and prosecute anyone caught selling a pirated work." In fact, under this law, the police already had made fifty-nine arrests before arresting the bookstore owner, all designed to encourage those engaging in piracy to stop doing it, because, as the NCC Director of Enforcement stated to the News Agency of Nigeria (NAN) in Minna: "Piracy has become a cankerworm that is eating deep into the fabric of the Nigeria economy . . . So let this serve as a warning to those engaging in piracy to desist from it, because there is no hiding place for them."[53]

In the United States, the use of the lawsuit may prove to be one of the tactics in the anti-piracy arsenal. For instance, Voltage Pictures—which worked with a Canadian company to locate and sue individuals who downloaded *The Hurt Locker*—filed a lawsuit in January 2014 in the Southern District of Texas against file sharers who downloaded a leaked DVD screener copy of the Oscar-nominated movie *Dallas Buyers Club*, one of the most-downloaded movies at the end of January. It started the process by identifying the illegal downloaders by their ISPs with plans to take them to trial by jury, although if it follows its past strategy, the aim is to obtain a cash settlement of several thousand dollars, which could be in the millions with thousands of defendants.[54] In fact, in Colorado alone, Voltage sued hundreds of people who illegally downloaded the movie. The company named up to twenty defends, so that as many as 320 people are facing lawsuits of $150,000 in penalties, though the company's lawyers have provided another option of settling for $8,000.[55]

The Many Different Worldwide Approaches to Combat Piracy

As revealed in this foregoing discussion of the extent of piracy, the forms it takes in various countries, and the strategies taken to combat it in different countries by the government, law enforcement, and private individuals and companies, piracy is like a mutating virus or weed spreading its roots everywhere. In the process, it lives off its host while sucking that host dry and then changes its form to find its victims somewhere else. The Internet has proved an easy venue for its expansion, since it is easy to spread creative content files electronically through uploading and downloading or file sharing, and multiple websites have proved ideal for promoting the pirated files and getting clients, like safe houses hidden from view. And then, should one website safe house be discovered, it is easy to create many more or restore the original site once again, like an ever-emerging and transforming Pirate Bay, one of the most notorious pirate sites, finally taken down only to rise again under a new coordinator.

At the same time, as an alternative to creating and distributing online files, some pirates are using an older popular method of scanning books, commonly textbooks, to sell on the streets or to the schools. This is the approach often used in the less technologically sophisticated and poorer countries, where Internet use is less common. So instead of providing free files, the pirates sell pirated copies of books to people on the streets, in bookstores, and through deals with college officials.

In turn, efforts in different countries have ranged from confiscating pirated books and other materials, to requiring websites to take down pirated material or shutting them down, to arrests, fines, and lawsuits against those who distribute, sell, or receive pirated materials in whatever form. Yet no matter what efforts are taken, more pirates appear, and those fighting them generally have a labor-intensive, daunting path to stop the pirates, much less recover any lost compensation or damages as a result of the piracy. Moreover, a part of the problem is that piracy is global in scope; pirates in one country launch websites, software, and services to facilitate the transfer of files or manufacture pirated books for shipment to another country.

Thus, a worldwide effort is needed more than ever to fight back against the pirates, who are like the pirates on the high seas attacking vulnerable ships, like viruses might victimize hosts or weeds might victimize gardens. But here the victims are the legitimate publishers, writers, and creators of other forms of creative content. As one victim put it in the article "Rant on E-book Piracy, Sociopaths and Rampant Criminality," without using his name to avoid further targeting:

"Like other criminals, pirates have a thousand ways to justify their crimes to themselves and others. One of the lies they tell is that piracy doesn't affect sales. They even have false surveys that they share online . . . to convince others that stealing books online is a victimless crime that doesn't cost. Some of these criminals even go so far as trying to make the case that stealing from writers and publishers helps them . . .

"(But) online piracy is organized crime and there is no justification for participating in it . . . 'Sharing' is a euphemism for counterfeiting . . .

"The unethical people who participate in this crime might be the same people who break into your house or rob banks, but they commit their crimes online mainly because they think there is less likelihood of getting caught and there is definitely considerably less likelihood of being physically injured or killed during the commission of their crimes.

"They are extremely well organized. Not only are their actual criminal enterprises, which are criminal conspiracies, well-organized, but their not-for-profit supporters are well-organized, as well. They have important sounding names and often disguise themselves as academics who support the freedom of information. But, these organizations and their criminally-minded members don't just want free information exchange within the boundaries of the law, they want to freely exchange what is the property of other people" (http://witchrants.wordpress. com/2013/03/13/rant-on-e-book-piracy-socopaths-and-rampant-criminality).

CHAPTER 11

The Battles of the Music and Film Industries Against Piracy

For the most part, the fight against piracy has been carried out by the music and film industry, compared to a relatively few limited efforts by writers and publishers, largely in the form of takedown notices. While one strategy has been the massive lawsuits against downloaders, such as by Voltage in various countries, one of the most successful approaches to reducing piracy has been creating an online pay-as-you-download or paid subscription system. Examples of this strategy can be found with iTunes and Netflix, which have provided low-cost alternatives that make it easier to pay a small amount to listen to music or view films, rather than obtaining them legally. But the system doesn't always work, most notably in the case of newly released films, where there is an incentive to download or share files before or while the film is in theaters and before it is released through subscription services or the home video market. This issue is reflected in the pirating of popular films and TV like *The Hurt Locker, Dallas Buyers Club*, and *Game of Thrones*, all pirated worldwide, as described in Chapter 10. Still, the music and film industries have benefited from being more organized and better financed in taking on the pirates, compared to the publishing industry. The following chapter discusses how they have organized and have been successful in some respects, while being very vulnerable in other cases.

The Potential for Damage from Pirates and the Sony Hack

The potential for damage, shown by the Sony hack in response to the film *The Interview*, goes far beyond just the loss of income due to illegally sharing films, music, or other types of creative content. This hack takes the threat of piracy to an entirely new level, demonstrating that not only can creative property be obtained and shared by pirates, but high-tech pirates can reach within the very innards of a company in order to steal copies of private materials—from employment and health records to information on company financial data and personal emails. In the news accounts of the hack, a lot has been made about the embarrassing emails released that showed CEO Amy Pascal and other company officials trashing various Hollywood celebrities, such as calling Angelina Jolie an untalented prima-donna director. While that may be titillating reading for the general public, what is more significant for the piracy battles is the way the pirates were able to locate and breach passwords to gain access to virtually anything they might want to steal, copy, and distribute publically or use for extortion to prevent the revelation of this material.

The Interview was widely pirated before Sony chose to release it through legitimate downloads and independent theaters—about 450,000 downloads within one week according to some media reports. The irony of this hack is that the focus on the film—a largely sophomoric comedy that likely would have disappeared within a week or two with relatively low-box office numbers—launched it into a must-see box office sensation. At the same time, media has mostly focused on the film's success showing that critics can't stop freedom of speech, on the embarrassing revelations about the emails and high salaries of Sony executives, and on the need to find blame for the hack, such as claiming North Korea behind it because the picture featured a successful plot to kill its Chairman Kim. Attention to these factors has obscured the broader threat of hacking into any system to pirate not only creative content but anything. This means that any company, any individual, could become fair game for piracy, linking the act to an invasion of privacy because once pirated, any information can be revealed. This goes beyond pirating books, films, music, and other creative content; virtually anything can now be pirated once a company or individual becomes the target of a hack. In a sense, then, the Sony hack might be seen as a kind of wake-up call to the very serious dangers of Internet piracy and its ability to steal not only property, but the very privacy and identity of its victims.

While much of the Sony hack story will be well known, a summary of the case may help to reflect the vast damages, apart from whether Sony can recoup its investment in the film that triggered the hack. Then again, maybe it could have been used as an excuse to hack into the company, given one of the theories that it may have been engineered by a disgruntled insider, along with some collaboration with high-tech hackers and operatives working with the North Korean government.

The hack began on November 24, shortly before the Thanksgiving holiday, when hackers calling themselves "The Guardians of Peace" accessed the computers at Sony Pictures, forcing the company to temporarily shut down its email and other systems until it was able to restore services on Monday. Meanwhile, the hackers apparently dug deeply into the Sony system, enabling them to steal copies of files and emails and pirate some of the studio's current and upcoming releases, which were soon circulated widely on file-sharing sites.[56]

Among the pirated films were Brad Pitt's war movie *Fury*, which was downloaded on peer-to-peer networks over 888,000 times in one day alone, November 27, as well as *Annie*, downloaded over 206,000 times, and *Mr. Turner, Still Alice,* and *To Write Love on Her Arms,* downloaded 100,000 times.[57] As of November 30, these numbers were over 1.2 million downloads for *Fury,* over 206,000 for *Annie*, about 104,000 for *Still Alice*, 63,000 for *Mr. Turner*, and 20,000 for *To Write Love on Her Arms.*

But the release of the films was just the beginning of the revelations from the hack attack, announced on Sony's computers with the image of a skeleton and a message that said: "Hacked by #GOP." The group also posted the chilling message that it would release "secrets and top secrets" of the company.[58] Additionally, without specifying demands, some screens showed a red skeleton with the warning: "If you don't obey us, we'll release data shown below to the world."[59] The first mystery was who was behind the hack, since on November 25, the website TheVerge reported an email from a hacker who identified herself as "Lena" and claimed, "We Want equality [sic]. Sony doesn't. It's an upward battle. Sony doesn't lock their doors, physically, so we worked with other staff with similar interests to get in. I'm sorry I can't say more, safety for our team is important [sic]."[60] So was this the disgruntled employee? Was this a cover for a more nefarious hack orchestrated by hackers in North Korea, since the North Korean government called *The Interview* an "evil act of provocation" that deserved "stern punishment"?[61]

So that became the beginning of the mystery to discover who was behind the hack. And then on Monday, December 1, the leak of internal documents began, initially published on Pastebin, an anonymous Internet posting site. Among other things, one of these documents contained the pre-bonus annual salaries of senior executives, showing that seventeen of them earned over $1 million a year. Moreover, at this point, the FBI got involved and issued a private bulletin to a wide range of companies about a malicious software threat that could remove data from its computers, which could not be recovered and confirmed that it was working with Sony to investigate the attack. And later that evening, the hackers released what they claimed were "tens of terabytes" of internal Sony data, described as a "Gift of the G.O.P." Among other things, the post included links to various Sony archives that included its employees' passwords, social security numbers, salaries, and performance reviews.[62]

Then, over the next weeks the hackers released even more, including lists of all the computers on the company's internal networks, as well as the locations, IP addresses, MAC addresses, Windows computer names, and usernames of over three thousand individual PCs in North America and over 7,700 more worldwide computers on the company's network. There was also a digital certificate issued by Sony's corporate certificate authority to Sony Pictures to create server certificates for Sony's Information Systems Service (ISS) infrastructure, which might have been used to sign later versions of the malware that took all of Sony's computers offline. Plus, there were other certificates associated with the Sony Pictures e-commerce site, with its intranet servers, and with its infrastructure provided from multiple telecommunications companies.[63] While most of the general public was fascinated by all of the gossip revealed about executive salaries and embarrassing emails, and then by the warnings of mayhem if theaters released the picture, within the very structure of Sony's computer and Internet infrastructure, the hackers/

pirates caused vastly more damage. There is evidence that much earlier, in February 2014, the hackers/pirates had already breached the system, beginning with an attack on the company's international theatrical sales and distribution system in Brazil—in which they obtained passwords to access stored invoice and payment information—though Sony disabled the two accounts involved.[64] After that, Sony was mainly concerned about potential denial of service attacks. Then the GOP launched its attack from inside Sony's own network, and after burrowing deep within the system, threatened Sony with even further damage. This was all made possible by its deep penetration, such as releasing the emails and private information about Sony employees and eventually causing Sony to go bankrupt.[65]

This potential for hackers/pirates to burrow deep within any company's network system is chilling. This action against Sony could be replicated in other companies around the globe, and it goes far beyond pirating films, music, books, software, or other creative content; it shows the potential of pirates to take much more than creative content to make or save money through what many pirates justify as sharing or helping others facing overpriced creative content, from films to music to books. For the most part, though, this wasn't the story of the Sony hack that spread like wildfire through the media. Instead, the focus shifted from the high executive salaries and their embarrassing emails to the story of *The Interview*. Many believe that the hack and threats to escalate the damage to Sony was due to hackers in North Korea acting on behest of the North Korean government, because the film—a comedy about two goofball journalists hired by the CIA to kill leader Kim Jong Un—was a gross offense of the nation.[66] So now the threat was that any theaters showing the film would be in danger of terrorist attacks.[67]

The widely known result is that Sony did pull the film, since the nation's five biggest theater chains refused to show it,[68] but within a week, independent theaters came to the rescue and were willing to open the film on Christmas day. These openings were carried out without incident, and thereafter the film was quickly released on Netflix and other online channels, and was subsequently pirated by over 450,000 illegal downloads the first day of its release. These numbers represent a kind of ironic coda to the original piracy of Sony's private information, including around forty-seven thousand social security numbers, plus network passwords. Then all of the hullabaloo turned a quickly forgettable film into a must-see feature that raked in over $15 million in sales.

So the story became more about free speech and Sony's initial cowardice in pulling the film from theaters in response to pressure from the owners. Prominent members of Hollywood's creative community expressed anger at Sony's feature to "make a stand for artistic freedom,"[69] though Sony sought to justify their response based on security concerns that someone could get injured or killed if there was an attack. There was also some blowback against Seth Rogen, the writer-director-star, and his filmmaking colleagues for exposing employees and the audience "to digital damage and physical threat by pushing his outrageous humor to the limit and backing the film to the last."[70] At the same time, the release of damaging emails by Amy Pascal, co-chairman of the studio, and Clint Culpepper, head of Sony's Screen Gems unit, led to criticism of their leadership; Pascal had traded racial jokes with producer Scott Rudin about President Obama's supposed taste in black-themed movies, while Culpepper called one of the few black moviemakers, Kevin Hart, a "whore" because of his growing salary demands.[71] And then it became a kind of patriotic duty to see this film to stand up to the terrorists and North Korea. President Obama even got into the act with threats of sanctions against North Korea, while the FBI claimed evidence that the hackers were from North Korea, although some alternate theories post that the takedown of Sony was the work of a former Sony employee who had been fired. Or maybe the former worker had teamed up with the North Korean hackers.

Whatever the source of the hack, the piracy of private data is what led some former Sony film production workers to file lawsuits against Sony. The grounds were that the company did not do enough to prevent hackers from stealing nearly fifty thousand social security numbers, along with salary and other personal information on current and former workers, or waited too long to tell employees about their stolen data. As described in the Associated Press article, "Sony Facing 2 Suits by Ex-Workers Over Data Breach," two employees sued in federal court alleging that "the company failed to secure its computer systems despite 'weaknesses that it has known about for years,' and instead made a business decision to accept the risk," since Sony had repeatedly been attacked over the years. And then two former movie production workers sued Sony in Los Angeles Superior Court, claiming that "the company waited too long to notify employees that their data had been stolen," in violation of a California law to protect sensitive financial and medical information, resulting in "likely damage [to] plaintiffs and class members for the rest of their lives." According to legal experts, these cases are likely to be among the many that are filed over this data breach, causing Sony to potentially face "tens of millions of dollars in damages from a class-action lawsuit." Plus, Sony could be likely to face fines from government regulators and lawsuits from actors, producers, and directors who may prefer not to work with the company anymore.[72]

Meanwhile, the US government has gotten involved in the fallout from the attack. Besides stating that it thought Sony "made a mistake" in releasing the film, it issued a stern warning to North Korea of sanctions due to its being behind the attack. These sanctions could run the gamut from cyber retaliation and financial sanctions to criminal indictments against individuals implicated in the attack, or even increased US military support of South Korea, which is still supposedly at war with North Korea.[73]

As of this writing, it is not clear where this attack will lead, but it shows the potential for an act of piracy to go far beyond the theft of creative content of films, books, music, and other materials. Then, if this is done on a large enough scale, as with the Sony hack, it could result in severe economic damage not only to that company, but multiple companies, and further undermine a country's economy. Already governments have sought to crack down on the piracy of creative materials because they threaten to undermine major industries, such as the film, music, and publishing industries producing these materials. But now—given the potential for piracy to go within these companies to steal private information, passwords, and undermine computer networks—the threat is that much greater. So the Sony hack is not just about the ability of a single film to antagonize a country with its material, if that is in fact the reason for the Sony hack. It's not just a convenient explanation provided by the hackers to cover up their other reasons for targeting Sony, perhaps in retaliation for other wrongs committed by the company. It's not just a way to show the prowess and power of hackers today. Rather, the hack reflects the potential damage of piracy to not just a single company or industry, but to the economy of the country as a whole, as the piracy of materials from multiple companies grows.

Other Battles by the Film and Music Industries Against the Pirates

While the Sony hack is the largest high-profile and most damaging act of piracy against the film and music industries, the battle of these industries against piracy goes back over a decade, and they have largely carried the banner in the fight. That's because the film and music industries have been more organized and consolidated than the vast number of small and medium-sized publishing companies, individual self-publishers, and authors of millions of books published each year, most self-published. Moreover, the major film and music companies have far larger warchests to bring to the battle.

For example, the more than twenty thousand lawsuits filed by the RIAA (the Recording Industry Association of America) against music fans who downloaded free songs online instead of buying CDs initially raised a ruckus from protesters who claimed these lawsuits were unfair—like an army of evil Goliaths hitting thousands of Davids who couldn't fight back. However, the strategy was ultimately successful. The RIAA hardline position was that anyone making unauthorized copies of copyrighted music recordings was stealing and "could be held legally liable for thousands of dollars in damages."

That's what one woman, Jammie Thomas, found after a trial before a federal jury in Minnesota in 2007. She was ordered to pay $220,000 to the big record companies—"9,250 for each of the 24 songs she was accused of sharing online" (www.washingtonpost.com/wp-dyn/content/article/2007/12/28/AR2007122800693.html). In his testimony before the Senate Committee on Governmental Affairs, CEO of the RIAA Mitch Bainol, whose members create and distribute 90 percent of all legitimate sound records in the US, argued that these lawsuits against peer-to-peer sharers were justified, given the drastic decline in record sales that was threatening the security of industry (http://amh500.edublogs.org/the-music-industrys-lawsuits-against-online-music-sharers-are-justified).

Besides, as he pointed out, although the peer-to-peer networks were well aware of the widespread illegal copying, they took no steps to stop it, and even encouraged and enabled this sharing, while "taking steps to shield themselves from liability."

Eventually, this strategy of going after both the consumers and networks was largely successful, resulting in the end of Napster and the emergence of companies like iTunes and Rhapsody, which offer individual sales or subscriptions to download services and pay royalties to the artists and companies.

Meanwhile, the movie industry has similarly targeted the file-sharing services and their customers to stop movie piracy. For example, in "The Long Lasting Battle Against Online Movie Piracy," Juan Matossian describes how one independent film company, Nu Image, backed by the US Copyright Group, announced the biggest file-sharing lawsuit ever filed in the United States in February 2011 in Florida, Washington, and Maryland. In the lawsuit, over twenty-three thousand IP addresses were cited for illegally downloading the Sylvester Stallone movie *The Expendables*, and a federal judge allowed Nu Image to subpoena Internet service providers to identify the customers at each IP address (http://nycultureblog.journalism.cuny.edu/2011/05/19/the-long-lasting-battle-against-online-movie-piracy). Although that suit ran into problems because many defendants didn't live where the case was filed, in February 2012, Nu Image filed a suit targeting 2,165 residents in Maryland who downloaded *Conan the Barbarian* (http://blogs.villagevoice.com/runninscared/2012/02/you_might_get_s.php).

While the major studios have largely decided not to use this approach because of the PR dangers and legal complications, they have turned to Washington for assistance in passing protective legislation, such as a bill introduced by Senator Patrick Leahy to prosecute the websites devoted to selling counterfeit products, including movies and TV shows. While Leahy's bill ultimately went down to defeat due to a growing chorus of defenders of Internet freedom, ultimately, much of the film industry's piracy problem disappeared with the emergence of video download and subscription services like Netflix, Amazon Prime, Hulu, and iTunes, which worked out arrangements with the major movie companies to pay them for the films added to their collections.

Now, to combat the remaining Internet services offering pirated music or films, these industries have been working with Internet providers to fight piracy. For example, as noted by technology editor Ian Bush, the music and movie industries have been teaming up with Comcast, Verizon, Time Warner, and several other Internet service providers "in a push to fight piracy that's expected to take a 'six strikes and you're out' approach." Basically, this six-strikes policy means you will get five chances in which the Internet provider will first tell you what you are doing is wrong and warn that further violations could create big problems for you—such as a lawsuit from the copyright holder (http://philadelphia.cbslocal.com/2012/10/17/music-and-film-industry-working-with-Internet-providers-to-fight-piracy).

Called the Copyright Alert System (CAS), this system joins the biggest copyright holders—including the Motion Picture Association of America, the Recording Industry Association of America, and the National Cable and Telecommunications Association—with the ISP organizations to jointly battle copyright infringement in an organized way. The way it works is that the Internet providers and copyright holders will use peer-to-peer (P2P) surveillance methods to determine when copyrighted content is uploaded or shared illegally. Then, any owner of copyright, which has so far primarily been moviemakers, musicians, and other content creators, can seek help from various powerful infrastructure companies. These might include Internet service providers, credit card processors, and search engines that can undermine sites that enable piracy by making it hard for them to operate and process transactions.[74] Once the copyright owners see their movies, music, TV shows, or other copyrighted materials shared without permission on a P2P site, they are able to notify the ISP of the Internet protocol (IP) addressed, whereupon the ISP notifies the individuals with that IP to stop the illegal file sharing. If they don't, the ISP can act to negatively impact the IP owner's Internet experience, such as by reducing their bandwidth or quality of service.[75]

For example, one company that helps content owners do this is MarkMonitor, owned by Thomson Reuters, a huge multinational corporation. It joins the BitTorrent networks, the most common method for illegally sharing files, to look for the names of copyright-protected movies, music, and TV shows. Once MarkMonitor finds a file that has been illegally uploaded or shared, it will find the IP address of the user and send it to the user's Internet provider, who will issue a series of increasingly dire warnings sent to the user's email address. By the fourth or fifth alert, the Internet provider can begin taking action against the user, such as reducing the speed of his or her connection, making it more difficult to download illegal files. Then, the sixth alert could result in a lawsuit (http://www.popsci.com/technology/article/2013-02/everything-you-need-know-about-piracy-battling-copyright-alert-system). Alternatively, upon getting such a notice, many IP service providers will ask the user to take down the infringing content, or they will take it down or remove access to it themselves.

However, the Copyright Alert System only affects peer-to-peer file sharing, such as the BitTorrent sites. It does not affect the cyberlockers, which host illegal content and enable individuals to access links to stream this material, leading to the use of litigation against some of these more blatant lockers, such as the notorious Megaupload case against Kim Dotcom.

In addition, some content owners, such as movie studios, are seeking help from law enforcement agencies, such as ICE, the US Department of Homeland Security Immigrations and Customer Enforcement's task force, or the FBI, and taking legal action against individuals pirating materials.[76]

Latest Developments in the Battle Against the Pirates by the Film and Music Industries

With these new tools, such as the Copyright Alert System and the assistance of law enforcement, there have been increased efforts to fight piracy, especially by the film and music industries. One example is the case against isoHunt Web Technologies, Inc. for "inducing users to illegally download and distribute copyrighted materials such as movies and TV shows." In March 2013, the US Court of Appeals for the Ninth Circuit issued a unanimous decision against the company, and another trial is expected to determine how much in monetary damages isoHunt has to pay the plaintiffs. Yet, while the court issued an injunction against the company, it has continued to operate through private servers located in Canada and is still "the fourth most popular torrent site on the internet," with approximately fifty-nine million file shares to nearly 11.8 million active users.[77]

Another recent development in the piracy wars has been the attempts to get some legislation passed to combat infringement, such as the Protect IP Act (PIPA) in the Senate and the Stop Online Piracy Act (SOPA) in the House, though they were defeated due to a highly vocal opposition and protests by those in the tech community. Among other things, they feared the power of law enforcement, ISPs, and other gatekeepers to restrict access to entire Internet domain names. Protests also claimed that the requirement of search engines to delete domain names went too far in that this action could be taken even if the infringement only occurred on a single webpage or blog.[78] Yet, while these bills failed, many services involved in providing Internet access began to take steps on a voluntary basis to curtail piracy. For example, as Claudia Kienzle notes in an article in *Streaming Media Magazine*, "Search engines volunteered to take down links to pirated content, and ISPs and large networks tried to be more rigorous in enforcing their standards, such as prohibiting advertising on sites that are engaged in piracy. Credit card processors volunteered not to process payments for sites that sell infringed materials."[79]

There has also been a growing business in companies seeking to track down and dissuade pirates primarily providing this service for the film and music industries. If the pirates don't desist, the next step might be litigation or assistance from law enforcement or legislation to penalize them. For instance, one such company that targets pirates and claims a 60 percent reduction in piracy for its clients is London-based KLipcorp. Using a proprietary technology, the company locates pirated content, identifies the pirates, and gathers evidence to show the extent of their piracy. Then, it takes action to discourage or stop these illegal activities by putting the perpetrators, rather than the individual consumers, on notice. The final step is to take legislative or legal action to stop them and penalize them. Additionally, the company tracks pirate sites' digital advertising that is placed around illegal content. Often the agencies are unaware that this is infringed-upon material, or the pirates can sell ads for a much lower amount than a traditional media company would because they aren't paying anything to the rights holders and have very low production and distribution costs. The goal is to get the advertisers to not advertise there.

Still another strategy has been for law enforcement to file charges against the most egregious pirates of films and music. For example, California Attorney General Kamala Harris filed charges against three brothers—Hop Hoang, 26; Tony Hoang, 23; and Huynh Hoang, 20—for one count each of conspiracy, four counts of receiving stolen property, and one count of grand theft for operating a website, mediamp4.com, which allowed users to stream over one thousand copyrighted TV and movie titles on their computers and mobile devices. Among the titles were the popular sitcom *How I Met Your Mother* and some box office hits, such as *Black Swan* and *Tangled*. Now the brothers face up to five years in prison.

The case began when the Motion Picture Association of America initially began investigating iphonetvshows.net and movieiphone.net and sent a cease and desist letter to Tony Hoang, who then continued the operation under the new name mediaamp4.com. Then, the Attorney General's office began an investigation into this site, with the assistance of the eCrime Unit of the California Attorney General's Office, the California Highway Patrol, and REACT, a law enforcement task force in Santa Clara, California, specializing in investigating technology crimes and identity theft. Among other things, the investigators executed a search warrant, seized property used to further the illegal operation, conducted a forensic analysis of the computer that was seized, and filed charges against the brothers.[80]

In investigating the case, Harris's office said that the brothers earned $150,000 in ad revenue during the eighteen months the site operated, much of the traffic resulting from Google search ads.[81] Though this case may seem like a drop in the bucket, considering the huge number of piracy websites and the millions earned by many of these, the prosecution is like a warning shot to dissuade other would-be pirates, given the serious economic damage caused by the crime. As Harris put it: "Digital piracy is theft. It is a serious crime that harms one of California's most important economic engines—our entertainment industry. This case sends a clear message that the California Department of Justice will investigate digital piracy and prosecute violators to the fullest extent of the law."[82]

However, there have recently been some court rulings that may make it more difficult to pursue lawsuits against multiple defendants, as some record labels and film studios have done in suing nearly 250,000 defendants for downloading and sharing copyrighted files in the last few years. Most of these suits end with settlements of about $2,000–$7,000 each. Such suits have been relatively inexpensive to bring, since most of these defendants have been combined together into a large case whereby the copyright holder can obtain the personal details of the alleged infringers via their IP addresses. These grouped cases have meant that the copyright holder doesn't have to pay a filing fee for each defendant. Instead, for a single fee they can sue hundreds or thousands of alleged infringers at the same time. But the latest rulings could make that impossible.[83]

As described in a January 2014 *Torrent Freak* article, a federal judge in Iowa ruled that copyright holders can't join multiple defendants in a single suit, since there is no proof that they shared files with each other. As Federal Judge Stephanie Rose ruled in judging several cases involving independent films—such as *Killer Joe*, *Sibling*, and *The Company You Keep*—the file sharers aren't acting in concert because they all "downloaded the same torrent file and joined the same swarm," as argued by the copyholders. Instead, Judge Rose ruled that in order to join multiple defendants in a single lawsuit, the copyright holder would have to show they were involved in the same series of transactions to demonstrate it was likely that they trade files with each other. But in the cases she judged, there were weeks or even months between the time the first and last defendant was observed sharing the film. So it appeared unlikely that all the defendants actually shared files with each other, even though they shared a torrent file with the same hash mark. Thus, Judge Rose concluded that all mass-BitTorrent lawsuits should be limited to one defendant, and she dismissed all of the other cases.[84]

Though other judges could still reach other conclusions, the rulings provide a warning that other movie studios, as well as music, book, and other copyright holders, will find it more difficult to use mass lawsuits as a strategy against copyright holders. In fact, defendants in other cases will be able to use these rulings as precedents in their own cases.

It's a trend that has continued, with other judges more carefully looking at these suits with multiple defendants. For example, in a *Mother*

Jones article titled "Why It's Getting Harder to Sue Illegal Movie Down-loaders," Dana Liebelson cites a series of cases where the judges have dismissed or become more wary about granting subpoenas to companies with only IP addresses to identify defendants. For example, in January 2014, one judge in the US District Court for the Western District of Washington in Seattle dismissed a case brought against 152 anonymous defendants by the studio that produced *Elf-Man*, a direct-to-video movie, stating that "simply identifying the account holder associated with an IP address tells us very little about who actually downloaded *Elf-Man*." And earlier a federal district judge in New York in 2012 and a federal district judge in Illinois in 2011 similarly dismissed the cases on the grounds that IP addresses "don't have a high degree of reliability, and they're not an accurate representation of who has control of the computer."[85]

The problem is that an IP address usually indicates the person who pays for the Internet account, but not the person doing the download-ing, since all the people using a single wireless router have the same IP address, and now over 60 percent of people use wireless routers in their house, which wasn't the case a decade ago. So a neighbor could easily be the person guilty of making the illegal downloads, as well as using another person's Internet IP router without permission.[86]

Thus, even while some judges have issued these rulings, there are still many lawsuits being filed, though the studios are no longer going after the tens of thousands of defendants at once as they were doing from 2011 to late 2012, as in the *Hurt Locker* case, where the producers sued nearly twenty-five thousand BitTorrent users for illegally downloading the film. However, they later claimed to have dismissed almost all of the claims, since it took them too long to find most of the defendants by their IP addresses. Instead, the claims are generally filed against no more than one hundred defendants who are the most active downloaders, who are more reasonable to pursue and more acceptable to the courts, as well as being better public relations with consumers generally.[87]

Aside from lawsuits, another strategy has been to go after the adver-tisers whose ads appear on the pirate sites, again with the sites with video and music content attracting the most attention. For example, in response to the Obama administration's request for private-sector actions to reduce piracy, the American Association of Advertising Agencies, also known as the 4A, and Association of National Advertisers (ANA) have sought to keep their members' ads off such sites. The value of these ads has been substantial, as a report from the Digital Citizen Alliance, a nonprofit focused on Internet safety issues, has shown: about $227 million in ad revenue in 2013. Moreover the report has pointed out that piracy not only is "a threat to the content creators whose material is being stolen but the reputations of the advertisers whose brands appear on the sites."[88] In fact, the 4As and ANA issued a statement of best practices for its members to follow to avoid supporting sites with exclusively or primarily pirated material:[89]

"The Association of National Advertisers (ANA) and the American Association of Advertising Agencies (4A's) strongly believe that U.S. advertisers must have confidence that their ads are not unintentionally providing financial support to, or otherwise legitimizing, "rogue" Internet sites whose primary and apparent purpose is to steal or facilitate theft of the intellectual property of America's innovators and creators. U.S. advertisers must also have confidence that their corporate brands and images are not being harmed by association with such unlawful activity. In order to help address this complex problem, our Associations believe that our members should each commit to take affirmative steps to avoid placement of their ads on such sites.

"At the outset, we emphasize that this commitment is not intended to foreclose advertising on legitimate social media or user-generated content sites, even if infringing content occasionally appears on such sites. Rather, this commitment addresses "rogue" sites that are dedicated to infringement of the intellectual property rights of others, in that they have no significant, or only limited, use or purpose other than engaging in, enabling or facilitating such infringement."

To develop the advisory, the Digital Citizens Alliances commissioned the media advisory firm Media Link to prepare the report, which it did by examining the content sites that were ad-supported and had many requests to take down stolen content. Eventually it ended up with 596 content sites, which included both BitTorrent sites like Pirate Bay and video-streaming sites like Alba File. And they looked at the number of ads on the sites, their audience size, and the cost-per-click and per-action pricing models to assess the likely revenue from the ads.[90] While this research reflects the extent of the problem, it can also be used as a guide for advertisers to avoid advertising on these sites.

Sometimes just the threat of legal action has worked to get pirates who think they are simply providing a public service to consumers, such as movie fans, to drop out, even though they may still feel that they had noble intentions. As an example, that's what happened with Popcorn Time, which shut down on March 14, 2014. The basic premise of the site was working with BitTorrent to let users download movies from the web completely free. They also had a large collection of films currently in theaters, even the year's Oscar winners, which might not later show up on Netflix. So instead of spending $10–$12 to see the movie in theaters, users could see any movie "instantly streamed in perfect high-definition quality," as described by Taylor Cast in a *Huffington Post* blog: "Popcorn Time Lets You Watch Any Movie for Free (P.S. It's Illegal)." And the app was designed much like a Redbox display, letting users readily find what they wanted rather than navigating through a confusing array of torrent sites. In effect, the app made stealing copyrighted material easier than ever, although the Popcorn Time creators thought they were not doing anything illegal, since they didn't actually host any copyrighted material on their site, and they provided the service free through open source.[91]

Yet those downloading and watching movies through the site were clearly at risk of being accused of, sued for, or criminally charged with copyright infringement. So shortly after this article about them appeared and Popcorn Time creators were slammed with threats of legal action, they decided to shut down the site, though they left a good-bye message on their website that expressed their view that they were doing nothing wrong. As the message stated:

"Popcorn Time is shutting down today. Not because we ran out of energy, commitment, focus or allies. But because we need to move on with our lives.

"Our experiment has put us at the doors of endless debates about piracy and copyright, legal threats and the shady machinery that makes us feel in danger for doing what we love. And that's not a battle we want a place in."[92]

Still another strategy to combat the pirates, despite the resistance of some judges to the multi-defendant BitTorrent lawsuits, is comprised of the mega-lawsuits, which are even more aggressive in attacking both the downloaders and the owners of the torrent sites.

One example of this is the movie studios suing the defunct Megaupload piracy site, seeking at least $175 million in damages, which the principals allegedly earned from the pirated materials they illegally shared on their cyberlocker site, even though the US law enforcement officials shut down the site in January 2012. The six major film studios—Twentieth Century Fox Film, Disney Enterprises, Paramount Pictures, Universal City Studio Productions, Columbia Pictures Industries, and Warner Brothers Entertainment—filed the complaint on April 7 in the US District Court for the Eastern District of Virginia, and they named as defendants Megaupload Ltd. and its founder Kim Dotcom, Vester, the majority shareholder of Megaupload, Mathias Ortmann, the site's chief technical officer, and Bram van der Kolk, in charge of programming. A reason for filing the suit is that according to the US government's indictment of the company, Megaupload not only obtained more than $175 million in proceeds, but they cost copyright owners more than $500 million by "enabling copyright infringement on a massive scale." It was, according to Steven Fabrizio, the senior executive VP and global general counsel of the Motion Picture Association of America, "the largest and most active infringing website targeting creative content in the world."[93]

Another example of this more aggressive attack on the pirates in the courts by the film industry is the Lionsgate lawsuit filed July 31, 2014, in California Federal Court. The suit was filed after learning on July 24 that a digital file with a high-quality reproduction of the film *The Expendables 3* had been stolen and uploaded to the Internet, resulting in over one million downloads at the time of its filing.[94] Among other things, they demanded a temporary restraining order and injunctions that prohibited the anonymous operators of the sites from "hosting, linking to, distributing, reproducing, performing, selling or making available copies of *The Expendables 3*." Moreover, their demands went even further than other lawsuits in seeking to have the defendants prohibited from "operating any of the websites" and ordered to "take all steps necessary to recall and recover all copies of the Stolen Film" as well as any parts of it that they had distributed. Further, Lionsgate sought to prevent the defendants from transferring any of their assets or circumventing the court orders, and they wanted their domain names placed on locked status. Plus, Lionsgate may issue subpoenas to the ISPs providing hosting and cloud storage, as well as to the banks and financial institutions providing support to the torrent sites.[95]

While the lawsuit didn't immediately prevent the torrent sites from continuing the downloads, which reached over two million by the following day, it reflects the approach of a major film studio to call for all-out war on the pirates, from those stealing the files to those permitting the downloads and anyone making the film available to spread illegally. For example, the suit targeted ten John Doe torrent downloaders and the owners of the main torrent sites involved in hosting, distributing, or otherwise making available copies of the film, including LimeTorrents. com, BillionUploads.com, HulFile.eu, Played.to, SwantShare.com, and Dotsemper.com. And while other Hollywood studios have gone after the pirates, many feel Lionsgate's attack takes the war on piracy to a whole new level. As Robin Parrish writes in *Tech Times*:

"This is hardly the first time a Hollywood studio has gone to war against piracy, but Lionsgate's lawsuit feels much more stern and resolute than any that's come before. The very nature of torrent file sharing would seemingly make it all but impossible for a film to be recalled from every computer or hard drive it's been downloaded to. Yet Lionsgate is adamant that these torrent sites 'take all steps necessary to recall and recover all copies of ['The Expendables 3'] or any portion thereof that they have distributed.'"[96]

The Development of Legitimate Alternatives

However, while one strategy is to defeat the pirates by eliminating the cyberlockers, restricting the sites, seeking damages through litigation, and reducing their profits, another that has proved fairly successful for the film and recording industries has been providing appealing alternate sites where material is available legally and at a low cost. For example, the music industry first created some legal digital access models—such as Spotify, YouTube, VEVO, Pandora, and Rhapsody—that grant consumers access to a legal marketplace for music whenever they want it, sometimes for free, and since 2007 these have gained an increasing proportion of the music marketplace, from 3 percent in 2007 to 15 percent in 2012, according to RIAA statistics.[97] At the same time, the RIAA has launched campaigns to not only make the public aware that they are breaking copyright laws when they illegally download and copy music, but also encourage music fans to go to the legal sites, though it has still taken steps to shut down the major piracy sites, such as LimeWire and Kazaa.[98] In short, it has combined a carrot and stick approach to provide a user-friendly source of copyrighted material, while finding other ways to strike back at the pirates through reducing their access or shutting down the sites of the biggest offenders.

Likewise, the film industry has taken much the same approach. Private companies are setting up sites like Netflix and Hulu that provide access for subscribers to see newly released or classic films and TV shows on demand, wherever and whenever they want, for a low price or even for free in some cases. For example, Netflix's service was only $7.99 a month after a one-month free trial when it first started its digital service and phased out its DVD-by-mail service; currently it is only $8.99 a month, allowing users to watch whatever they want, and even share the service with others in their household.

However, in one of the many ironies in the battle against piracy, Netflix is actually looking to the pirates to decide what films and TV shows to add to its service. It regularly checks out the illegal file-sharing platforms to see what is most popular with the online pirates, and the more popular the films and TV shows, the more likely these are to be added to its roster, including its Watch Instantly section.[99]

And even the major studios regard illegal downloads as a measure of success, as much as they may want to destroy the pirates. For instance, David Kaplan, head of Warner Brothers' anti-piracy wing, had this to say on the website of the annual Anti-Piracy and Content Protection Summit for 2013: "Generally speaking, we view piracy as a proxy of consumer demand. Accordingly, enforcement related efforts are balanced with looking at ways to adjust or develop business models to take advantage of that demand by offering fans what they are looking for when they are looking for it."[100] In other words, while the companies are still trying to stop illegal file-sharing and regularly monitor the BitTorrent sites, such as Pirate Bay, to identify pirates as the enemy, they are still looking to the pirates for market insights they can use in developing content to appeal to their audience.

Still another example of this trend to find alternate channels: In 2013, the Motion Picture Licensing Corporation (MPLC), representing over four hundred distributors from studios and independent producers and the "world leader in motion picture copyright compliance," set up a partnership with the Copyright Clearance Center (CCC)—a global rights broker that works with large corporations, research, government, and medical institutions, universities, government agencies, and others—to facilitate the licensing of all types of copyrighted material, including books, ebooks, trade journals, magazine articles, and newspapers. Under this program, the CCC worked with the MPLC to license films and video programs to corporate clients to use in motivating and training employees and appealing to prospective customers.[101]

The effectiveness of the CCC as an alternative to piracy is reflected in its payout of $1.3 billion in royalties to right holders in the ten-year period from 2003 to 2013.

Intriguingly, the publishing industry has largely been left out of the music and film industry battle, even though publishers and writers are similarly affected by the pirates. Perhaps this lack of involvement has occured because the book writers and publishers are much less organized, and so many writers publish books themselves or give out free content in order to build a platform for convincing agents to represent them and publishers to publish their books.

But now writers and publishers have much to learn from these earlier battles. There seems to be a growing concern, primarily from publishers, to take some action to protect their books, while writers individually feel there is little they can do aside from sending out takedown notices, which they believe have little effect. They feel powerless to do more. After all, they want to write, not spend time locating pirate sites and trying to get their books removed. But now there are some growing alternatives in the form of services that help publishers, writers, and other content creators find the pirates, send them warnings, and even institute litigation against them. The next chapter deals with the way in which the publishers and writers are increasingly fighting back or finding alternative ways to deal with piracy, too.

CHAPTER 12

How Publishers Are Beginning to Battle the Pirates

WHILE THE MUSIC AND FILM industries battled the Internet pirates with lawsuits, legislation, and new marketing models to get consumers to pay for downloading or streaming music and films, publishers were left on the sidelines. But now they seem to finally be ready to do battle. While they have sent out cease and desist letters resulting in some takedowns, now some publishers are acting more aggressively to take on the pirates in court and shut down some of the worst offenders.

The Problem of Book Piracy

Such an effort is long overdue, because individual writers, aside from the most successful, generally don't have the resources to seriously combat pirates individually. And rampant piracy can not only decimate the earnings of victimized writers, but also undermine the publishing industry's ability to successfully market and promote its books, leading to fewer professional authors and publishers. As author Karen Dionne writes in "E-Piracy: The High Cost of Stolen Books," "Lost book sales can't be quantified, making it impossible to calculate the full cost of e-piracy, but the sheer number of illegal copies available for download gives an idea of the scope of the problem . . . they still translate into a staggering amount of royalties that have been stolen from authors." Moreover, if the authors' sales dry up, so do their prospects for future books. As Dionne observes: "Publishing is a business, and authors whose titles don't sell well aren't offered follow-up contracts . . . Meanwhile, (the authors') existing titles will likely go out of print, further degrading their bottom line. Even if authors dodge that worst-case scenario and continue to publish, there's no doubt the widespread availability of illegal digital copies affects their income."[102]

But piracy does more than just reduce income. As a growing community of individuals are recognizing, book piracy is not just a cost of doing business but a crime, so writers and publishers need to go after the criminals to seek damages and penalties. As A. Giovanni writes in "Online Book Piracy," "Among a certain class of online Internet users there is a perception that piracy is acceptable and normal. But, no matter how common it may be, it is certainly not normal. It is theft. It is criminal. It's extremely costly to copyright holders, and the only way to put an end to this culture of crime and recoup losses is for more authors and publishers to pursue damages and criminal charges against pirates."[103]

The Efforts of Publishers to Take Legal Action

Publishers are finally taking action to combat this. One of the first efforts occurred on February 4, 2010, when six publishers of educational, scientific, and professional books—Bedford, Freeman & Worth, an educational publisher and subsidiary of Macmillan, Cengage Learning, Elsevier, McGraw-Hill, Wiley, and Pearson Education—combined together to obtain an injunction against RapidShare, based in Switzerland. They sought an injunction to stop RapidShare from file sharing their works, and in its February 10 judgment, a German court ordered RapidShare to take steps to prevent the illegal file sharing of the 148 copyrighted works cited in the lawsuit. Among other things, the court ruled, "RapidShare must monitor its site to ensure the copyrighted material is not being uploaded and prevent unauthorized access to the material by its users. The company will be subject to substantial fines for non-compliance."[104] It was, according to an interview with Maria Danzilo, Wiley's Legal Director, a "great victory" to show pirates that there would be consequences for pirating the work of writers and publishers, who relied on numerous support staff to make a book happen.[105]

As noted by CEO of the Association for American Publishers Tom Allen, speaking on behalf of the publisher plaintiffs, "This ruling is an important step forward. Not only does it affirm that file-sharing copyrighted content without permission is against the law, but it attaches a hefty financial punishment to the host, in this case RapidShare, for noncompliance. Consider this a shot across the bow for others who attempt to profit from the theft of copyrighted works online."[106]

He then went on to elaborate on the importance of legal action to protect writers and publishers from copyright infringement, since otherwise it could lead to fewer books written and published due to the reduced income of the writers and publishers. Or as he put it:

"Without the ability to earn a living from their work, authors will not have the incentive to create books in the first place. Moreover, publishers won't be able to develop powerful content resources and educational tools that help to improve the academic and professional performance of the people who use them. Quality and readability would suffer, and distinguishing credible, quality information from that which is unreliable and untrustworthy would become a gargantuan task. If that happens, we all lose."[107]

Then, after a long investigation to identify the site owners, a February 2012 international coalition of seventeen publishers, including John Wiley, began legal proceedings in Ireland and Germany against two site operators of two websites, library.nu and iFile.it. The industry considered the latter to be "one of the largest pirate web-based businesses in the world," as Jeff John Roberts noted in his posting, "Updated: Book Publishers Force Down Piracy Sites."[108] Library.nu itself offered over four hundred thousand copyrighted titles, and the site operators reportedly earned millions in advertising revenues. The result was that on February 13 a Munich judge granted injunctions against the illegal posting or sharing of these two websites. Among other things, library. nu was alleged to have posted links to hundreds of thousands of illegal PDF copies since December 2010, and the majority of these uploads went through the iFile.it website. The ruling came after seven months of investigations by private investigators led by a German publishing association, Börsenverein des Deutschen Buchhandels, and the International Publishers Association.[109]

At the time, this joint action by publishers was considered unusual, since their usual response was to send a takedown notice from their lawyers ordering the website company to take down copyrighted material. But in this case, these two websites were doing more than hosting a small number of book files. Instead they were "allegedly hosting and providing links to illegal PDF files of more than 400,000 books," which included some well-known authors, among them Salman Rushdie and Jonathan Franzen, and many expensive textbooks.[110]

What made investigating this case difficult is that the owners of Library.nu had used false names and addresses in registering its web domain names. To find them, the publishers' lawyers hired private investigators with the help of an organization in Ireland—the Irish National Federation Against Copyright Theft (http://infact.ie)—since the registered addresses for the owners of both sites were based in Ireland. Initially, they couldn't prove a link between the owners of both companies, but eventually they got their break on PayPal where users could donate to Library.nu in order to gain access for more files. Then, after they got an email from PayPal stating that admin@library.nu has received your donation, they found a real receipt from PayPal with the real names of the owners of the account, which matched the owners and directors of iFile.it. So with the proof that both sites were owned by the same individuals, the judge granted injunctions against both, after which Library.nu was shut down and visitors were directed to Google Books, while iFile.it could no longer allow unregistered users to upload files.[111]

Meanwhile, John Wiley began domestic efforts to retaliate against the individuals who downloaded its *For Dummies* books through a series of John Doe suits, beginning in October 2011. It filed the first of seven of these suits in New York against unknown defendants only identified by their IP addresses, and in December, January, and February 2012, it filed additional suits. One of its reasons for launching the suit was to get contact information for hundreds of sharers so it could offer them settlements—about $3,000 per person—and the courts were generally amenable to these requests, enabling the company to subpoena the Internet service providers for the information they needed.[112] As noted by their attorney Bill Dunnegan of Dunnegan & Scileppi in New York, the litigation was designed to "demonstrate or educate people that this type of infringement is not a no-risk proposition," and thereby "dry up the demand for (pirated) ebooks."[113]

Wiley also won a default judgment against one BitTorrent sharer of *WordPress for Dummies* for $7,000–$5,000 for copyright violation, plus $2,000 for violating counterfeiting Wiley's trademarks—substantially less than the $150,000 Wiley requested, but twice as much as the average settlement amount.[114]

A reason Wiley fought the *For Dummies* infringers was because the amount of revenue lost was enormous, with over seventy-four thousand copies of its *Photoshop CS5 All-In-One for Dummies* guide stolen over a sixteen-month period. Plus, it went after infringers for *WordPress for Dummies, Hacking for Dummies*, and *Day Trading for Dummies*.[115] It took four people to court, since they refused to settle, after Wiley asked the infringers to pay the minimum due under the Copyright Act as statutory damages: $750 versus a potential of loss of $150,000 per infringement.[116] Then, in January 2013, it won a lawsuit against another two downloaders, who were found guilty as charged and fined $7,000 in damages.[117]

While Wiley's lawsuit was successful in getting some small damages, it also put pirates on notice that the publishers might sue them. This led to some blowback, such as from author John Paul Titlow, who complained in his article, "Why Winning a $7,000 Piracy Lawsuit Could Be the Worst News Ever for Book Publishers." He suggested Wiley's strategy would only anger the most avid book readers, much like the RIAA's earlier attack on thousands of music pirates angered the "most avid, dedicated music fans."[118] But the strategy proved effective in that it eventually contributed to the music industry's success in creating another model for fans to pay. Moreover, Wiley's approach has differed from the music industry's shotgun approach, since it more narrowly targeted "the worst of the worst and people who are profiteering," thereby distinguishing between large-scale operators and small-scale downloaders.[119]

Other Strategies to Fight the Pirates

On another front, leading independent ebook publisher RosettaBooks achieved success in using Attributor's Digimarc Guardian system (http://www.digimarc.com/guardian) to prevent online piracy of its catalog of backlist and original titles. As described in its presentation at the Digital Book World Convention in New York, January 2013, the company began using the Guardian system in June 2011 to identify infringing websites and then send them takedown notices and warning letters. If the site didn't comply, the next step was contacting the hosting provider and the site might be delisted from search engines. Finally, payment providers and advertising networks were notified of the violation as well as domain registrars. The result was that legal action was only necessary in less than 5 percent of cases.[120]

In March 2013, Simon & Schuster entered the battle by sharing piracy statistics with authors and agents. Since 2011, the company also used Attributor, a company that scans hundreds of millions of web pages every day, including peer-to-peer networks, to fight ebook piracy by sending the infringing sites takedown notices to remove pirated content.[121] When Simon & Schuster began sharing its privacy stats, it enabled authors and agents to report piracy by using its online piracy report (http://www.simonandschuster.biz/online_piracy_report). The way it works is that you put in your email, publisher, book title, author, the offending URLs, and any comments, after which the offending sites are quickly notified to remove that content. Additionally, Simon & Schuster CEO and president Carolyn Reidy compiles these into a report that provides "information about the number of infringements identified and takedown notices sent to infringing sites, success rates in removing infringements, the types of sites where infringement is occurring, the specific URLs and geographic distribution of sites where unauthorized copies are offered, and more."[122]

Then, in June 2013, several large publishers—among them Wiley, Elsevier, and McGraw-Hill—filed a joint lawsuit against file-sharing system Usenet, forcing them to reveal the names of two members who uploaded illegal ebooks under the user names "Hockwards" and "Rockhound." Presumably, anyone who downloaded anything from them could become a part of this suit.[123]

However, such lawsuits are actually quite rare. According to a 2012 study by the American Assembly at Columbia University, 46 percent of Americans and 70 percent of young Americans eighteen to twenty are copyright pirates. Though copyright holders can sue them for a lot of money—up to $150,000 in statutory damages per copyright infringement—these laws are mostly unenforced. Aside from the cases involving Wiley, with multiple defendants settling for a few thousand dollars, there have only been a few headline cases in which some unfortunate individuals have been targeted for punishment. An example is the case of thirty-seven-year-old Jammie Thomas-Rasset, a mother of four in Minnesota, who was ordered to pay record labels $222,000 for downloading and sharing two dozen copyrighted songs on the file-sharing network Kazaa, which is now out of business. Her case even went to the Supreme Court, which upheld the lower court's verdict in 2013.[124]

To some extent, federal agencies have contributed to reducing the number of pirates of books, films, games, and software, since the US government's action led to the closure of Megaupload, which was one of the biggest cyberlockers in the world.[125] Though similar sites sprung up or continued to operate, there was a decline in the number of users; however, these agencies have done little to go after the book pirates, as well as those pirating music and films. This is perhaps because they are focused on other types of Internet crime, most recently on the hacks into major corporations resulting in the theft of all types of data, including customer and personal information.

The Growing Difficulty of Battling the Pirates

But other publishers have felt powerless to do anything to stop the pirates. as Rick Townley addresses in a *Washington Times* article, "Frustrated Publishers Find There Are No Easy Solutions to Book Piracy." According to Townley, digital editions of Stephen King's new book *Joyland* were pirated and began circulating on the Internet within days of its publication by Hard Case Crimes. But the publisher felt that it was impossible to do anything, as is the opinion of a growing number of publishers because, as Townley points out: "With a little online searching you can find unlicensed copies of most current bestsellers and thousands of backstock books. Pirates seem to pride themselves on variety and selection."[126] And in some countries, book pirating is especially rampant, such as Russia, Spain, Nigeria, Pakistan, Germany, Peru, and India; in fact, in some of these countries, the number of pirated books are greater than the number of legitimate books being sold, such as in Russia and Peru. For example, in Russia, in 2012, over one hundred thousand pirated ebooks were available online; in Peru, more people are employed in pirate firms than legitimate publishers; in India, children on the streets earning $2 for each pirated book they sell average three sales a day and earn more than a father who works at a trade job, such as plumbing, though the children themselves cannot read the books they sell.[127]

And some types of piracy are worse than ever, such as the piracy of books by students. Science and engineering books are the most pirated, due to the high costs of new editions released annually, along with the big increase in tuition fees, the scarcity of jobs, and a lessening reliance on hardcover copies. And even some lecturers using out of print book titles encourage students to download illegally.[128]

No wonder the publishers feel frustrated. It is like they are snuffing out a few weeds in a garden, but then the rains come and the weeds are out in even greater force. Even the lawsuits targeting hundreds of users and some of the biggest piracy offenders have done little to stem the tide. Now that the technology is available for ebooks and scanning technology is even better for copying legitimate books to make illegal copies, piracy is easier and more rampant than ever. Like traffic tickets, the lawsuits may have stifled some pirates, but many return to the business under another name, while other eager pirates return to continue to distribute the pirated books, whether through uploads and downloads, streaming services, scanning counterfeit copies, or other means.

So while legal efforts have gained some monetary return and stopped some pirates, the high cost of an investigation and lawsuit, which often involves tracking down piracy sites in other countries and downloaders around the world, means that this is a response limited to those with means—namely the biggest publishers. But writers and small publishers generally can't afford this approach, and because of the vast number of pirates, these efforts can only take down a few of the most notorious pirates and individuals obtaining pirated materials from these sites. These legal battles may result in winning a particular battle, but it doesn't have much effect in losing the larger war.

Some Technological Responses to Piracy

It's possible that some technological responses may provide an answer to reducing piracy. One is the sticks approach of making it harder to find or duplicate pirated books or watermarking them to indicate this book has been pirated and by whom. The other is the carrots approach of providing easier and cheaper ways to obtain legitimate books, similar to the music and film industries providing services like iTunes, Netflix, and Redbox for inexpensively obtaining music and videos. Though the problem is not completely eliminated, it is much reduced. David Price, the director of piracy analysis for the online data monitoring company NetNames, explains: "The best way to beat piracy is to get your content out there, to give it to people in some way or make them buy it in some simple, cheap, easy way."[129]

The takedown notice, which has long been a standard approach, advises the owner of a website or the hosting service to take down the site or else be subject to penalties for copyright infringement. And mostly the services, if not the website owners, do take down the material, though it may pop up again elsewhere, and these notices can be a prelude to subsequent litigation. However, this is a labor-intensive, time-consuming process that can take publishers and writers away from publishing and writing books. So now a number of piracy-protection companies have emerged that can send out automated notices for its clients. The way this works is that these companies use algorithms to find illegal copies of books and other materials. Then, they send out the DMCA takedown notices, which include the links to specific URLs, hosting sites, Internet service providers, and search engines. The result is that in a day or two, the notice recipients will take down the offending files and the search engines will remove their links from their search results pages.[130]

Muso, one of these companies, has removed over 580,000 illegal files for its publishing clients in 2014. This is a substantial savings for the companies, since the average file is downloaded three hundred times, and even with a low estimate of one hundred downloads per file, that is potentially almost sixty million downloads, according to Muso's client manager for publishing.[131] In turn, this removal process has tangible results in reducing piracy. For instance, to take just the results of one company, ebook publisher Rosetta Books experienced a 15 percent increase in its sales as a result of Digimarc's piracy protection program of sending out takedown notices.[132]

Technology has also come to the rescue in a copyright alert system agreed to by some major ISPs—including Comcast, Verizon, and AT & T—which notifies subscribers in a series of six warnings when they are downloading or streaming illegal content.[133]

Another strategy involves using technology to reduce the visibility of the piracy sites. Google took this route in August 2012 by adjusting its algorithm to give sites with a high number of piracy notices a lower ranking, as noted by Jason Boog in "Google Gives Lower Search Rankings to Piracy Sites." The number of complaints Google has reviewed is huge. In September 2012 alone, the company received 4.4 million requests to take down URLs for copyright violations, though unless Google receives a valid copyright removal notice from the rights owner, it won't remove any pages from its search results.[134]

But more than just lowering the search rankings, Google will remove the violator's links entirely from its search-engine results pages through its Trusted Copyright Removal Program. This program streamlines the process of eliminating infringing sites for its members, which include a number of piracy protection companies, such DMCA Force, Muso, and Digimarcs. In fact, some companies, such as DMCA Force, have found that this delisting works even more efficiently than sending notices to both the search engines and offending sites.[135] Here's how the program works for trusted submitters: The member sends in a notice to report content they would like removed, and many of these requests are added to a Chilling Effects project, which Google has entered into with US law schools. The project creates a database and information on the requests to remove information from the Internet, though the submitter's personal contact information is redacted. Additionally, the information from the notice is added to Google's Transparency Report, which indicates the number of URLs to remove. Google may also send a notice to the alleged infringer, and if Google should suspect the validity of the complaint, a notice will go to the rights holder as well. Among other things, members of the program submit not only their own name, company name, country, and email, but also the copyright owner or owners they represent, the identity and description of the copyright work, the location (URLs) of the infringing material, and where they can see an authorized example of the work. Then, this information is used to remove material from Google's search engine and then sent to YouTube, Blogger, and Picasa, a photo-sharing site.[136]

The number of removal requests per month is amazing, according to Google's Transparency Report. For example, the number of URLs requested to be removed from Google's Search was 35,787,908 URLs in one month from 56,595 specified domains representing 4,893 copyright owners and 2,124 reporting organizations![137] Also, the Transparency Report includes information on the top reporting organizations—Degban, BPI (the British Recording Music Industry), Takedown Piracy, Skywalker Digital, and Unidam—which have requested between 2.5 to 5.9 million URLs with offending content, on the top copyright owners who had infringed upon material with nearly 2 million to 3.5 million URLs each, and the top domains that were described as having illegal material with 500,000 to 1.4 million URLs on them: unblocked.pw, unblock.re, vmusice.net, uploaded.net, and rapidgator.net.[138]

Google has also participated in the effort to stem piracy by prohibiting publishers to use its AdSense program to put ads on pages of websites that contain pirated content. In turn, piracy-protection companies and the law firms hired by publishers have contributed to knowing which websites do this by creating lists of domain names for websites with pirated content.[139]

Another approach has been to introduce Digital Rights Management (DRM) strategies. One has been to put a lock on ebooks, so they can't be shared on any devices other than the one the book was originally uploaded on, although tech-savvy pirates have been able to readily disable these locks to share the book. At the same time, some publishers resist this method since it could antagonize customers. For example, if a customer has purchased an ebook copy for one device, such as a Kindle, and then that device breaks or is stolen, so they have to get another, they would be locked out of a book they have previously purchased.[140]

On the other hand, Tor Books UK, one publisher who tried dropping its copy protection from ebooks, found there was no "discernable increase in piracy" on any of their titles, though possibly that resulted from Tor having a close-knit science-fiction/fantasy reader community with a very large online presence.[141] Thus, being a part of this community, readers might not feel comfortable seeking out illegal copies of these books.

Another approach that has contributed to reducing piracy goes beyond just offering a good product at a fair price. It's also important to make it easy to buy, like Apple and Amazon have done by creating a single click-to-buy button.[142] So if the price is reasonable, the ease of making a purchase reduces the chance an individual will look for an illegal copy of the book elsewhere.

A more recent strategy developed by German researchers at the Fraunhofer Institute is to change the wording in a book to combat piracy. The idea behind this version of DRM, called SiDiM, is to provide a digital watermark[143] that is unique to each ebook when it's sold, so it can be tracked and linked back to the person who first purchased it. Theoretically, this watermark will scare consumers away from illegal sharing for the fear of getting caught, which might subject them to criminal or civil penalties. However, the approach has been criticized by some writers who don't like the technology changing their work, like switching the order of words or changing one word into another with a similar meaning, such as turning the word "unhealthy" into "not healthy."

Still another approach, launched in July 2014 by the piracy protection company Digimarc, involves putting invisible watermarks known as Guardian watermarking on individual ebooks. While Digimarc is putting these marks on the ebooks with select partners, such as Harper Collins, it is an approach that others can use to identify individuals pirating their books.[144] The system enables publishers to track down those who are uploading ebooks to torrenting websites, enabling the publishers to take action against and prevent piracy reoccurrence. But unlike DRM, which restricts consumers from using a book on another system, the watermark has no negative impacts on legitimate consumers, since it only tracks people who are illegally uploading or downloading the books. In addition, Digimarc claims the watermark is very difficult to remove, so it will be expensive for the pirates to fund removal.[145]

NPR writer James Glynn outlines another approach developed in Russia, a country where digital piracy has run rampant. The strategy involves creating a streaming service, like a Netflix or Spotify for books.

The Russian company Dream Industries created Bookmate, a subscription reading service that provides access to its library of over 225,000 books in English and Russian for only about $5 a month. The app is designed to work on multiple devices and operating systems.[146]

However, unlike the piracy sites that are charging subscription services but not paying writers or publishers, Bookmate has created partnerships with publishers in the US and UK in order to bring English-language books to Russia, Turkey, Nigeria, Pakistan, India, and the Philippines, which have huge numbers of native and other English speakers—about 380 million of them, even more than in the US, UK, and Canada combined. Moreover, these readers tend to be more educated, have smartphones, and want to read.[147] But according to Bookmate's head of global development, James Appell, these readers "aren't being served through traditional sales channels." So the goal is for publishers to use Bookmate to reach readers who "previously either read pirated copies of these books or who didn't read them at all because they were unaffordable."[148] Another advantage of this streaming service for publishers is that it provides insight into customers' reading habits and behaviors, so publishers can better reach out to them and use this data for publicity and communication purposes.

The Bookmate book-streaming service has been available in Russia since 2009 and has partnered with all of the major Russian book publishers; in addition to its over two hundred thousand Russian language titles, the company has reached out to other devices and markets. For instance, besides reaching out to customers directly to buy subscriptions, it has sought to partner with a number of device manufacturers, telecommunication companies, and retailers to get Bookmate bundled with other services.[149] For example, it might be included in the price of a handset, so readers feel comfortable to pay. The advantage of such a subscription service, according to Simon Dunlap, CEO of Dream Industries, is that it "can provide copyright owners with some level of protection, as it makes content much harder to copy." But this also means that the publishing industry, which has shown very little innovation during the digital revolution, needs to be more innovative in how they sell their books, rather than simply selling a book for $10 on a digital service that might sell for $10 in a store. In this view, the publishing industry needs to "rip up the business model" and "start to sell fractions of the book for smaller prices and with different ways of paying—maybe give 100 different ways that I can access and pay for that experience—that's innovation."[150]

Another approach from writers has been posting warnings about certain companies, which include pirated copy along with legitimate writing calling for better policing of their site to get rid of pirated material. For example, in a blog post on *Writer Beware*, a writers' support website sponsored by the Science Fiction and Fantasy Writers of America, Michael Capobianco complained about the new subscription ebook service and many illegally uploaded copyright files available on Scribd, which doesn't pay writers for those uploads. In describing the problems with Scribd, he used screenshots of the site to show how, with the addition of the preview service, Scribd now offers nonsubscribers previews of both legal and illegal content. And then once a person had subscribed, he or she had access to numerous illegally uploaded copyrighted files, which could only be read in their entirety through full-text access if a person became a Scribd subscriber.

In response, Scribd's VP of Content Acquisition, Michael Weinstein, acknowledged the issue and said that the company was trying to deal with the problems on an individual basis with takedown notices, as well as through the development of a technological solution.[151] For instance, in November 2013, he spoke with the Association of American Publishers about the company's four-point program to deal with pirated content on Scribd. The program included the following plans for action, which might provide a model for other sites with pirated content that are trying to offer legal material:

- posting clear legal terms of use banning the uploading of copyrighted material by others;

- using a technical solution, such as a document fingerprint system, in which publishers provide an unencrypted copy of content to enable Scribd software to reject unauthorized uploads that match the original copy;

- developing a "robust process of reaction" by offering a copyright link with instructions and guidelines for writers or publishers to use to report pirated content and then reacting within one day or less to take steps to remove that content;

- working with content management services, such as Attributor, a service that monitors online content, to help these companies do the bulk DMCS takedown notices and seek other ways to help them find infringing content.[152]

While this may be a workable method, the copyright fingerprint system is still an imperfect one and it depends on publisher buy-in for the system to work at all, and this hasn't happened yet, according to Scribd VP Weinstein. One barrier has been obtaining unencrypted content from publishers to help prevent pirates from uploading illegal content. Also, since Scribd doesn't have relationships with all publishers, there is a great deal of copyrighted material that the system can't recognize. Plus, there has been a lack of communicating about Scribd's approach to authors about what it has been trying to do, so there is a perception that Scribd is one more site pirating their work.[153]

The Growing Call for Alternatives to Piracy

Since 2014, it seems like some of the debate about what to do about book piracy has changed to reflect its pervasiveness and the difficulty of fighting pirates to the need to find new models of getting consumers to buy legal books inexpensively, which will cause piracy to decline. After all, if the pirates are making less money, the reasoning goes, there will be less piracy and fewer pirates. It's a matter of economic supply and demand. While some of the same tired pro-piracy arguments—that pirates help new writers get discovered, and that not everyone who steals your book would buy it if piracy weren't an option—still exist, the hope is for a shift to providing individuals with another way to get the material they want in a less costly way, thereby undermining the economic model that helps piracy flourish.

In a February 2014 article, "The Pointlessness of Fighting E-Book Piracy," Matt Forney argues exactly that. After pointing out that DRM and other anti-piracy measures don't work well—since they punish people who legally buy books by restricting how they can use them—he asserts: "The simple reality is that if you want to sell anything today, you have no choice but to put up with piracy."[154] He suggests that piracy can be an indicator that people like your work, and the vast majority of customers will buy your books to support you and see you succeed, even if it is on pirate sites like *The Pirate Bay*, as long as they can buy your book for a reasonable price and see value in it. For example, Matt puts out a lot of quality work for free and finds that people are then willing to buy his books because they figure they are worth the money, after seeing value in his free material.[155]

While noting the major threats pirated books pose to consumers, writers, and publishers, in an April 2014 column, Naturi Thomas-Millard makes a similar argument in an April 2014 column. He believes that the industry needs to adjust its pricing to make the purchase price more reasonable given the technology changes of the digital age. As he points out, with the rise of e-readers and digital bookstores, it's easy to strip the DRM protections or digital locks from files, so pirates can mass distribute books—not like the old days when pirated books had to be manually scanned before being uploaded or sold in a counterfeit edition. But there are strategies writers can use to sell books, such as offering free material as a loss leader or making ebooks more inexpensive, given the much lower costs of publishing digital books.[156]

Thomas-Millard describes how Neil Gaiman noticed that his work was being pirated around the globe, but sales went up in the countries where his work was illegally distributed. So he tried an experiment with his publisher's approval. He made his entire novel free for a month as a way of "beating the pirates at their own game,"[157] and he found that this tactic resulted in more sales in the future, because the free book helped to spark purchasing interest in the future after the free promotion was over. Thus, as he describes, he is a strong advocate for publishers lowering their pricing to make books more widely available. As he puts it:

"One of the surest ways to curtail digital piracy is to make the materials such as eBooks and movies legally available and accessible the world over. Neil Gaiman's pirated books, for example, were largely found in Russia, where his books were difficult to obtain.

"The publishing industry also needs to catch up and play fair. Sites like Spotify and Netflix allow fans to access music and movies while respecting the rights (and copyrights) of those whose work is involved. While it's to be assumed that there are costs engendered with the manufacture of eBooks, it's hard to believe that these costs could be anywhere near those of producing paper books. If this is the case, why are eBooks almost as expensive (and in some cases, more so) than physical copies of new releases? If they were priced more reasonably, consumers might be more likely to purchase them legally, and authors would see more of the profits."[158]

Another suggested approach is working with the pirates to actually gain publicity and sales of the legitimate version of the book. For example, in an April 2014 article on AuthorMedia.com, Thomas Umstattd argues to authors that "Piracy Is Not Your Enemy." Rather, the biggest enemy is obscurity. One author even gained success by uploading his book to some bit torrent pirate sites, which resulted in tens of thousands of legal downloads and increased sales. Umstattd writes:

"If a million people 'steal' your book, you win. As long as you get credit, you win when people share your book with others. Books that sell well spread from person to person like a virus. The harder you make it to share your work, the more obscure you will be."[159]

In fact, Umstattd suggests several ways that authors can win from piracy:

"You win because your platform grows; you can book more speaking engagements at higher prices . . .

"Your publisher wins free marketing. Your publisher spends a lot of time and money trying to get people to talk about your book. Books sell from word of mouth. Allowing people to share your work turns them into evangelists for free! More talk = more sales."[160]

Still another argument in favor of making ebooks cheap and convenient to reduce piracy is from David Gaughran, author of "Let's Get Digital," directed to self-publishers on how to sell more books. By contrast, he points out the failure of the approach of many big publishers to use DRM, the proprietary software owned by Amazon, to protect their ebooks, sold only through Kindle. Not only does it prevent publishers from bundling print and digital book offerings to customers, it also restricts authors who want to give free copies to reviewers. But worse, the technology doesn't work to combat piracy, since any hacker can easily crack DRM in a few seconds, and all it takes is cracking the code of a single book to put it out on the torrent sites where it can be copied repeatedly by anyone. Or a hacker can easily strip off the lock, since publishers have to give readers the key so they can open the lock. So hackers can readily obtain a key, and presto, the file with the book is easy pickings. The result, as Gaughran notes, is that "publishers' insistence on DRM prevents them from competing with Amazon, selling direct, and bundling." Even worse is using DRM, "antagonizing legal, playing customers," since all they have to do is switch devices (such as from a Kindle to a Nook), and they could lose their entire library, because they can no longer access their books that they already paid for. The result: Many readers learn to crack DRM or turn to the torrent sites to download the book.[161]

Thus, the solution to the piracy problem, he asserts, is to recognize that there is "no way to get rid of piracy" because "once you make a digital product available to the public, it will be pirated by someone, somewhere." But there are ways to reduce piracy that actually work. How? By "making your books available everywhere, in all formats. And price means making your books cheap enough that piracy is more hassle than it's worth." While major publishers took the opposite approach to hold back the digital revolution in various ways, such as taking a go-slow approach to digitizing their backlist, engaging in an illegal conspiracy to fix the price of ebooks, and using an unworkable DRM system, self-publishers don't have to do that. The solution is to "price cheaply" and not "waste time and money hunting down pirates."[162]

In short, don't worry about the excuses and explanations of the pirates claiming what they are doing is not wrong because they are just sharing or it is only fair that they can use the books freely, because otherwise they are priced far too high. Instead, for economic reasons, the best way for the publishers and writers to fight back is by pricing their work cheaply, so there is no economic incentive to put the time and effort into finding pirated books. Under this model, it is pointless to take an active approach to combating piracy and there are many ways that piracy might be beneficial to authors. For example, piracy might help them rise from obscurity into becoming well known, or it might help sell more books, assuming they are priced reasonably.

In keeping with this approach of making ebooks more accessible to reduce piracy, some Internet bookstores and e-text portals are liberalizing sharing permissions to create a lending library online.[163] What this means is that there is a subscription fee or a per-book lending charge, with some of the earned amount going back to the publishers and writers, based on the number of times their books are borrowed.

Another approach is for an educational campaign. These campaigns can alert pirates about how their acts are harming writers, providing ways in which they might legally obtain books as well as supporting the writers with good reviews and comments on social media. For example, in a June 2014 blog about book piracy, Lucy Powrie had this to say:

"I understand why people may feel the need to pirate books, I really do. After all, books can be incredibly expensive and to some people buying them just isn't an option. That, however, does not make piracy acceptable.

"Every time somebody pirates a book, part of that book dies. Do you want to be responsible for the book deaths, you murderer? . . .

"Many authors have to work second and third jobs to allow them to do what they love. By pirating books, you're completely disrespecting them . . . Pirating means that you're lowering the chance of the author getting any royalties in the first place, and increasing the time it will take them to earn those royalties.

"There are so many other options: visiting your local library to take out books, second hand bookshops, borrowing from friends, trading books. The difference is that all of the books have been paid for beforehand in some form and so, whilst you're not contributing, you're still supporting the author. Feel bad? You can help the author even more by leaving reviews on websites and talking as much as you can about the book via the social media and offline.

"Most people wouldn't go into a shop and walk out without paying, so how is a book any different. It's not. **Piracy is theft**."[164]

Another educational strategy is for publishers, writers, and the media to advise readers that there are risks of getting a free ebook, such as the possibility of getting a virus-infected computer, or the ebook could be used as a come-on to get personal information from one's computer. For example, Harper Collins Chief Digital Officer Chantel Restivo-Alessi says that the industry needs to communicate the risks more to readers "so that people start to think, 'I might be saving a few bucks, but do I really want to risk spending $100 or $200 [on repair] and losing my existing content in the process?'"[165]

In short, all kinds of alternatives have been developed to reduce piracy outside of the criminal justice and civil litigation model, because the war against them seems unwinnable. It's like prohibition in the 1920s or the drug wars from the 1940s to the present. So many people are doing it, that it doesn't make sense to continue to enforce laws or litigate against it in what is an expensive, time-consuming strategy of targeting individual consumers, rather than using strategies to take down the piracy sites, make it difficult to find them, or offer less expensive legal alternatives so consumers can buy legal copies conveniently and at a reasonable price. This is not to deny that piracy is an economic problem, because it definitely has resulted in declines in sales and the loss of hundreds of thousands of jobs—an estimated 750,000 in the entertainment industry, including books, music, and films, in recent years. But instead, as John Aziz suggests in a July 2014 article in *The Week,* since one can't eliminate the pirates, the entertainment industry has "moved on to another, smarter proposition," based on offering a service that is "better quality, more reliable, and more accessible." He writes:

"Internet piracy is a messy game—files are often incorrectly labeled, sound quality can be poor, download speeds can be unreliable, and those who choose to pirate risk downloading spyware and malware. Services like Spotify, iTunes, Rdio, Beats Music, Netflix, Hulu, Sony, and Amazon are offering shed-loads of high-quality legal entertainment for a reasonable price that—importantly—goes to compensate the creators. These services are already making big inroads, and piracy is falling as a result."[166]

It is an approach that is gaining support worldwide, based on the notion that the pirates on the Internet will always be a step ahead as they find ways around the latest technological steps to defeat piracy. So the solution to piracy will include "better pricing and availability," which will have an effect on the market, while educational campaigns will help "to sway some of those sitting on the fence" to not pirate copyrighted material. And here the ISPs can help with a "notice-and-notice scheme to warn and educate consumers."[167]

And so the war on piracy goes on, although it has most recently seemed to shift from a focus on suing the pirates or pursuing them through law enforcement action to finding ways to work with them. Examples include using the pirated materials as a kind of marketing tool to increase visibility and sell other materials, or work around them by creating more attractive ways to entice buyers through lower pricing, convenience, and quality materials so they are less likely to seek this material from pirates.

So what should you do if you discover your own work has been pirated? There is a chapter in the final section on what you can do. The following sections provide a more detailed description of the protections provided by the copyright law and what law enforcement has done in the past to fight back against the pirates.

PART III

The Copyright Law and Infringement

CHAPTER 13

The Remedies for Infringement under US Copyright Law

Suppose you do have a book or other material that has been pirated. What exactly are your rights? Generally, assuming you have registered a copyright that permits statutory damages up to $150,000—not just damages you can prove—the basic remedy is to send a takedown notice to the owner of the website. If they do not respond, the notice goes to the service hosting the website, or to both at the same time. Normally, if the website owner doesn't take down the copyrighted material, the website service provider will, and sometimes that will mean the whole website will come down. And usually that will be the end of it, unless you choose to take some legal action for damages and statutory penalties.

So far, these legal actions have mainly been taken by the larger publishers, individually or as part of a collective of publishers. But these actions are very time consuming and expensive, and then there may be appeals and difficulties in collecting the judgment. So a growing trend for writers and publishers, especially the smaller independents, is to give up on taking any legal action and send out takedown notices themselves, through piracy protection services or through others acting on their behalf, to get the infringing material removed from websites and search engines, or find ways to benefit from what the pirates are doing to promote one's own website and books and sell other materials.

Still, it helps to understand the different laws that can be used like weapons to combat the pirates, accomplices, and supporters. Then, you can use that in your strategy in deciding what to do, as well as how to use the various tools to protect your work. It also helps to know what lawyers and government officials might do to help you figure out the legal strategies and criminal codes they can use to fight the battle. Perhaps individually you may not be able to do much beyond sending out takedown notices or working with a privacy protection service to do that for you. But if collectively enough publishers or writers get together after they have had their work pirated by the same pirates or group of pirates, they might take some legal action—or they might interest law enforcement in taking some action against the pirates, too.

The following chapters deal with understanding the major copyright laws to help you decide how these laws protect you and what to do when you discover an infringement and want to get the infringer to stop doing it—or want to pursue damages for the infringement individually or part of a group lawsuit. A copy of a sample takedown notice is included in the Appendix.

The Remedies for Copyright Infringement

One of the most basic weapons is the US Copyright Law 17 USC #504, which provides remedies for infringement based on actual damages and profits or statutory damages. As provided in the law, if you own the copyright, you can choose which option, though you need to have already registered the copyright within a three-month window of publication to opt for statutory damages.

To recover actual damages and profits, you have to show what damages you suffered due to the infringement, along with the infringer's profits, based on his or her gross revenue, while the infringer has to show any deductible expenses and what profits came from sources other than the copyrighted work.

In the case of statutory damages, you can recover between $750 to $30,000, based on what the court considers just, from one or more infringers who are liable jointly and severally for each work—a common approach applied to those downloading the work. Should the infringement be considered willful, as in the case of the site owners or those providing multiple uploads, the court can increase the damages up to $150,000. It is up to the violator to show that the infringement was not committed willfully, since it is a rebuttable presumption that a violation was willful.

The US Copyright Code with Remedies for Infringement

Following is the exact language of the law in Title 17, #504 of the US Copyright Law, as provided by the US Copyright Office (http://www. copyright.gov/title17/92chap5.html). You can include a reference to this code to strengthen your argument in asking violators to remove your copyrighted material posted online without your permission, in seeking a settlement from them, or in participating in litigation to claim damages and/or profits.

§ 504. Remedies for infringement: Damages and profits

a. IN GENERAL. — EXCEPT as otherwise provided by this title, an infringer of copyright is liable for either —

   1. the copyright owner's actual damages and any additional profits of the infringer, as provided by subsection (b); or

   2. statutory damages, as provided by subsection (c).

b. ACTUAL DAMAGES AND PROFITS. — The copyright owner is entitled to recover the actual damages suffered by him or her as a result of the infringement, and any profits of the infringer that are attributable to the infringement and are not taken into account in computing the actual damages. In establishing the infringer's profits, the copyright owner is required to present proof only of the infringer's gross revenue, and the infringer is required to prove his or her deductible expenses and the elements of profit attributable to factors other than the copyrighted work.

c. STATUTORY DAMAGES. —

   1. Except as provided by clause (2) of this subsection, the copyright owner may elect, at any time before final judgment is rendered, to recover, instead of actual damages and profits, an award of statutory damages for all infringements involved in

the action, with respect to any one work, for which any one infringer is liable individually, or for which any two or more infringers are liable jointly and severally, in a sum of not less than $750 or more than $30,000 as the court considers just. For the purposes of this subsection, all the parts of a compilation or derivative work constitute one work.

2. In a case where the copyright owner sustains the burden of proving, and the court finds, that infringement was committed willfully, the court in its discretion may increase the award of statutory damages to a sum of not more than $150,000. In a case where the infringer sustains the burden of proving, and the court finds, that such infringer was not aware and had no reason to believe that his or her acts constituted an infringement of copyright, the court in its discretion may reduce the award of statutory damages to a sum of not less than $200. The court shall remit statutory damages in any case where an infringer believed and had reasonable grounds for believing that his or her use of the copyrighted work was a fair use under section 107, if the infringer was: (i) an employee or agent of a nonprofit educational institution, library, or archives acting within the scope of his or her employment who, or such institution, library, or archives itself, which infringed by reproducing the work in copies or phonorecords; or (ii) a public broadcasting entity which or a person who, as a regular part of the nonprofit activities of a public broadcasting entity (as defined in section 118(f)) infringed by performing a published nondramatic literary work or by reproducing a transmission program embodying a performance of such a work.

3. A. In a case of infringement, it shall be a rebuttable presumption that the infringement was committed willfully for purposes of determining relief if the violator, or a person acting in concert with the violator, knowingly provided or knowingly caused to be provided materially false contact information to a domain name registrar, domain name registry, or other domain name registration authority in

registering, maintaining, or renewing a domain name used in connection with the infringement.

B. Nothing in this paragraph limits what may be considered willful infringement under this subsection.

C. For purposes of this paragraph, the term "domain name" has the meaning given that term in section 45 of the Act entitled "An Act to provide for the registration and protection of trademarks used in commerce, to carry out the provisions of certain international conventions, and for other purposes" approved July 5, 1946 (commonly referred to as the "Trademark Act of 1946"; 15 U.S.C. 1127).

d. ADDITIONAL DAMAGES IN CERTAIN CASES. — In any case in which the court finds that a defendant proprietor of an establishment who claims as a defense that its activities were exempt under section 110(5) did not have reasonable grounds to believe that its use of a copyrighted work was exempt under such section, the plaintiff shall be entitled to, in addition to any award of damages under this section, an additional award of two times the amount of the license fee that the proprietor of the establishment concerned should have paid the plaintiff for such use during the preceding period of up to 3 years.

CHAPTER 14

The Limitations on Liability for Service Providers

BESIDES US COPYRIGHT LAW: 17 USC #504, which provides remedies for infringement based on actual damages and profits or statutory damages, other laws provide exceptions from liability for service providers. By knowing about these laws, you can both better know the steps for notifying the infringers yourself, and know what to expect in response to a takedown notice when piracy protection services or others act on your behalf.

The key provisions in the US Copyright Code that carve out this exception are #512 (a) (b) and (c), which provide limitations of liability for certain online providers who are not the actual infringers and don't know about the infringement. More specifically, under #512(a), those who transmit, route, or provide connections for the infringing material are excluded, if the transmission was initiated by or at the direction of someone other than the service provider, if the transmission occurred through an automatic technical process without any selection or modification of the content, or if the transmitter made no copy of the material beyond the time needed to transmit it.

Under #512(b), a service provider has no liability for storing any material in the system if someone besides the service provider makes this material available online and the storage occurs through an automatic technical process to make the material available to those using the system. Then, too, under #512(c) the service provider isn't liable if he or she is unaware that the material on the system or network is infringing and, once aware of the infringement, quickly responds to remove or disable any access to material which is claimed to be infringing, after receiving a notification of this claimed infringement.

In other words, a website hosting service or communications provider like Hostcentric, Yahoo, or Google won't be liable for a website hosted or listed by them, when they are unaware that the website is posting copyrighted material, unless they are notified about the claim of infringement. Then, their responsibility is to remove the material or disable access to it, After that they will commonly notify the alleged infringer about the removal or denial of access, so the alleged infringer has an opportunity to file a counterclaim that the infringement claim is a mistake or a misidentification, though counterclaims are unlikely when you own the material.

Moreover, to avoid liability, a service provider has to have a designated agent to receive notifications of a claimed infringement and must provide this information through its service, such as on its website where the public can readily see it. In addition, it has to provide the Copyright Office with the agent's name, address, phone number, email address, and any other contact information required by the Register of Copyrights. In turn, the Register of Copyrights keeps a current directory of agents available, including on the Internet, for the public to inspect.

Following is the law as stated in Title 17, Chapter 512, (a)(b) and (c) of the US Copyright Law (http://www.copyright.gov/title17/92chap5.html). You might include a reference to this code in your initial letter to a service provider to strengthen your claim. Then, if they don't immediately respond to take down or remove access, they will become liable, and you can use their failure to act in seeking a settlement from them or in including them in litigation to claim damages and/or profits.

§ 512. Limitations on liability relating to material online

a. TRANSITORY DIGITAL NETWORK COMMUNICATIONS. — A service provider shall not be liable for monetary relief, or, except as provided in subsection (j), for injunctive or other equitable relief, for infringement of copyright by reason of the provider's transmitting, routing, or providing connections for, material through a system or network controlled or operated by or for the service provider, or by reason of the intermediate and transient storage of that material in the course of such transmitting, routing, or providing connections, if —

1. the transmission of the material was initiated by or at the direction of a person other than the service provider;

2. the transmission, routing, provision of connections, or storage is carried out through an automatic technical process without selection of the material by the service provider;

3. the service provider does not select the recipients of the material except as an automatic response to the request of another person;

4. no copy of the material made by the service provider in the course of such intermediate or transient storage is maintained on the system or network in a manner ordinarily accessible to anyone other than anticipated recipients, and no such copy is maintained on the system or network in a manner ordinarily accessible to such anticipated recipients for a longer period than is reasonably necessary for the transmission, routing, or provision of connections; and

5. the material is transmitted through the system or network without modification of its content.

b. SYSTEM CACHING. —

1. LIMITATION ON LIABILITY. — A service provider shall not be liable for monetary relief, or, except as provided in subsection (j), for injunctive or other equitable relief, for infringement of copyright by reason of the intermediate and temporary storage of material on a system or network controlled or operated by or for the service provider in a case in which —

A. the material is made available online by a person other than the service provider;

B. the material is transmitted from the person described in subparagraph (A) through the system or network to a person other than the person described in subparagraph (A) at the direction of that other person; and

C. the storage is carried out through an automatic technical process for the purpose of making the material available to users of the system or network who, after the material is transmitted as described in subparagraph (B), request access to the material from the person described in subparagraph (A), if the conditions set forth in paragraph (2) are met.

2. CONDITIONS. — The conditions referred to in paragraph (1) are that —

A. the material described in paragraph (1) is transmitted to the subsequent users described in paragraph (1)(C) without modification to its content from the manner in which the material was transmitted from the person described in paragraph (1)(A);

B. the service provider described in paragraph (1) complies with rules concerning the refreshing, reloading, or other updating of the material when specified by the person making the material available online in accordance with a generally accepted industry standard data communications protocol for the system or network through which that person makes the material available, except that this subparagraph applies only if those rules are not used by the person described in paragraph (1)(A) to prevent or unreasonably impair the intermediate storage to which this subsection applies;

C. the service provider does not interfere with the ability of technology associated with the material to return to the person described in paragraph (1)(A) the information that would have been available to that person if the material had been obtained by the subsequent users described in paragraph (1)(C) directly from that person, except that this subparagraph applies only if that technology -

i. does not significantly interfere with the performance of the provider's system or network or with the intermediate storage of the material;

ii. is consistent with generally accepted industry standard communications protocols; and

iii. does not extract information from the provider's system or network other than the information that would have been available to the person described in paragraph (1)(A) if the subsequent users had gained access to the material directly from that person;

D. if the person described in paragraph (1)(A) has in effect a condition that a person must meet prior to having access to the material, such as a condition based on payment of a fee or provision of a password or other information, the service provider permits access to the stored material in significant part only to users of its system or network that have met those conditions and only in accordance with those conditions; and

E. if the person described in paragraph (1)(A) makes that material available online without the authorization of the copyright owner of the material, the service provider responds expeditiously to remove, or disable access to, the material that is claimed to be infringing upon notification of claimed infringement as described in subsection (c)(3), except that this subparagraph applies only if —

i. the material has previously been removed from the originating site or access to it has been disabled, or a court has ordered that the material be removed from the originating site or that access to the material on the originating site be disabled; and

ii. the party giving the notification includes in the notification a statement confirming that the material has been
removed from the originating site or access to it has
been disabled or that a court has ordered that the material be removed from the originating site or that access
to the material on the originating site be disabled.

c. INFORMATION RESIDING ON SYSTEMS OR NETWORKS AT DIREC-
TION OF USERS. —

1. IN GENERAL. — A service provider shall not be liable for monetary relief, or, except as provided in subsection (j), for injunctive or other equitable relief, for infringement of copyright by
reason of the storage at the direction of a user of material that
resides on a system or network controlled or operated by or for
the service provider, if the service provider -

A. i.   does not have actual knowledge that the material or an
         activity using the material on the system or network is
         infringing;

   ii.   in the absence of such actual knowledge, is not aware
         of facts or circumstances from which infringing activ-
         ity is apparent; or

   iii. upon obtaining such knowledge or awareness, acts
         expeditiously to remove, or disable access to, the
         material;

B. does not receive a financial benefit directly attributable to
the infringing activity, in a case in which the service provider has the right and ability to control such activity; and

C. upon notification of claimed infringement as described in
paragraph (3), responds expeditiously to remove, or disable
access to, the material that is claimed to be infringing or to
be the subject of infringing activity.

2. DESIGNATED AGENT. — The limitations on liability established
in this subsection apply to a service provider only if the ser-

vice provider has designated an agent to receive notifications of claimed infringement described in paragraph (3), by making available through its service, including on its website in a location accessible to the public, and by providing to the Copyright Office, substantially the following information:

A. the name, address, phone number, and electronic mail address of the agent.

B. other contact information which the Register of Copyrights may deem appropriate.

The Register of Copyrights shall maintain a current directory of agents available to the public for inspection, including through the Internet, and may require payment of a fee by service providers to cover the costs of maintaining the directory.

CHAPTER 15

Notifying the Infringers and Website Hosts

Once you identify any copyright infringements of your work along with the service providers making it available, the next step is notifying the site owners and service providers to take down this material or prevent access to it. The infringers must then respond immediately to take down your copyrighted material. While the service provider must do so to avoid liability, the person uploading the material and the company offering the infringed-upon material are still liable for any damages and profits. While you can do this yourself, a piracy protection service can draw on its own lists and algorithms to find the pirated copy and send out the takedown notices to the site owners and service providers on your behalf.

These service providers are like enablers, accomplices, or associates who are giving the actual infringers a platform to use in giving away or making a profit from copyrighted material. While they provide a channel for distributing the work, they may not be aware that the copyrighted work has been uploaded without permission, so they have an opportunity to escape liability if they have properly registered an agent with the Copyright Office to be in a public directory and receive notifications, and they promptly remove or deny access to this copyrighted material. However, if they don't do either of these actions, they can then become liable for damages and profits, just like the company offering the infringed-upon material. Accordingly, it is important to monitor their response to a takedown request; if they don't respond to quickly take down the material or deny access to it, they can be included in any litigation or criminal prosecution, along with the primary offender, since they are now knowingly aiding and abetting the act of piracy.

According to the copyright law, a notice to be effective must be in writing and include these key elements:

- a physical or electronic signature of the victim of the infringement,

- an identification of the copyrighted work or a representative list of such works and a request to remove or disable access to it,

- contact information so the service provider can contact you, such as an address, phone number, and email,

- if you are acting on behalf of the copyright owner, a statement that you have a good faith belief that the material is not authorized by the copyright owner and that you are authorized to act on behalf of the owner

Then, the service provider has to reply promptly to such a notification to avoid liability. More specifically, as provided for in Title 17, Chapter 512, (c)(3)(a and b) of the US Copyright Law (http://www.copyright. gov/title17/92chap5.html), the notification and response requirement is as follows. Again, you might refer to this code in your initial letter to such a service provider, and if they don't immediately respond to take down or remove access, they will become liable, and you can use this information in seeking a settlement from them, or in including them in any litigation to claim damages and/or profits.

3. ELEMENTS OF NOTIFICATION. —

 A. To be effective under this subsection, a notification of claimed infringement must be a written communication provided to the designated agent of a service provider that includes substantially the following:

  i. A physical or electronic signature of a person authorized to act on behalf of the owner of an exclusive right that is allegedly infringed.

ii. Identification of the copyrighted work claimed to have been infringed, or, if multiple copyrighted works at a single online site are covered by a single notification, a representative list of such works at that site.

iii. Identification of the material that is claimed to be infringing or to be the subject of infringing activity and that is to be removed or access to which is to be disabled, and information reasonably sufficient to permit the service provider to locate the material.

iv. Information reasonably sufficient to permit the service provider to contact the complaining party, such as an address, telephone number, and, if available, an electronic mail address at which the complaining party may be contacted.

v. A statement that the complaining party has a good faith belief that use of the material in the manner complained of is not authorized by the copyright owner, its agent, or the law.

vi. A statement that the information in the notification is accurate, and under penalty of perjury, that the complaining party is authorized to act on behalf of the owner of an exclusive right that is allegedly infringed.

B. i. Subject to clause (ii), a notification from a copyright owner or from a person authorized to act on behalf of the copyright owner that fails to comply substantially with the provisions of subparagraph (A) shall not be considered under paragraph (1)(A) in determining whether a service provider has actual knowledge or is aware of facts or circumstances from which infringing activity is apparent.

ii. In a case in which the notification that is provided to the service provider's designated agent fails to comply substantially with all the provisions of subparagraph (A) but substantially complies with clauses (ii), (iii), and (iv) of subparagraph (A), clause (i) of this subparagraph applies only if the service provider promptly attempts to contact the person making the notification or takes other reasonable steps to assist in the receipt of notification that substantially complies with all the provisions of subparagraph (A).

CHAPTER 16

Copyright Laws Affecting References Sources and Educational Institutions

INDIVIDUALS OR COMPANIES THAT PUT together reference tools—such as a directory, index, pointer, or list of hyperlinks to the locations which have infringing materials—have certain exemptions from liability. So do public or private nonprofit institutions of higher education, which are service providers, and their faculty members and students have certain exemptions from liability. However, these individuals, companies, and institutions have to be unaware of the infringing content and act to remove or disable any infringing content to remain free of liability. If they don't, they can be held responsible for damages and profits, like any knowing infringer.

These details are spelled out in Title 17, Chapter 512, (d) and (e). More specifically, a service provider who refers or links users to an online location containing infringing material or activity—such as through a directory, index, reference, pointer, hypertext link, or other information tools—must not have actual knowledge that the material or activity is infringing. Then, once made aware of this infringement, he or she must quickly remove or disable any access to that material. Additionally, the service provider cannot receive a financial benefit directly due to that infringing activity or the ability to control that activity, lest he or she become liable like the original infringer.

In the case of an educational institution, the provisions affecting other service providers about being unaware of any infringement and removing or disabling access to any infringing material apply. The institution also has to comply with and promote compliance with the copyright laws to its faculty and graduate students. These faculty members and students are considered separate from the institution, and they cannot knowingly engage in any infringing activities themselves, such as by requiring, recommending, or providing online access to infringing materials. To avoid liability for the actions of its faculty and graduate students, the institution has to act promptly to stop the infringement, since it can become liable if it receives more than two notifications over a three-year period of an infringement by a faculty member or graduate student.

More specifically, as provided for in Title 17, Chapter 512, (d) and (e) of the US Copyright Law (http://www.copyright.gov/title17/92chap5.html), the special provisions covering service providers offering referrals or links and educational institutions and their faculty members or graduate students are the following. Again, you might refer to this code in your initial letter to such a service provider, educational institution, faculty member, or graduate student. Then, if they don't immediately respond to take down or remove access, they become liable, and you can use this information in seeking a settlement from them, or in participating in litigation against them to claim damages and/or profits.

d. Information Location Tools. — A service provider shall not be liable for monetary relief, or, except as provided in subsection (j), for injunctive or other equitable relief, for infringement of copyright by reason of the provider referring or linking users to an online location containing infringing material or infringing activity, by using information location tools, including a directory, index, reference, pointer, or hypertext link, if the service provider —

1. A.   does not have actual knowledge that the material or activity is infringing;

B.   in the absence of such actual knowledge, is not aware of facts or circumstances from which infringing activity is apparent; or

C.   upon obtaining such knowledge or awareness, acts expeditiously to remove, or disable access to, the material;

2. does not receive a financial benefit directly attributable to the infringing activity, in a case in which the service provider has the right and ability to control such activity; and

3. upon notification of claimed infringement as described in subsection (c)(3), responds expeditiously to remove, or disable access to, the material that is claimed to be infringing or to be the subject of infringing activity, except that, for purposes of this paragraph, the information described in subsection (c)(3)(A)(iii) shall be identification of the reference or link, to material or activity claimed to be infringing, that is to be removed or access to which is to be disabled, and information reasonably sufficient to permit the service provider to locate that reference or link.

e. LIMITATION ON LIABILITY OF NONPROFIT EDUCATIONAL INSTITUTIONS. — (1) When a public or other nonprofit institution of higher education is a service provider, and when a faculty member or graduate student who is an employee of such institution is performing a teaching or research function, for the purposes of subsections (a) and (b) such faculty member or graduate student shall be considered to be a person other than the institution, and for the purposes of subsections (c) and (d) such faculty member's or graduate student's knowledge or awareness of his or her infringing activities shall not be attributed to the institution, if —

A. such faculty member's or graduate student's infringing activities do not involve the provision of online access to instructional materials that are or were required or recommended, within the preceding 3-year period, for a course taught at the institution by such faculty member or graduate student;

B. the institution has not, within the preceding 3-year period, received more than 2 notifications described in subsection (c)(3) of claimed infringement by such faculty member or graduate student, and such notifications of claimed infringement were not actionable under subsection (f); and

C. the institution provides to all users of its system or network informational materials that accurately describe, and promote compliance with, the laws of the United States relating to copyright.

2. For the purposes of this subsection, the limitations on injunctive relief contained in subsections (j)(2) and (j)(3), but not those in (j)(1), shall apply.

CHAPTER 17

Making Accurate Takedown Requests and Dealing with Counterclaims

THE VAST MAJORITY OF PIRACY victims can probably ignore the clauses in the copyright law that deal with making misrepresentations in an infringement claim or what to do if the infringer fights back and claims no infringement. Generally, the Internet listing itself provides a clear-cut case of piracy and in most cases, the infringer and service provider will either honor or ignore your request to stop the infringement by removing or denying access to the material. But just in case, you should know about the infringer's or service provider's options to counter your claim.

These situations are covered in Title 17, Chapter 5, sections (f) and (g) of the Copyright Code. Section (f) deals with misrepresentation; section (g) deals with replacing removed or disabled material should the infringer claim a mistake was made in claiming an infringement.

Based on section (f), you, a piracy protection service, or other representative acting on your behalf need to be accurate in claiming an infringement. Anyone who knowingly misrepresents that a material or activity is infringing, or causes any material or activity to be removed or disabled by mistake, can be liable for any damages, including costs and attorney fees incurred by the alleged infringer, copyright owner or licensee, or service provider. An example of a mistake might be a writer making an infringement claim if the publisher has actually posted the material for sale on the site. A misrepresentation might be if an angry ex-wife wants to get back at her ex by claiming an infringement to get his book removed from sale.

Whatever the reason for the mistake or representation, the costs for damages might include responding by removing or disabling access to the material, or later replacing or ceasing to disable access to it. In other words, if a writer wrongly claims an infringement when the publisher has given permission to publish copy on a site, that would be a mistake, subjecting the writer to any damage claims. That is why it's important to check with a publisher who may have rights to the material at the time the book was placed on the site, even though the rights were subsequently returned to the writer. Some of the sites do intermix both legally obtained and pirated material, so it is important to clarify who has the rights before proceeding beyond sending a notification to take down the material.

Section (g) refers to the situation where an alleged infringer claims there was no infringement, so the service provider is in the middle. In such a case, the service provider has no liability for acting in good faith by removing or disabling access to material subject to an infringement claim which is subsequently contested, whether or not the material is ultimately determined to be infringing or not.

Basically, upon getting a notice of infringement, the service provider is required to notify the subscriber that he or she has removed or disabled access to the material. Then, upon receiving a counter notification that the subscriber in good faith believes the material was removed or disabled due to a mistake or misidentification, the provider has to advise the person providing the original notification that there has been a counter notification. Further, the provider must advise the initial notifier that it will replace the removed material or cease disabling access to it within ten business days. Then, the provider has to do so within ten to fourteen days, unless the initial notifier sends a notice that he or she has filed an action seeking a court order to prevent the subscriber from keeping the infringing material on the provider's system or network.

To be valid, such a counter notification has to be prepared much like the original notification with a physical or electronic signature, identification of the material that has been removed or disabled, and the location where it was before being removed or disabled, along with the subscriber's name, address, phone number, and other contact information required for service of process.

In short, there is the potential that an infringer can deny any infringement or delay the process with a counterclaim. But as long as you have correctly identified the work that is being pirated and you have the right to that work, any such response is unlikely, since it will only increase the pirate's damages, and any legitimate service provider wants to quickly disassociate itself from a pirated work. Moreover, you can respond to a counter notification with a court order showing why the subscriber has infringed upon your work, which will add to the infringer's costs.

More specifically, as provided for in Title 17, Chapter 512, (f) and (g) of the US Copyright Law, http://www.copyright.gov/title17/92chap5.html, the codes related to misrepresentation, mistakes, and the service provider's responsibility in the case of a counter notification are the following:

f. MISREPRESENTATIONS. - Any person who knowingly materially misrepresents under this section —

1. that material or activity is infringing, or

2. that material or activity was removed or disabled by mistake or misidentification, shall be liable for any damages, including costs and attorneys' fees, incurred by the alleged infringer, by any copyright owner or copyright owner's authorized licensee, or by a service provider, who is injured by such misrepresentation, as the result of the service provider relying upon such misrepresentation in removing or disabling access to the material or activity claimed to be infringing, or in replacing the removed material or ceasing to disable access to it.

g. REPLACEMENT OF REMOVED OR DISABLED MATERIAL AND LIMITATION ON OTHER LIABILITY. —

1. No liability for taking down generally. — Subject to paragraph (2), a service provider shall not be liable to any person for any claim based on the service provider's good faith disabling of access to, or removal of, material or activity claimed to be infringing or based on facts or circumstances from which infringing activity is apparent, regardless of whether the material or activity is ultimately determined to be infringing.

2. Exception. — Paragraph (1) shall not apply with respect to material residing at the direction of a subscriber of the service provider on a system or network controlled or operated by or for the service provider that is removed, or to which access is disabled by the service provider, pursuant to a notice provided under subsection (c)(1)(C), unless the service provider —

   A. takes reasonable steps promptly to notify the subscriber that it has removed or disabled access to the material;

   B. upon receipt of a counter notification described in paragraph (3), promptly provides the person who provided the notification under subsection (c)(1)(C) with a copy of the counter notification, and informs that person that it will replace the removed material or cease disabling access to it in 10 business days; and

   C. replaces the removed material and ceases disabling access to it not less than 10, nor more than 14, business days following receipt of the counter notice, unless its designated agent first receives notice from the person who submitted the notification under subsection (c)(1)(C) that such person has filed an action seeking a court order to restrain the subscriber from engaging in infringing activity relating to the material on the service provider's system or network.

3. Contents of counter notification. — To be effective under this subsection, a counter notification must be a written communication provided to the service provider's designated agent that includes substantially the following:

A. A physical or electronic signature of the subscriber.

B. Identification of the material that has been removed or to which access has been disabled and the location at which the material appeared before it was removed or access to it was disabled.

C. A statement under penalty of perjury that the subscriber has a good faith belief that the material was removed or disabled as a result of mistake or misidentification of the material to be removed or disabled.

D. The subscriber's name, address, and telephone number, and a statement that the subscriber consents to the jurisdiction of Federal District Court for the judicial district in which the address is located, or if the subscriber's address is outside of the United States, for any judicial district in which the service provider may be found, and that the subscriber will accept service of process from the person who provided notification under subsection (c)(1)(C) or an agent of such person.

4. LIMITATION ON OTHER LIABILITY. — A service provider's compliance with paragraph (2) shall not subject the service provider to liability for copyright infringement with respect to the material identified in the notice provided under subsection (c) (1)(C).

CHAPTER 18

Finding Out the Infringer's Identity

FINDING OUT WHO IS THE infringer can sometimes be tricky when you do it yourself, although the piracy protection services have a system for identifying website owners and service providers, so they can automate the process. But if your material is only on a limited number of sites, you can still do it yourself. For example, I did this by putting in the name of one person who had claimed my copyrighted material as her own. I readily found her website through a Google search, learned the name of her domain name provider and the ISP that hosted her site, and sent out a single takedown notice, with a copy to the provider and ISP, and that did the trick. The whole site was down within a few days, and after a year hasn't reappeared anywhere else. However, if your book or other material is posted on numerous sites, then it can be time consuming to find them all, as well as send out notices, which is when a priracy protection service can help.

In any case, if you do it yourself, there is a way to find the pirates and the service providers. In some cases, this information will be on the site, particularly when the infringer is intermixing pirated and legally posted material offered for free. For example, this is the case with www.scribd.com, launched in 2007 by Trip Adler and Jared Friedman. The site invites people to submit their own material to share with others, and it has a section of the website where people can report copyright violations and they will take down any violating material. The company even cites the Digital Millenium Copyright Act (DMCM)

(Title 17 Section #512) in its statement of legal policies and says it will terminate the accounts of those who are repeat infringers (http://support.scribd.com/entries/22981-DMCA-copyright-infringement-takedown-notification-policy). It also has arrangements with mainstream publishers like Random House and the *New York Times*, as well as any publisher who wants to make its material available for free or for sale.

However, with millions of books contributed by members of the community, who can upload any kind of document in dozens of formats, it is hard to police what's on the site. As a result, individuals can easily upload copyrighted material without permission, and unless a writer is vigilant, he or she won't discover his or her book is up there.

For example, when I did a search on my own name, I discovered 664 results, many uploaded by individuals without permission to do so. One of these, *The Survival Guide to Working with Humans*, was even accompanied by the news that the book had nearly five thousand readers of what was available for free. Needless to say, I wasn't pleased at the loss of royalty income, nor was my publisher when I reported my many books on Scribd that had received this free upload treatment.

Other blatant pirate sites may be harder to track down, especially when they don't post easily accessed contact information or are based in other countries. For example, when John Wiley and an international coalition of publishers went after the library.nu and iFile.it sites, they had to conduct a long investigation to identify the site owners. They had to take legal action against them in Ireland and Germany before the owners took down the sites (http://paidcontent.org/2012/02/15/419-book-publishers-take-down-piracy-sites).

There are various strategies for finding out both the owners and the uploaders of copyrighted material. One is to find out the owners of the IP addresses associated with the website and the uploaders. A number of companies now can do this. One example is IPTrackeronline (www.iptrackeronline.com); when I put in my own address, which was already identified when I checked out the company, the company's site immediately reported that I was in San Francisco, California, at postal code 94121 and I was hosted by Comcast Cable. From there, one could obtain more specific details from Comcast Cable through a subpoena. Another such company is Whoer.Net (http://whoer.net/ext), which provided similar information on my location.

Likewise, you can discover the email sender's IP address, since it is stored in an email header (http://compnetworking.about.com/od/workingwithipaddresses/qt/ipaddressemail.htm). Companies can also find out the IPs or emails of those uploading files to their servers. Then, with this information you can notify the infringing website owner or uploader and follow up with a notification or lawsuit from there.

Finally, you can find out the identification of an infringer with a subpoena to a service provider, as provided by section (h) of Title 17, Chapter 5, #512 of the Copyright Code (http://www.copyright.gov/title17/92chap5.html). Basically, the way the subpoena process works is you request that the clerk of any district court issue a subpoena to a service provider to identify an alleged infringer. You make this request by submitting a copy of the notification described in subsection (c)(a)(3), which requires a signed document in which you identify the copyright work or works claimed to be infringed, along with sufficient identification, so the provider can locate the material. Additionally, you include your contact information, such as your address, phone number, and email address. Lastly, you provide a proposed subpoena and a sworn declaration that your purpose in seeking the subpoena is to obtain the identity of the alleged infringer, and that you will only use this information to protect your rights in the copyright.

As for the content of the proposed subpoena, this should authorize and order the service provider to quickly disclose to the copyright owner or the owner's agent the necessary information to identify the alleged infringer as described in the notification.

If this notification and proposed subpoena are in the proper form, the clerk of the court will quickly issue and sign the proposed subpoena and return it to the requester in order to deliver it to the service provider. Once the service provider receives the subpoena, he or she has to expeditiously disclose the requested information. The basic procedures for issuing and delivering the subpoena and the remedies for noncompliance are governed by the Federal Rules of Civil Procedures. You can check with the district court clerk for more specifics on what to do or with a local lawyer familiar with this process.

More specifically, as provided for in Title 17, Chapter 512, (h) of the US Copyright Law (http://www.copyright.gov/title17/92chap5.html), here are the steps for getting a subpoena to identify an infringer.

h. SUBPOENA TO IDENTIFY INFRINGER. —

1. REQUEST. — A copyright owner or a person authorized to act on the owner's behalf may request the clerk of any United States district court to issue a subpoena to a service provider for identification of an alleged infringer in accordance with this subsection.

2. CONTENTS OF REQUEST. — The request may be made by filing with the clerk —

A. a copy of a notification described in subsection (c)(3)(A);

B. a proposed subpoena; and

C. a sworn declaration to the effect that the purpose for which the subpoena is sought is to obtain the identity of an alleged infringer and that such information will only be used for the purpose of protecting rights under this title.

3. CONTENTS OF SUBPOENA. — The subpoena shall authorize and order the service provider receiving the notification and the subpoena to expeditiously disclose to the copyright owner or person authorized by the copyright owner information sufficient to identify the alleged infringer of the material described in the notification to the extent such information is available to the service provider.

4. BASIS FOR GRANTING SUBPOENA. — If the notification filed satisfies the provisions of subsection (c)(3)(A), the proposed subpoena is in proper form, and the accompanying declaration is properly executed, the clerk shall expeditiously issue and sign the proposed subpoena and return it to the requester for delivery to the service provider.

5. ACTIONS OF SERVICE PROVIDER RECEIVING SUBPOENA. — Upon receipt of the issued subpoena, either accompanying

or subsequent to the receipt of a notification described in subsection (c)(3)(A), the service provider shall expeditiously disclose to the copyright owner or person authorized by the copyright owner the information required by the subpoena, notwithstanding any other provision of law and regardless of whether the service provider responds to the notification.

6. RULES APPLICABLE TO SUBPOENA. — Unless otherwise provided by this section or by applicable rules of the court, the procedure for issuance and delivery of the subpoena, and the remedies for noncompliance with the subpoena, shall be governed to the greatest extent practicable by those provisions of the Federal Rules of Civil Procedure governing the issuance, service, and enforcement of a subpoena *duces tecum*.

CHAPTER 19

Stopping the Infringement with an Injunction

MOST SERVICE PROVIDERS WILL RESPOND to a takedown notification if they are innocently and unknowingly enabling the infringer to host or send out infringing material. This is likely because they want to remain compliant with copyright law and avoid being shut down themselves. However, in some cases, a further legal process may be necessary, getting an injunction. Such a document will order a service provider to deny access to any infringing material on an online site in their system or network. This order will also prevent a subscriber or account holder who is allegedly infringing on copyright materials from accessing the service by terminating his or her account.

These rules to obtain an injunction only apply under the following circumstances: The service provider must not be subject to monetary remedies because the transmission of the material was initiated by or at the direction of another person; the service provider is only transmitting, providing the connection, or providing storage through an automatic process; and the service provider does not make any modifications to the material going through its system, as described in section (a) referring to transitory digital network connections. The injunction is designed to stop any automated transmission that is not controlled by the service provider.

In deciding whether to grant this injunction, the court will consider various factors. These include whether the injunction will seriously burden the provider's operations of the system or network, the degree of harm likely to be suffered by the copyright owner if the injunction isn't granted, whether the injunction will be effective technically and not interfere with access to noninfringing material going through the system, and whether there might be a less burdensome and comparably effective way to prevent or restrain access to the infringing material.

Before the court grants the injunction, the service provider must receive a notice and be given an opportunity to appear in court. In short, you can get injunctive relief under certain circumstances from the transmission of your copyrighted material via an automated system.

More specifically, as provided for in Title 17, Chapter 512, (J) of the US Copyright Law (http://www.copyright.gov/title17/92chap5.html), here are the codes related to how to get an injunction to stop infringement by transmission over an automated system.

j. INJUNCTIONS. — The following rules shall apply in the case of any application for an injunction under section 502 against a service provider that is not subject to monetary remedies under this section:

1. SCOPE OF RELIEF. — (A) With respect to conduct other than that which qualifies for the limitation on remedies set forth in subsection (a), the court may grant injunctive relief with respect to a service provider only in one or more of the following forms:

   i. An order restraining the service provider from providing access to infringing material or activity residing at a particular online site on the provider's system or network.

   ii. An order restraining the service provider from providing access to a subscriber or account holder of the service provider's system or network who is engaging in infringing activity and is identified in the order, by terminating the accounts of the subscriber or account holder that are specified in the order.

   iii. Such other injunctive relief as the court may consider necessary to prevent or restrain infringement of copyrighted material specified in the order of the court at a particular online location, if such relief is the least burdensome to the service provider among the forms of relief comparably effective for that purpose.

B. If the service provider qualifies for the limitation on remedies described in subsection (a), the court may only grant injunctive relief in one or both of the following forms:

   i. An order restraining the service provider from providing access to a subscriber or account holder of the service provider's system or network who is using the provider's service to engage in infringing activity and is identified in the order, by terminating the accounts of the subscriber or account holder that are specified in the order.

   ii. An order restraining the service provider from providing access, by taking reasonable steps specified in the order to block access, to a specific, identified, online location outside the United States.

2. CONSIDERATIONS. — The court, in considering the relevant criteria for injunctive relief under applicable law, shall consider —

A. whether such an injunction, either alone or in combination with other such injunctions issued against the same service provider under this subsection, would significantly burden either the provider or the operation of the provider's system or network;

B. the magnitude of the harm likely to be suffered by the copyright owner in the digital network environment if steps are not taken to prevent or restrain the infringement;

C. whether implementation of such an injunction would be technically feasible and effective, and would not interfere with access to noninfringing material at other online locations; and

D. whether other less burdensome and comparably effective means of preventing or restraining access to the infringing material are available.

3. NOTICE AND EX PARTE ORDERS. — Injunctive relief under this subsection shall be available only after notice to the service provider and an opportunity for the service provider to appear are provided, except for orders ensuring the preservation of evidence or other orders having no material adverse effect on the operation of the service provider's communications network.

PART IV

The Criminal Crackdown on Internet Piracy

CHAPTER 20

The Beginning Criminal Attack On Internet Piracy

ALTHOUGH ONLINE BOOK PIRACY HAS been going on for over a decade, made possible by file-sharing programs and websites for uploading and downloading files in PDF and other formats, it is only in the last few years that law enforcement agencies have taken notice. A key reason is that piracy has become a billion-dollar business, involving millions of individuals and companies affected by the theft of their intellectual property. While the initial impetus to go after the pirates started in the music and film industries, writers and publishers are finally waking up to take action, and law enforcement agencies have begun to crack down on book piracy, along with other intellectual property thefts, including software, music, and films.

Despite bumps in the road, when the pirates fight back—claiming they weren't doing anything illegal or that law enforcement used inappropriate tactics to bring them to justice—the growing pressure is helping to draw attention to the crime of Internet piracy. People are becoming increasingly aware that it is a crime, and law enforcement agencies are seeking to target and eventually reduce the number of perpetrators. These include website operators, service providers, uploaders, and downloaders of infringed-upon material, though this effort may have slowed since mid-2014, given the complications in gaining convictions in these cases when the defendants have huge economic resources and are located in other countries.

One of the biggest and longest cases is the Megaupload case, in which Kit Dotcom and three other Megaupload executives face criminal copyright violations and related charges, although they have been fighting the extradition requests to go to the United States to be tried on these charges. Now defunct, the Megaupload site, launched in 2005 in New Zealand, was a web storage service where millions of users around the world uploaded and downloaded unauthorized copies of books, films, songs, and other digital entertainment. Before it was shut down, it was one of the 100 most popular websites, with about fifty million visitors each day. At its peak it had over 150 employees, earned $175 million in revenues—$42 million in 2010 alone—and became the thirteenth most visited site on the Internet, accounting for 4 percent of all Internet traffic (http://en.wikibooks.org/wiki/Professionalism/ Kim_Dotcom_and_Megaupload).

According to the DOJ, it cost the film studios and record companies more than $500 from users who shared their copyrighted materials, though Dotcom claims to be innocent on the grounds that Megaupload sought to make sure that users did not share copyrighted material and that he and the company's executives had no criminal intent (https:// news.vice.com/article/internet-mogul-kim-dotcoms-extradition-trial- begins-over-megaupload-copyright-case).

One of the big breakthroughs in the case came on January 19, 2012, when the FBI and dozens of armed New Zealand police busted the alleged operators of Megaupload, a locker service that made millions by helping millions of people store and distribute pirated feature films, TV shows, songs, software, porn, and some books (http://news.cnet. com/8301-31001_3-57362152-261/fbi-charges-megaupload-operators- with-piracy-crimes). Besides arresting Dotcom, the authorities confiscated millions of dollars worth of cars, laptops, and weapons (https:// news.vice.com/article/internet-mogul-kim-dotcoms-extradition-trial- begins-over-megaupload-copyright-case).

It named seven people in the indictment and took four suspects into custody, charging them in Virginia, since one of their servers was there, with crimes related to online piracy. Among those arrested by the New Zealand police in Auckland was the colorful founder of Megaupload, Kim Dotcom (a.k.a. Kim Schmitz), a German national, and three others, under arrest warrants requested by the United States. As reported by Greg Sandoval in a CNET News article, "FBI charges Megaupload operators with piracy crimes," "racketeering conspiracy, conspiring to commit copyright infringement, and conspiring to commit money laundering" (http://news.cnet.com/8301-31001_3-57362152-261/fbi-charges-megaupload-operators-with-piracy-crimes). In the raid, the FBI seized $50 million in assets and charged Dotcom and six others with "running an international enterprise based on Internet piracy that cost copyright holders at least $500 million in lost revenue" (http://robot6.comicbookresources.com/2012/01/comics-a-m-fbi-shuts-down-megaupload-file-sharing-site).

According to a statement issued by the US Justice Department and FBI, this action was truly a breakthrough in pursuing piracy as a crime. As the statement put it: "This action is among the largest criminal copyright cases ever brought by the United States . . . [It] directly targets the misuse of a public content storage and distribution site to commit and facilitate intellectual property crime" (http://news.cnet.com/8301-31001_3-57362152-261/fbi-charges-megaupload-operators-with-piracy-crimes). The United States had jurisdiction to act since Megaupload's servers were located in Virginia, although Dotcom and the other operators were arrested in New Zealand.

The raids caused Megaupload to close, although the fight has continued, since Dotcom has been fighting extradition. He recently won access to evidence seized during the raids, since the New Zealand high court decided that the warrants used to grab the material were illegal, according to a May 31, 2013, BBC News/Technology article, "Megaupload wins access to data seized in police raid." So now the New Zealand police have to look through the evidence grabbed during the raid and return any data files considered "irrelevant" to the case, as well as destroy any clones of this information created by the investigators and return any relevant information to Dotcom's legal team (http://www.bbc.co.uk/news/technology-22716718).

Meanwhile, as Dotcom fought back against the FBI with a team of twenty-eight lawyers, he defiantly created a new storage service, called Mega, launched on January 20, 2013, a year after Megaupload crashed (https://mega.co.nz). Within a month it was up to over three million registered users and growing at 30 percent a week, according to Andy Greenberg in a *Forbes* magazine article, "Inside Mega: The Second Coming of Kim Dotcom" (http://www.forbes.com/sites/andygreenberg/2013/04/17/inside-mega-the-second-coming-of-kim-dotcom). As Greenberg describes, this new site is designed to completely encrypt the stored files, so the only person who can decrypt the files is the user, making it impossible for the FBI or even Mega to unlock the file. The theory behind this approach is that the service can't be responsible for filtering or making available copyrighted content, because the company can plausibly claim it has no way to identify copyrighted material on its servers. The strategy is one of "willful blindness," whereby Mega might have to provide law enforcement with non-content data, such as IP addresses, but not the data itself. Will this strategy work? Will it make it even harder for the victims of infringement to know who's sharing their files with others? Only time will tell. And as of this writing the Mega site still exists.

Yet, despite Dotcom's global fight against criminal charges with his battery of lawyers—including plans to sue the US government and the studios that triggered the raid with "misinformation and corruption" —the raid has showed that criminal justice agencies are finally serious about pursuing Internet piracy by initially going after the worst of the worst. And despite Dotcom's counterattack, the bust has cost him a small fortune from the millions he once earned from Megaupload. As Greenberg notes, Dotcom had to fire forty-four of his fifty-two house staff and hundreds of Megaupload employees. All but two of his cars were seized or sold. He owes millions to defense lawyers, and all of his bank accounts were frozen, permitting him only a $20,000-a-month government allowance (http://www.forbes.com/sites/andygreenberg/2013/04/17/inside-mega-the-second-coming-of-kim-dotcom).

The takedown also showed the detrimental effect of these piracy sites on the market. There was an increase in movie rental and sales in the months after Megaupload was discontinued—evidence that piracy does reduce the sales of the infringed-upon work. As noted by Dara Kerr in a March 2013 CNN article, a new study by Carnegie Mellon's Initiative for Digital Entertainment Analytics showed that after Megaupload was shut down, online movie revenue increased by 6 to 10 percent, based on researching the revenues of two major movie studies from users in twelve different countries. The researchers concluded, "Shutting down MegaUpload and Megavideo caused some customers to shift from cyberlocker-based piracy to purchasing or renting through legal digital channels" (http://news.cnet.com/8301-1023_3-57573195-93/megauploads-closure-boosts-movie-rentals-and-sales).

The Megaupload takedown is also significant in showing the pirates that the government and law enforcement are getting serious about intellectual property crimes. While the raid may have been instigated by the film studios, it might be considered an opening salvo in the war against the pirates by the United States and other governments, which can help the book industry, too. While there may be hundreds of active pirates with websites, servers, storage lockers, or accounts for uploaded files, along with millions of individuals downloading the pirated files, the actions against Megaupload and Dotcom serve as a warning to all that law enforcement is now actively pursuing the pirates. So an enforcement action could potentially come after anyone next.

However, complications could undermine the case. For example, Megaupload filed a request to dismiss the indictment against it on the grounds that it is a foreign company and the government was required to serve the company in the United States, so it was not properly served. In response, in May 2014, the US government submitted its objections to Megaupload's motion to dismiss the case,[168] and in June, a US District Court granted Kim Dotcom's request to put the MPAA and RIAA civil actions against him for millions on hold to avoid him incriminating himself in the US government criminal case.[169] Yet, while the authorities froze his worldwide assets of over $40 million US dollars at the time of his arrest and he was jailed for a month, he earned another 40 million in New Zealand dollars (£20 million) from new ventures, including two more file-sharing sites—Mega and a music venture, Baboom. At the same time, he managed to delay extradition hearings several times, which have finally gone to trial in September 2015, though his bail conditions were retightened so he can no longer travel by private helicopter or boat and has to report to the police twice a week.[170] And so the biggest case of Internet piracy downloading drags on, with an appeal from the defense or prosecution almost certain whatever the court's decision.

Given Kim Dotcom's assets, it would seem this case could be prolonged, though he now claims the case has drained him of legal resources and he is broke, but is now returning to court to seek to have some of his frozen assets released to pay his legal fees and expenses.[171]

But since this big case, it appears that US law enforcement agencies have not been as aggressively pursuing Internet piracy cases involving the theft of books, films, and music, though there have been a sprinkling of smaller cases, perhaps due to a shift in priorities, given the growing concern with hacking and cybersecurity crimes.

However, on the international front, the big story was the December 2014 takedown of The Pirate Bay website—by far the biggest source of international pirating—by the Swedish police, with some pressure from the US government. The story actually dates back to the first police arrest in 2006, when Hollywood sought the government's help in cracking down on the site, after claiming that piracy cost it $6.1 billion in 2006 alone. In response, the United States threatened to impose trade sanctions against Sweden through the World Trade Organization if the site wasn't shut down. And so the Swedish police raided the site in 2006, which included "confiscating enough servers and computer equipment to fill three trucks and making two arrests." But three days later, the site was back up again, and was more popular than ever due to coverage by the mainstream media.[172] Instead of being based in Sweden, it moved its operation to cloud-hosting in two different countries with several virtual machines handling operations, and the original cofounders, Fredrik Neij, Peter Sunde, and Gottfrid Svartholm, sold the site to a possible shell company.

By 2008, the site was the ninety-seventh most-visited website on the entire Internet, and at the time of their 2009 trial, when the site reportedly had twenty-two million users, the cofounders received $3.6 million in fines along with time behind bars for copyright infringement. The way the site worked is that it didn't actually host any of the copyrighted material. Instead it maintained a database of tracker files so users could download the torrents, rather than the actual copyrighted content, and users needed a separate piece of software to actually use the torrent file, which consists of a set of instructions on how a computer should reassemble a large file from the relatively small pieces shared by many hosts, and illegally download the content. Essentially, this is distributed file sharing, so in effect, multiple pirates are to blame for a single completed file that is opened by the user.[173]

And then on December 9, the Swedish police raided a server room in the Stockholm area and left with several servers and computers, which took down not only The Pirate Bay, but also some related sites—bayimg.com, pastebay.net, and a few other torrent sites—in response to a complaint by the Rights Alliance, a Swedish anti-piracy site. But it would seem that the raid had little impact on piracy. According to *Variety*, on December 8, almost 102 million IP addresses were downloading movies and TV shows using the torrent sites, and that dropped to 95 million on December 9. But a few days later, the downloads were up to 100.2 million, perhaps because The Pirate Bay site was quickly replaced by the uTorrent site.[174] Plus, it was relatively easy to re-create the same service, since The Pirate Bay's database of torrent links was freely available for download, so another organization just had to upload this base and be ready to respond to the high level of traffic. And that's what happened. The operators of Isohunt, one of the torrent search websites blocked in many countries, including the UK, re-created a new version of The Pirate Bay on the oldpiratebay.org site.[175] As of this writing, while the original site is gone, there are a number of proxy sites (https://thepiratebay-proxylist.org) and it is still considered the top site for torrent downloads.[176]

While the Megaupload saga drags on and The Pirate Bay seems to have found new life to outwit the law, the decline in law enforcement actions against piracy sites could mean that there is a kind of exhaustion setting in, since for all the effort to take down the worst of the worst pirates, the practice of piracy still goes on, making these few takedowns seem like a hopeless effort—like tilting at windmills, only to find they are still popping up everywhere. Or perhaps law enforcement efforts have targeted other, more dangerous Internet criminals, such as those hacking into corporate servers and stealing masses of data and intellectual property, such as in the Sony case. Or then again, the anti-piracy measures could be working through the growing number of private efforts to combat piracy. Seppala concludes his article, "The Pirate Bay Shutdown: The Whole Story (So Far):

"Perhaps, though, the anti-piracy measures we've seen are working. After all, Google has said that it gets over a million Digital Millennium Copyright Act takedown requests *per day*. A recent *PC Pro* report notes that US BitTorrent traffic had dropped by 20 percent over the course of six months last year. What's more, it says that unique visitors to The Pirate Bay dropped dramatically between 2012 and 2013, from 5 million to 900,000 by last year's end.

"This can likely be attributed to how easy it's become as of late to access content legally. It's no mistake that Netflix offered UK customers episodes of *Breaking Bad*'s final season the day after they aired in the US. Or, that it's pushing to stream movies the same day they arrive in theaters. Same goes for Hulu Plus' entire business model of streaming shows the day after they air.

"Sure, you're going to have a minority of folks who'll pirate anything and everything as their own means of anarchy, but for the most part, by offering an all-around better *legal* experience (not having to worry about downloading a virus; better video quality) most people aren't going to bother pirating in the first place."[177]

So it may be that the major push in the criminal justice arena has shifted away from going after the book, film, and music pirates, given the growing private alternatives to reduce piracy—from lawsuits to restrictions on piracy websites, and in some cases using the pirates to help promote and market one's books. And perhaps another reason is the shift in focus to digital piracy of software and mobile apps, which have had a high rate of illegal app downloads for years—perhaps as high as 60 percent of these apps have been illegally downloaded.[178]

For example, in January 2014, the Justice Department filed its first criminal charges against the people accused of being behind popular Android piracy websites—Snappzmarket and Appbuket—which offered large catalogs of free app downloads. By downloading these apps, individuals could avoid paying for premium apps on Google play.

Originally, the two sites were seized by the government in 2012, and after assembling the case, the government charged four men with a conspiracy to commit criminal copyright infringement, providing a maximum sentence of five years in prison. In the course of the investigation, the government found that between May 2011 and August 2012 the site allegedly facilitated one million illegal downloads worth $1.7 million, and in one chat log between the head of Snappzmarket, Kody Peterson from Clermont, Florida, they found Peterson and his conspirators agreeing to ignore DMCA copyright takedown requests.[179]

And since then the Justice Department has been investigating other potential mobile app pirates rather than leaving it up to copyright holders to use the traditional civil suits or cease-and-desist letters to shut down the sites hosting copyrighted movies, music, computer software, as well as books. The rationale is to protect the legitimate app developers. Or as the acting head of the Justice Department's criminal division, Mythili Raman, put it: "These crimes involve the large-scale violation of intellectual property rights in a relatively new and rapidly growing market."[180]

So this seems to be the new focus of criminal justice prosecutions in Internet piracy cases. In short, there is a continuing crackdown on piracy as a crime. But for the most part this criminal crackdown doesn't involve books.

CHAPTER 21

The FBI's Role in Combatting Internet Piracy

GIVEN THE GROWING THREAT OF online book piracy in the United States as well as globally, a number of government agencies are taking steps to stop this, though since 2013, these prosecutions of the pirate sites seem to have slowed down. This is perhaps due to other priorities, the extensive time and effort required to pursue a piracy case in the courts, the vast number of pirates, and the increasing use of private efforts to reduce piracy, such as the takedown notices and the delisting of pirate sites in search engines.

Though now mired in appeals and court arguments, the FBI raid on Megaupload and Kim Dotcom with the help of the New Zealand police, one of the more high-profile efforts, shut down the biggest storage locker. The raid also raised the issue of whether a website can blindly allow its site to be used by others who are illegally uploading and downloading infringed-upon files to evade civil liability and criminal responsibility, since many services combine legal and illegal uploads, making the policing problem even more difficult.

Despite this shift to private actions to reduce piracy, among the law enforcement agencies that have participated in the anti-piracy battle are the FBI and its Internet Crime Complaint Center (IC3), the National White Collar Crime Center, the Bureau of Justice Assistance, and the National Intellectual Property Rights Coordination Center, as well as the Department of Homeland Security and the Immigration and Customs Enforcement Agency. While much of the attention has focused on other types of online piracy, such as movies, games, business software, and music, these law enforcement operations can easily go after book pirates, too.

Following is an overview of what the different agencies are doing in the battle against piracy, and how victims and other citizens who know of piracy violations can report them. This first section deals with the efforts of the FBI.

The FBI's Internet Crime Complaint Center has played a central role in pursuing the Internet criminals. The Center was created in 2000 as a partnership between the FBI, the National White Collar Crime Center (NW3C), and the Bureau of Justice Assistance (BJA). As described in the IC3 2012 crime report, the IC3 "has become a mainstay for victims reporting Internet crime and a way for law enforcement to be notified of such crimes." These reports are forwarded on to the federal, state, tribal, local, and international agencies that are working together to combat Internet crime, including book piracy. According to the IC3 report, the IC3 received and processed 289,874 complaints, averaging more than twenty-four thousand complaints per month, with unverified losses up 8.3 percent over the previous year (http://www.fbi.gov/news/pressrel/press-releases/ic3-2012-internet-crime-report-released).

In another approach to stopping piracy, the FBI created an FBI Anti-Piracy Warning (APW) Seal, which all copyright holders can place on their books and other copyrighted materials, including films, audio recordings, electronic media, software, and photographs. The purpose of the seal is to remind media users about "the serious consequences of pirating copyrighted works." Individuals can simply download the file to put it on their material.

Previously, after designing the seal in 2003, the FBI required anyone using it to sign a memorandum of understanding (MOU) agreement for using it, and it worked out agreements with five associations—the Motion Picture Association of America (MPAA), the Recording Industry Association of America, (RIAA), the Software and Information Industry Association (SIIA), the Business Software Alliance (BSA), and the Entertainment Software Association (ESA)—to use the seal. But beginning on August 12, 2013, the FBI allowed all copyright holders to use its seal without executing a written agreement. However, if you use the seal, it should be placed next to the following authorized warning language enclosed by a plain box border that states: "The unauthorized reproduction or distribution of a copyrighted work is illegal. Criminal copyright infringement, including infringement without monetary gain, is investigated by the FBI and is punishable by fines and federal imprisonment" (http://www.fbi.gov/about-us/investigate/white_collar/ipr/conditions-regarding-use-of-the-fbi-anti-piracy-warning-apw-seal).

While anyone with a copyright can now use the seal, it cannot be used to indicate the FBI's approval, endorsement, or authorization, and it cannot be used on any work whose production, distribution, sale, public presentation, or mailing would violate US laws, such as pornography. Thus, pirates can't simply put the seal on their own work to claim it is protected with this warning. Rather, to cite the FBI's statement, the seal "simply serves as a widely recognizable reminder of the FBI's authority and mission with respect to the protection of intellectual property rights." But the seal offers no protection beyond a warning, so a copyright holder should use any other industry-recognized copyright protection techniques to discourage copying, such as registering a copyright with the US Copyright Office.

According to the FBI, this APW Seal program is part of a larger anti-piracy effort, which the FBI is conducting independently and in partnership with other federal agencies and the National Intellectual Property Rights Coordinator Center (IPR Center). A goal is increasing public awareness of "the issues related to copyright piracy and other intellectual property theft," since the FBI has made investigating and preventing IP theft a top priority. The reason, as the FBI states, is that "Intellectual property rights theft is not a victimless crime. Because of piracy of media and other commercial goods, US businesses lose millions of dollars each year, threatening American jobs and negatively impacting the economy . . . . and often times, it fuels global organized crime." So now the FBI, along with the US Attorney's Office, has been pursuing those who violate these laws by reproducing or distributing copyrighted work, with or without monetary gain, and such crimes can be punished by fines and federal imprisonment (http://www.fbi.gov/about-us/investigate/white_collar/ipr/anti-piracy).

The verdict on the Megaupload case is still out, but the FBI has had some notable successes in the past in cracking down on intellectual property crimes. For example, in Operation Fastlink, a major Department of Justice initiative to combat online piracy worldwide, the US Attorney's Office secured sixty felony convictions as of March 6, 2009. To this end, the Operation, conducted by the FBI along with the US Attorney's Office for the District of Connecticut, and the Criminal Division's Computer Crime and Intellectual Property Section (CCIPS) executed over 120 search warrants in twelve countries and confiscated over $50 million worth of illegally copied business software, games, movies, and music from illicit distribution channels.

As an example of its success, the defendant in its sixtieth prosecution, Bryan Thomas Black of Waterloo, Illinois, pleaded guilty in March 2009 to one count of conspiracy to commit criminal infringement of a copyright for his participation in a multinational software piracy organization. When sentenced, he could face up to five years in prison, a $250,000 fine, and three years of supervised release (http://www.fbi.gov/newhaven/press-releases/2009/nh030609b.htm)—a common penalty for copyright infringement.

In a more recent case, a Florida man pleaded guilty to nine felony counts of a twenty-eight-count case for unauthorized access to protected computers to engage in wiretapping and wire fraud and unauthorized damage to protected computers. In doing so, between November 2010 and October 2011, he hacked into the email accounts of celebrities, including Scarlett Johansson and Mila Kunis, by taking the victims' email addresses, clicking on the "forgot your password?" feature, and resetting the victims' passwords by correctly answering their security question using publically available information on the Internet. Then, while in exclusive control of the victims' email accounts, he was able to access all of their emails, and he found email addresses of potentially new hacking targets from their contact lists. Additionally, he used the forwarding feature so he got a duplicate copy of all incoming emails to the victims, including any attachments, and even after the victims regained control of their accounts, he continued to get copies of their emails and attachments for weeks or months. He even hacked into some accounts again when a victim reset his or her password. Then, as his hacking scheme grew, he used a proxy service called "Hide My IP," since he knew his hacking was illegal and wanted to "cover his tracks" to prevent law enforcement officials from tracing the hack back to his home computer. Ironically, even after law enforcement agents used a federal search warrant and seized his home computers, but before his arrest, he used another computer to hack into another victim's email account. As a result, he obtained numerous private communications, photos, and confidential documents, including scripts, business contracts, letters, drivers licenses, and social security information. Afterwards, on several occasions, he sent emails from the hacked accounts to the victim's friends, posing as the victim to request more private photos. After downloading many of the confidential documents and photos to his home computer, he emailed many of the stolen photos to others, including another hacker and two gossip websites. The result was that some of these photos, including some explicit ones, ended up on the Internet.[181] After nine months in custody, he was sentenced to ten years in federal prison, and is required to pay $66,179 in restitution.[182] While he wasn't specifically involved with book piracy, his theft did involve some scripts, and it reflects the way any kind of hack can reach far beyond stealing book files to anything in a private email. This opens up the door to still further access to everything in an individual's life or within a company, as reflected in the aforementioned Sony hack.

While it appears that other FBI cases dealing with the Internet since 2013 have not involved book, film, or music piracy—at least according to their weekly press releases about current cases—the FBI has cracked down on the sharing of trade secrets. This could, under circumstances, apply in a book, film, or music piracy case if a company's strategy for developing, marketing, or promoting the book was compromised. For example, in a more recent February 2013 case, former Silicon Valley engineer Suibin Zhang was convicted on five felony counts of the theft of Marvell Semicomputer's trade secrets. Zhang had downloaded those secrets onto a laptop provided by his new employer, the Broadcom Corporation, which happened to be Marvell's chief competitor, when he was employed as a Project Engineer at Netgear, giving him access to Marvell's secure database. Using his Netgear account, he downloaded dozens of documents, datasheets, hardware specs, design guides, application notes, board designs, and other confidential and proprietary items. He was found guilty at a two-and-a-half-week trial lasting from October 24 to November 9, 2011, and was eventually sentenced on February 25, 2013, to three months in prison, followed by a three-year term of supervised released, which included two hundred hours of community service. Plus, he was ordered to pay $75,000 in restitution to Marvell Semiconductor by May of that year.[183]

Though these more recent cases aren't directly focused on book, film, or music pirates, they do show the FBI's continued efforts to fight intellectual property crimes on the Internet, such as in investigating cases of obtaining confidential information from private emails or from company databases. In turn, such arrests and convictions can help to make many people think twice about engaging in piracy, because they risk not only civil litigation but criminal prosecutions. At times, the battle against piracy may seem like a "whack-a-mole" approach that involves a lot of time and expense to take down just one of a great many bad actors, who are readily replaced by still more intellectual property pirates. But at least the effort to go after the worst of the worst may help to take some of the pirates out of circulation for a time. This sets an example of the potential dangers of piracy and contributes to dissuading some pirates, just as some of the efforts in the private sector can contribute to reducing the damage of piracy.

CHAPTER 22

How Two Crime Centers Are Taking On the Pirates

BESIDES THE FBI, A NUMBER of other organizations are a part of the growing fight, including the National White Collar Crime Center (NW3C) and the Internet Crime Complaint Center (IC3). Others include the Bureau of Justice with its Intellectual Property (IP) Theft Enforcement Program and the National Intellectual Property Rights Coordination Center (IPR Center).

Much of this increased effort dates back to two key developments: the passage of the Prioritizing Resources and Organization for Intellectual Property Act of 2008, and the 2010 Joint Strategic Plan on Intellectual Property Enforcement. As described in an Intellectual Property Theft white paper (http://www.nw3c.org/docs/whitepapers/intellectual_property_theft_september_201008B6297ECEB4FAE7EAA79494.pdf?sfvrsn=3), the 2008 Intellectual Property Act greatly increased both the civil and criminal penalties for trademark and copyright infringement. It also dramatically increased the role of the federal government in policing intellectual property issues by creating an organizational framework to support the United States' interest in protecting the rights of intellectual property holders throughout the world. As stated in the paper:

"The act established a separate enforcement division with the United States Department of Justice, created a representative position within the executive branch on all IP enforcement matters, and provided United States embassies with intellectual property representatives abroad to protect the IP interests of corporations internationally."

Through these strategies, the act was designed to enable the federal government to better enforce and maintain intellectual property law through divisions in the government dedicated to these issues.

Then, in 2010, the United States government issued a Joint Strategic Plan on Intellectual Property Enforcement outlining a national plan to combat both domestic and international IP piracy, along with fraudulent products. A special concern was the pervasiveness of these illegal acts over the Internet. The many US government organizations that have sprung up and taken a more active approach to fighting online piracy can trace their roots to these initiatives.

One of the most active of these organizations is the National White Collar Crime Center (NW3C), which describes itself as a "nationwide support system for law enforcement and regulatory agencies involved in the prevention, investigation and prosecution of economic and high-tech crimes," which include book piracy. The Center's primary tasks include providing training in computer forensics, cyber and financial crime investigations, and intelligence analysis. Among other things, the Center helps other agencies in investigating white collar and related crimes, including by conducting original research. It also partners with the Internet Crime Complaint Center (IC3), which enables the victims of cybercrimes, including book piracy, to report these incidents to law enforcement (http://www.nw3c.org).

The NW3C's vision is to be "the national and international leader in the prevention, investigation and prosecution of economic and high-tech crimes," and its mission is to "provide training, investigative support and research to agencies and entities" involved in these activities (http://www.nw3c.org/about). To this end, the Center has over two dozen partners, including the Department of Justice (DOJ), Bureau of Justice Assistance (BJA), FBI, Regional Organized Crime Information Center (ROCIC), National Sheriff's Association, International Association of Chiefs of Police, National Association of Attorney Generals, Virginia State Police, National Economic

Security Group, and the aforementioned Internet Crime Complaint Center (IC3). The list goes on and on (http://www.nw3c.org/about/key-partnerships).

The IC3, in cooperation with the NW3C, invites anyone victimized by Internet crime to report this to them, so they can notify the appropriate law enforcement agencies of this complaint. Whenever a victim files a report, it goes into the extensive IC3 database. The Center's analysts then review and analyze individual complaint data by identifying and grouping the complaints with similar information. Next, the IC3 collates and refers these complaints to the appropriate state, local, federal, tribal, and international law enforcement agencies (http://www.ic3.gov/media/annualreport/2012_IC3Report.pdf).

In order to collate and refer the information, the IC3's analysts use automated matching systems to identify the links and commonalities between the complaints it receives. Then, the analysts organize the complaints into referral groups by type, such as impersonation email scams, intimidation/extortion scams, using computer scareware to extort money from Internet users, and other crimes (http://www.nw3c.org/news/press-releases/article/2013/05/14/ic3-2012-internet-crime-report-released).

Since the IC3 offers remote access capability, this data is available to law enforcement anywhere, and these agencies can use that data to combine the number and types of victims and their losses in their area of jurisdiction and better develop their cases (http://www.ic3.gov/media/annualreport/2012_IC3Report.pdf). Or even if the IC3 doesn't immediately turn all of its complaints into referrals, these complaints contribute to identifying trends and building statistical reports, which are posted on the Center's website (www.ic3.gov) as a public service to educate the general public on the continually changing nature of cyber scams and crimes. For example, in April 2014, the National White Collar Crime Center joined forces with Symantec to enable cybercrime victims, including Internet piracy, to use its VOICE website (www.victimvoice.org) to report Internet-related crimes. Then this site provides information and resources not only to help victims know what to do after experiencing online crime, but also to help prevent victimization of such crimes in the future.[184] The website enables victims to easily file a complaint, which takes them directly to the Internet Crime Complaint Center (IC3).

Primarily the complaints are about different types of scams, such as marketing scams, loan scams, fraudulent tech support scams, and wire fraud.[185] However, ebook or any other kind of piracy is not listed as a separate category; this may be due to law enforcement's focus on Internet scams and fraud, or to the public's general lack of awareness of the problem and where victims can go for help. Presumably, with a growing awareness of the pervasiveness of piracy and increasing litigation and private efforts to reduce it, more and more individuals will report these crimes to the National White Collar Crime Center or Internet Crime Complaint Center, as well as to other organizations that stand ready to combat piracy and other online intellectual property crimes, such as the National Intellectual Property Rights Coordination Center and the Bureau of Justice's Intellectual Property Theft Enforcement Program.

It may seem like an alphabet soup of agencies are involved. But it would seem that multiple efforts are needed, since there are millions of victims and billions of dollars in losses at the hands of pirates stealing intellectual property all over the globe.

CHAPTER 23

How the Bureau of Justice Assistance Is Combatting Piracy

BESIDES THE FBI, NATIONAL WHITE Collar Crime Center, and Internet Complaint Center, another agency taking on the online pirates is the Bureau of Justice's Intellectual Property Theft Enforcement Program. While virtually all of the cases involving investigations, arrests, convictions, and jail sentences have involved the piracy of films, software, and counterfeited DVDs with films and software on them, they could pave the way for similar investigations and arrests in book piracy cases.

Along with many other programs, including corrections, counterterrorism, crime prevention, justice information sharing, and mental health and substance abuse programs (https://www.bja.gov/topic.aspx), the Bureau manages the Intellectual Property Theft Enforcement Program, in coordination with the Department of Justice's Computer Crime and Intellectual Property Section and its Task Force on Intellectual Property. Through working with these different units, the IP Theft Enforcement Program is designed to help state and local criminal justice systems better enforce intellectual property laws through increased prosecution, prevention, training, and technical assistance. Among other things, the program provides expenses for criminal enforcement operation, and educates the public and law enforcement professionals about IP crimes in order to prevent, deter, and identify criminal violations of IP laws. In addition, the IP Theft Program establishes task forces to conduct investigations, analyze evidence, and prosecute crimes, and it acquires equipment to conduct investigations and analyze evidence (https://www.bja.gov/ProgramDetails. aspx?Program_ID=64).

The Bureau of Justice Assistance also has established a Grant Program, which helps local jurisdictions around the United States better detect and respond to intellectual property crimes in their communities. It has launched a national training program to increase knowledge and awareness about the impact and cost of IP theft. In its November 2012 report posted on its website, the BJA describes the grantees and the amounts from 2009 through June 2012. Commonly, the grants were for about $200,000, and among the major grantees were the City of Los Angeles, the LA County Sheriff's Department (for three years), the New York City Criminal Justice Coordinator's Office, the New York County District Attorney's Office, New York City, and the New York City Police Department, several New York counties, including the Bronx County District Attorney (three years) and Suffolk County. Many grantees were also located in several California counties, including Fresno (two years), Sacramento (two years), San Francisco, and Marin. A sprinkling of grants also went to law enforcement offices in a few other states, most notably: North Carolina, Virginia, Oregon, and Texas (https://www.bja. gov/Publications/IPEP_PPR_2012Q3.pdf).

Still another program supported by the IP Theft Enforcement Program is the World Intellectual Property Day, held every April 26, since 1970 (http://www.wipo.int/ip-outreach/en/ipday/2013). The purpose of the event is for people around the world to discuss "the role of intellectual property in encouraging creativity and innovation."

A key reason the BJA is involved in these many IP protection programs is because the US Department of Justice (DOJ) has made protecting intellectual property "a major law enforcement priority." As the BJA notes in its description of the IP Theft Program, "the DOJ recognizes that innovation is a central pillar of our nation's economy and crucial to enabling American businesses to remain competitive in a global market. Our entrepreneurs require protection from criminals here and abroad who would copy their creations with less expensive and dangerous imitations." While this concern with protection extends broadly to cover all kinds of pirated goods and services, it includes book piracy, too (https://www.bja.gov/ProgramDetails.aspx?Program_ID=64).

Another motivator for acting forcefully to stop piracy is that research has shown that "intellectual property crimes are closely related to and support other crimes, including violent crime." For example, a Rand Corporation report found that counterfeiting was widely used to generate cash for a number of criminal organizations, while criminal groups were moving to control the entire supply chain for DVD film piracy. This ranged from manufacture to distribution to street sales, thereby creating a lucrative black market producing wealth and influence throughout the world. Thus, cutting down on such piracy could help to limit the ability of these criminal gangs from engaging in other types of crimes. Then, too, the DOJ considers IP a central component of the US economy, especially since the United States is a global leader in creating intellectual property, contributing to US competitiveness and prosperity. Thus, aggressively enforcing the existing IP laws is seen as being in the interests of American economic prosperity, job creation, and economic recovery (https://www.bja.gov/ProgramDetails.aspx?Program_ID=64).

Though these programs have approached the crackdown on IP theft broadly, they are one more avenue for protecting writers and publishers from piracy. For example, just like film piracy has spawned a huge black market industry, so might books, as a result of pirates expanding the book piracy sites already in place to create a kind of black market Amazon. For now, most writers and book publishers are using takedown notices based on the Digital Millennium Copyright Act (DMCA) to ask sites to take down their pirated material, with some success. The problem is that it is hard to locate all of the infringing sites, and these requests are often ignored or the books are soon replaced. But books are increasingly endangered, especially ebooks, since they can readily be accessed online, downloaded, or distributed on DVDs replacing hard copies. So the financial incentive is there to create even larger and more lucrative pirated book empires.

But now that government programs, such as the BJA's IP Theft Enforcement Program, are in place to assist local law enforcement and other agencies target book and other IP pirates, writers and publishers need to increasingly register their complaints with these agencies to raise awareness of the issue. In addition, the writers and publishers might organize consortiums to urge the government agencies to take action, much as the Motion Picture Association of America and the Recording Industry of America Association, which worked with the FBI on earlier piracy cases. Then, with increased complaints and organized pressure, these agencies might more actively pursue the book pirates, too.

CHAPTER 24

How Still Other Agencies Are Going After the Pirates

STILL OTHER ORGANIZATIONS INVOLVED IN the piracy battle include the National Intellectual Property Rights Coordination Center (IPR Center), a collaborative effort of fifteen US government agencies and two international governments. Even the US Immigration and Customs Enforcement (ICE) is involved in the effort to go after pirates, since the IPR Center is managed by ICE's Homeland Security Investigations (HSI).

Based in Virginia, IPR acts primarily as a task force to assist other agencies that are members of the team. As IPR describes its efforts: "As a task force, the IPR Center uses the expertise of its member agencies to share information, develop initiatives, coordinate enforcement actions, and conduct investigations related to IP thefts" in order to "protect the public's health and safety, the US economy, and the nation's war fighters" (www.iprcenter.gov).

Especially relevant for book piracy is IPR's Operation in Our Sites program, which targets websites that distribute pirated and counterfeit items over the Internet, including pirated movies, TV shows, music, software, and other merchandise, including books. Once identified, the IPR Center and its partner agencies aggressively pursue the pirates, whether they operate out of a storefront or on the web, since they are violating federal criminal laws. Should the IPR Center receive credible information about an IP violation and an investigation determines there has been criminal wrongdoing, the IPR Center works with the US Department of Justice "to prosecute, convict, and punish individuals as well as seize website domain names, profits, and other property from IP thieves" (http://www.iprcenter.gov/reports/fact-sheets/operation-in-our-sites/view). It uses a three-pronged approach of "interdiction, investigation, and outreach and training to combat IP theft" (http://www.iprcenter.gov/reports/fact-sheets/intellectual-property-right-theft-enforcement-teams/view).

Among other activities, its investigations are used to develop the evidence necessary to obtain seizure warrants from federal judges. Then, based on this warrant, the website domain names are seized, and anyone going to the site will see a seizure notice, which explains that the site has been seized because it has been in violation of federal IP law (http://www.iprcenter.gov/reports/fact-sheets/operation-in-our-sites/view).

The reach of the IPR Center is extensive. It consists of seventeen key US and international agencies involved in intellectual property theft enforcement. The IPR Center additionally works closely with a number of key officials, agencies, and departments, including the Intellectual Property Enforcement Coordinator, DOJ's Computer Crimes and Intellectual Property Section, and US Attorney's offices around the country (http://www.iprcenter.gov/reports/fact-sheets/operation-in-our-sites/view).

For its training program, the IPR Center has created IP Theft Enforcement Teams (IPTETs) led by the Homeland Security Investigation unit, which provides training to combat IP theft. In addition, the IPR Center works with the International Anti-Counterfeiting Coalition's Foundation, the National Association of Attorneys General, and the National White Collar Crime Center to support its training efforts. The Center also provides training for the IPTETs and acts as a resource to support the IPTETs' investigations. These trainings are designed to assist state and local officers, detectives, prosecutors, and their federal partners to inform them about the IPR Center, federal and state IP laws, investigative techniques and tools, and product identification (http://www.

iprcenter.gov/reports/fact-sheets/intellectual-property-right-theft-enforcement-teams/view).

To conduct its investigations, the IPR Center has twenty-six HSI Special Agent in Charge (SAC) offices around the country that use the best practices, as identified by the IPR Center, partner agencies, and private industry to investigate thefts, working with federal, state, and local law enforcements partners in each area (http://www.iprcenter.gov/reports/fact-sheets/intellectual-property-right-theft-enforcement-teams/view).

As for outreach and training, the Center's Outreach and Training Unit has partnerships with public and private sectors to combat IP theft through its Operation Joint Venture initiative. To this end, it contacts the copyright and other rights holders, manufacturers, importers, and others in the public to increase their awareness of IP theft and other trade violations, and it acts as a point of contact for investigative leads. Thus, writers and publishers might contact this unit to advise them about copyright violations (http://www.iprcenter.gov/reports/fact-sheets/outreach-and-training/view).

The IPR Center also participates in international training programs by working closely with its partners' international attaché networks and local US embassies, as well as with international organizations such as the World Customs Organization and INTERPOL. Plus, it hosts visits by international law enforcement and customs officers, who are participating in various International Visitor Programs, to increase cooperation, skill sets, and relationships to help to deal with IP theft overseas (http://www.iprcenter.gov/reports/fact-sheets/outreach-and-training/view).

Along with the organizations already mentioned, the IPR Center's task force includes the following partners, who share their resources and skills so the IPR can better provide a comprehensive response to IP theft. These include:

- Immigration and Customs Enforcement (ICE)

- US Customs and Border Protection (CBP)

- Federal Bureau of Investigation (FBI)

- Food and Drug Administration (FDA)

- US Postal Inspection Service (USPIS)

- Department of Commerce International Criminal Investigative Service

- US Army Investigative Command – Major Procurement Fraud Unit

- General Services Administration – Office of Inspector General (GSAIG)

- Consumer Product Safety Commission (CPSC)

- Defense Logistics Agency – Office of Inspector General (DLA)

- INTERPOL

- Royal Canadian Mounted Police

- Government of Mexico Tax Administration Service

- Department of Justice (DOJ) Computer Crime and Intellectual Property Section

(http://www.iprcenter.gov/reports/fact-sheets/national-intellectual-property-rights-ipr-coordination-center-ipr-investigations).

Within the IPR Center, its Field Support Unit takes the lead in coordinating multijurisdictional, large-scale field investigations. Among other things, the Center coordinates the sharing of leads to avoid investigative overlap, mounts some undercover operations to investigate the sale and distribution of counterfeit and substandard products over the Internet, and works closely with the DOJ to prosecute violators both domestically and internationally (http://www.iprcenter.gov/reports/fact-sheets/national-intellectual-property-rights-ipr-coordination-center-ipr-investigations).

Additionally, since the FBI's IP headquarters are housed at the IPR Center, the Field Support Unit oversees the FBI's IPR field agents. The IPR Center also manages and supports the ICE commercial fraud program, since criminals involved in IPR violations are often involved in other types of commercial fraud violations (http://www.iprcenter.

gov/reports/fact-sheets/national-intellectual-property-rights-ipr-coordination-center-ipr-investigations).

These coordinated efforts have, in turn, led to some major accomplishments in the battle against IP piracy. Though the IPR Center's efforts don't yet focus on book piracy, its actions, along with these other agencies, set the stage for identifying, investigating, and going after the book pirates. These agencies just need more leads of book pirates and support from writers and publishers to make it another priority.

CHAPTER 25

Major Accomplishments in the Battle Against Piracy Crimes

Now that numerous federal, state, local, and international organizations have teamed up to take on the intellectual property pirates, with much of the leadership from the FBI and Intellectual Property Rights Coordination Center, what are their major accomplishments? While the January 2012 Megaupload/Kim Dotcom takedown made big headlines, numerous other website seizures, arrests, and convictions have occurred. However, due to little notice from the major media, the general public is unaware of these actions. But in the future, more media attention and a greater public awareness would help to increase involvement by the public, such as in providing leads to websites featuring pirated books.

To date, much of this law enforcement effort has targeted the pirates of counterfeit goods, films, and software, not books. But these successes show what is possible, setting the stage for focusing on book pirates in the future. As described in a series of IPR Center, DOJ, and ICE reports and press releases, these are the major results in the battle against online piracy since 2010, when this war against Internet piracy heated up:

1.   In 2010, the DOJ and ICE launched the first-ever US government program for seizing websites—called Operation In Our Sites— that provided pirated content or sold counterfeit products. ICE

had five major operations, resulting in the seizure of 125 domain names, and over half of them (eighty-four) were forfeited to the US government. Then, based on a court order permitting a banner display, a banner was placed on each site announcing seizure by the US government and explaining that willful copyright infringement is a federal crime subject to punishment for copyright theft and distribution or trademark violations. Since June 2010, when these sites were first seized, the sites showing the warning banner had over fifty million hits (http://www.iprcenter.gov/reports/ipr-center-reports/2011-joint-strategic-plan-on-intellectual-property-enforcement/view).

2.   In February 2010, President Obama signed Executive Order 13565 establishing two intellectual advisory committees chaired by the Intellectual Property Enforcement Coordinator (IPEC). These committees included "a Cabinet-level committee comprised of the heads of the departments responsible for intellectual property enforcement and a committee comprised of Senate-confirmed Government officials from those departments" (http://www.iprcenter.gov/reports/ipr-center-reports/2011-joint-strategic-plan-on-intellectual-property-enforcement/view).

3.   Also in February 2010, US Attorney General Eric Holder announced the formation of a Department of Justice Task Force on Intellectual Property to fight intellectual property crimes "by coordinating with State and local law enforcement partners, and with international counterparts" (http://www.iprcenter.gov/reports/ipr-center-reports/2011-joint-strategic-plan-on-intellectual-property-enforcement/view).

4.   In October 2012, the Department of Justice made an increased commitment to protecting intellectual property by announcing $2.4 million in grants to thirteen jurisdictions around the United States to help them enforce the criminal laws related to intellectual property theft (http://www.justice.gov/css-gallery/gallery-ip-towson2012.html#1).

5.   Ambassador Ronald Kirk and the Office of the United States Trade Representative issued a 2012 Special 301 Report, drawing on information obtained from global US embassies and interested stakeholders. The report provided information on the state of intellectual property protection and enforcement around the world, showing how the battle had become a worldwide effort. For example, some of the major events occurring in 2011 and early 2012 were the following:

- Malaysia passed copyright amendments that significantly strengthened its protection of copyrights and its enforcement against piracy, such as establishing a mechanism for Internet service providers to cooperate against piracy over the Internet.

- The US removed Spain from its Watch List because of Spain's recent efforts towards IPR protection and enforcement, such as adopting the "Ley Sinde," a law to combat Internet copyright piracy.

- The Philippines enacted specialized IPR procedural rules to improve judicial efficiency in IPR cases.

- Russia enacted a law to establish a special IPR court by February 2013 and amended its Criminal Code to reduce the criminal threshold for copyright. It also began criminal proceedings against interfilm.ru, an infringing website, and the court made civil findings against vKontakte, Russia's largest social networking site, for copyright infringement.

- China established a State Council–led leadership structure, headed by Vice Premier Wang Qishan, to lead and coordinate IPR enforcement across China. Additionally, China's leadership began measuring the performance of province level officials in enforcing intellectual property rights in their regions.

- In 2011, the Global Intellectual Property Academy (GIPA), a division of the US Patent and Trademark Office, designed to produce education and training on IPR protection and enforcement, trained over 5,300 foreign IP officials from 138 countries through 149 separate programs. Among the attendees were IPR policy makers, judges, prosecutors, customs officers, and examiners. Post-training surveys indicated that 79 percent of the attendees reported taking some steps to implement policy changes in their organizations to support IPR efforts.

- In 2011, the Department of Homeland Security's Bureau of Customs and Border Protection conducted regional border training programs that focused on IPR enforcement in Morocco, El Salvador, Thailand, and India.

- The National IPR Coordination Center worked with Interpol to conduct training programs in eleven countries and conducted three advanced IPR training sessions at the US International Law Enforcement Academies (ILEAs) in Thailand and El Salvador for participants from twenty-two countries.

6. The Department of Commerce's Commercial Law Development Program (CLDP)—which provides training to foreign lawmakers, regulators, judges, and educators—worked with over thirty-five governments and conducted cooperative programs in Central and Eastern Europe, the Commonwealth of Independent States, the Middle East, Africa, and Asia to better adjudicate IPR cases. The CLDP also organized interagency IPR enforcement programs in the Ukraine and Pakistan, as well as regional programs with Armenia, Georgia, Turkey, Kenya, and the East African Community member states (http://www. iprcenter.gov/reports/digital-and-online-ip-theft/2012-special-301-report/view).

While it may seem surprising that the US agencies are making such a widespread outreach to work with countries around the world on IPR training and enforcement strategies, such efforts are necessary because all piracy, including book piracy, is now a global problem. For example, Megaupload was based in New Zealand, but had servers in Hong

Kong as well as Virginia. The Bookos.org website, which illegally listed eighteen of my books, is based in Panama. And the Internet piracy gangs have outposts and representatives all over the world.

As the 2012 Special 301 Report describes the problem:

"Piracy over the Internet is a significant concern in many U.S. trading partners . . . U.S. copyright industries also report growing problems with piracy using mobile telephones, tablets, flash drives, and other mobile technologies. In some countries, these devices are being pre-loaded with illegal content before they are sold. In addition to piracy of music and films using these new technologies, piracy of ring tones, apps, games, and scanned books also occurs. Recent developments include the creation of 'hybrid' websites that offer counterfeit goods, in addition to pirated copyright works, in an effort to create a 'one-stop-shop' for users looking for cheap or free content or goods. The United States will work with its trading partners to combat these growing problems, and urges trading partners to adequately implement the WIPO (World Intellectual Property Organization) Internet Treaties, which provide tools necessary for protecting copyrighted works in the digital environment" (http://www.iprcenter.gov/reports/ipr-center-reports/2011-joint-strategic-plan-on-intellectual-property-enforcement/view).

In particular, the United States is seeking to work with numerous trading partners to strengthen their legal regimes, enhance enforcement, and encourage them to implement the WIPO Internet treaties, which provide protection against circumventing technological protection measures. Additionally, the US is encouraging its trading partners to enhance their enforcements efforts, such as by "strengthening enforcement against major channels of piracy over the Internet, including notorious markets; creating specialized enforcement units or undertaking special initiatives against piracy over the Internet; and undertaking training to strengthen capacity to fight piracy over the Internet" (http://www.iprcenter.gov/reports/ipr-center-reports/2011-joint-strategic-plan-on-intellectual-property-enforcement/view). The list of trading partners singled out for special encouragement for improvement includes about two dozen countries that range from larger countries like Canada, China, India, Italy, Switzerland, Mexico, and Russia to smaller countries like Belarus and Brunei. And the selected countries span the globe, including countries in North, Central, and South America, Europe, and Asia.

In turn, these efforts show a major commitment by US government agencies to fight the Internet pirates, although the general public has little awareness of these efforts. This government commitment, in the United States and other countries, has been building in the last few years and is much needed, since intellectual property theft has become such a big global business. To some extent, individuals and publishers can fight back through takedown notices and litigation; but the problem has become so big that a crackdown on pirates as criminals is needed by governments across the globe.

Now this global crackdown seems to be happening, as international teams increasingly act together against some of the worst criminals. In effect, these battles in individual nations have become a global war on piracy. Governments are realizing the need to work together, given the negative effect of piracy on not only individual victims, but on the society as a whole. Piracy results in huge amounts of money lost not only from the lack of legitimate sales but as well as unpaid taxes to the government. Numerous other problems arise from individuals buying substandard counterfeit merchandise, which can include books plagiarized from authors and reissued under other names.

CHAPTER 26

Arrests and Convictions for IP Crimes: the Imagine and Ninja Video Cases

ASIDE FROM THE FANFARE THAT accompanied the raid on Megaupload and arrest of Kim Dotcom associates, many other arrests and convictions have occurred with little public notice due to the investigations by ICE—the US Immigration and Customs Enforcement agency—the largest investigative arm of the Department of Homeland Security. Commonly, ICE is associated with immigration fraud and uncovering and deporting illegal immigrants, but they have also played a major role in discovering copyright infringement and other intellectual property crimes, which have resulted in arrests, prosecutions, convictions, and sentences to jail time.

As described in a series of press releases, about 20 percent of their cases involve IP infringement (33 out of 174 cases between September 1, 2011, and June 3, 2013), while others mainly involve counterfeit products, including phony drugs. So far, these arrests do not include pirated books, but in the future, ICE investigators could easily go after the book pirates, using the same kinds of techniques used to obtain these other convictions   (http://www.ice.gov/news/releases/index.htm?top25=no

&year=all&month=all&state=all&topic=12). The following are some examples of these copyright infringement cases:

1. Numerous members of the "IMAGINE" piracy group were sentenced to prison terms after an ICE investigation. Beginning on April 18, 2012, four leading members of the IMAGINE group, described as "an organized online piracy group seeking to become the premier group to first release Internet copies of new movies only showing in theaters," were indicted. Before they were shut down, the group operated between September 2009 and September 2011 as the most prolific motion picture piracy release group on the Internet.

   One of the first to plead guilty on May 9 was Sean M. Lovelady, of Pomona, California, who admitted that he went to movie theaters near his home and secretly used receivers and recording devices to copy the audio track of the movies. Then, he synchronized the audio with an illegally obtained video file of the movie to create a complete movie file to share over the Internet among the IMAGINE group members and others. The case was successfully prosecuted by attorneys in the Criminal Division's Computer Crime and Intellectual Property Section; Lovelady faces up to five years in prison, a fine of $250,000, and three years of supervised release.

   On June 22, Willie O. Lambert of Pittston, Pennsylvania, pleaded guilty to similarly capturing the audio track, soon to be followed on July 11 by, Gregory A. Cherwonik of Canandaigua, New York; they face the same punishment. Then, August 29, the group leader Jeramiah B. Perkins of Portsmouth, Virginia, pleaded guilty to conspiring to willfully reproducing and distributing tens of thousands of infringing copies of movies before they were commercially released on DVD, and he faces the same penalties as the others. Among other things, Perkins took the lead in renting computer servers in France and elsewhere and registered domain names for the group. He opened email and PayPal accounts to receive donations and payments from persons downloading or buying the pirated copies. Plus,

Perkins directed and participated in using recording devices in movie theaters to secretly capture the audio soundtracks and synchronize them with the illegally recorded files. One additional conspirator, Javier E. Ferrer of New Port Richey, Florida, was charged on September 13.

On November 2 and 29, the four were sentenced—Lambert to thirty months in prison, three years of supervised release, and $449,514 in restitution; Lovelady to twenty-three months in prison, three years of supervised release, and $7,000 in restitution; Cherwonik to forty months in prison; and Perkins, the group leader, to sixty months in prison, three years of supervised release, and $15,000 in restitution. Subsequently, Ferrer pleaded guilty on November 12 and was sentenced on April 10, 2013, to twenty-three months in prison, three years of supervised release, and $15,000 in restitution.

2. In another big case, part of the first phase of an Operation in Our Sites investigation, five individuals were charged on September 9, 2011, in Alexandria, Virginia, for their involvement with the NinjaVideo website, which operated from February 2008 until law enforcement shut it down in 2010. According to the indictment, the site provided millions of website visitors with the ability to illegally download infringing copies of copyright-protected movies and television programs in high-quality formats. Many of the movies were still playing in theaters, while others had not yet been released. Reportedly, the website offered many copyrighted movies free of charge, while customers had access to a greater selection of copyrighted materials for a "donation" of at least $25. In addition, the website gained significant revenue through advertising. Allegedly, the defendants collected more than $500,000, while the website operated for 2.5 years and infringed upon millions of dollars of copyrighted movies, TV programs, and software products.

    Among those charged were Hana Amal Beshara of North Brunswick, New Jersey, and Matthew David Howard Smith of Raleigh, North Carolina, identified as the service's founders and administrators; Joshua David Evans of North Bend, Washington and Zoi Mertzanis of Greece, allegedly two of the most active uploaders of copyrighted material; and Jeremy Lynn Andrew of Eugene, Oregon, who allegedly headed up security for the website. Over the next few months, Beshara and Smith pleaded guilty to conspiracy and criminal copyright infringement, and faced sentences of up to five years on each count. The remaining defendants opted for a jury trial, scheduled for February 6, 2012. Beshara, who had personally received over $200,000 from the operation, also agreed to forfeit any earnings that had been seized, which included cash, an investment brokerage account, two bank accounts, a PayPal account, and one Internet advertising account. Eventually, Evans—called the "Head God" of the uploaders—also admitted to both uploading his own content and supervising other uploaders, pleading guilty to one count each of conspiracy and criminal copyright infringement; he agreed to pay back the $26,660 he received from the operation. Two other men, Jeremy Lynn Andrew of Eugene, Oregon, who earned $5250 from the scheme, and Justin A. Dedemko of Brooklyn, New York, who earned $58,0004, pleaded guilty to a single count of conspiracy for their role in uploading infringing content on the Internet. Additionally, Dedemko played a role in marketing and talking to companies about placing ads on the NinjaVideo website. As part of his plea, he agreed to return the $58,004 he received. Meanwhile, an arrest warrant was issued for Zoi Mertzanis of Greece.

Then, in January 2012, Beshara, known as "Queen Phara" on the Internet and the public face of NinjaVideo, was sentenced to twenty-two months in prison for criminal copyright conspiracy, along with two years of supervised release, five hundred hours of community service, repaying the $209,827 she personally received from her work at NinjaVideo, and forfeiting several financial accounts and computer equipment involved in the operations. Subsequently, Matthew Smith received fourteen months in prison, two years supervised release, and was ordered to pay back about $172,000 that he earned from the site. Though the government sought a prison term for Andrew, the court eventually sentenced him to three years probation, finding that he wasn't motivated primarily by monetary rewards (http://torrentfreak.com/tag/ninjavideo).

Ironically, when Beshara was released from prison in April 2013 to a half-way house with a requirement that she find a job, stay in home detention for two months, and spend the next two years under supervised release, she came out defiant. She attacked Hollywood for its inflated budgets and ridiculous salaries, blaming Hollywood's practices for the prevalence of piracy. In fact, she announced plans to remain an advocate for the free media movement (http://arstechnica.com/tech-policy/2013/04/ninjavideo-link-site-founder-out-of-prison-wants-to-lead-free-media-movement).

However, regardless of the apologists for piracy, these ICE investigations of two major operations show the ability of the government to successfully go after the big piracy operations, serving as a warning to those seeking to earn money on the piracy black market. And even smaller, more independent pirates aren't safe, as numerous other ICE operations show, to be described in the next section.

CHAPTER 27

Arrests and Convictions of Independent Pirates

ALTHOUGH THE BIGGER BUSTS, ARRESTS, and convictions involve more investigators, multiple suspects, and more media attentions, such as the IMAGINE, NinjaVideo, and earlier Megaupload cases, ICE and other investigators have gone after smaller IP violators on the Internet, too. In many instances, these cases involve only one or two defendants, and typically they plead guilty and are subjected to a few years in prison and restitution. These cases also commonly involve downloading copyrighted material, though the Internet is also used to take orders, such as in many DVD/CD infringement cases. However, in some of those cases the defendants used flea markets, storefronts, and personal contacts to make sales, but only the Internet sales cases are included here.

While some of the cases in the ICE news releases only note the indictments and upcoming sentencing dates, trials are unlikely in most cases, since investigators have clear-cut evidence of the infringed materials and purchases. Moreover, the investigators have already shut down the sites and confiscated accounts, so these small-time defendants have little ability to mount a defense, unlike multimillionaire Kim Dotcom in the Megaupload bust. Most defendants have little money and little ability to earn more, once their sites are closed and their accounts are frozen. Often they have to face the consequences of piracy, usually spending some time in prison and paying back any ill-gotten gains.

Here are some examples of these cases between September 2011 and February 2013: (http://www.ice.gov/news/releases/index.htm?top25=no&year=all&month=all&state=all&topic=12)

1. After running a large-scale bootleg operation, Saidou A. Dia of St. Louis pleaded guilty to one felony count of copyright infringement, along with one felony count of failing to register as a sex offender. On November 10, 2011, he was sentenced to fifty-seven months in federal prison and a lifetime of supervision, based on an investigation by ICE, Homeland Security Investigations, the US Marshals Service, and the St. Louis Metropolitan Police Department. Among other crimes, Dia created, distributed, and sold bootleg copies of movies from his residence, his House of Beauty business, and other locations where he received materials for making counterfeit movies and stored his inventory. During the investigation, the investigators seized about 6,400 counterfeit movies, ten DVD-burning towers that were able to produce nearly ninety bootleg movies simultaneously, and numerous counterfeit movie labels and related packaging materials.

2. Two Seattle-area men, Sang Jin Kim of Everett, Washington, and Eugene Yi of Bothell, Washington, were charged on November 30, 2011, with operating websites that sold pirated copies of movies, TV shows, and software, after an investigation by ICE and Homeland Security Investigations. Kim and Yi received a profit by requiring a fee from the website users. Among other things, the investigators seized two of the websites, 82movie.com and 007dsk.com, and the servers supporting them. As part of the investigation, undercover agents posed as interested buyers, and Kim told them that when he got complaints from movie companies about his site, he removed the movies for a time, but put them back a few weeks later. Some of these movies were still showing in theaters or not yet released on DVD. The potential sentence was up to five years in prison and a $250,000 fine, though his actual sentence wasn't announced in the releases.

3. James Clayton Baxter of Wichita Falls, Texas, was sentenced on February 28, 2012, to fifty-seven years in federal prison and

ordered to pay $402,417 in restitution after he pleaded guilty to copyright infringement. According to documents filed in the case, he infringed on the copyrighted works of Adobe Systems between June 8, 2006, and April 9, 2007, by reproducing copies of its computer software. The case was initiated in May 2007 after investigators working for Adobe notified ICE and HSI that they had purchased infringing computer software from TechKappa. com, a website that sold copies of software titles via Internet downloads. Around that time, the Wichita Falls Police Department notified the FBI that Baxter was selling pirated software, after they previously investigated him for credit card abuse and warned him that he could not sell pirated software on his website. But Baxter continued to do so anyway.

The ICE and HSI investigation revealed that he owned and operated a half-dozen websites, which he advertised online, to offer backup copies of software from Adobe, Microsoft, and Autodesk, Inc. for sale at about one-fifth of the manufacturers' retail value. He also provided counterfeit product registration serial numbers, so the customer could install the software. To further the scheme, Baxter used at least seventeen business names with accompanying merchant bank accounts to process credit card payments for software orders. Altogether, he sold more than ninety copies of copyrighted software and received more than $66,000, while causing the software companies an actual loss of $400,000 to $1 million.

4.   In another software piracy case, Quynh Trong Nguyen of Annandale, Virginia, was sentenced on November 9, 2012, to thirty-six months in prison, three years of supervised release, restitution of $2.5 million, and a forfeiture of $1.4 million, partially satisfied by $650,000 in already-seized liquid assets. As investigators from ICE, HSI, and the US Postal Inspection Service found over the course of 2.5 years, Nguyen sold $2.5 million in copyright-infringing software featuring popular titles such as Adobe Acrobat, Microsoft Office, and Autodesk AutoCAD, using Internet websites operated from his home to defraud

over two thousand customers. In addition, Nguyen falsely told suppliers that he was eligible to purchase and resell educational software in connection with George Mason University. Then, he altered the educational software by painting over labels and modifying the product packaging, so he could sell the software at a higher price.

5.   Still another computer software fraudster, Collier Bennett Harper, of Lakewood, California, was sentenced on October 16, 2012, to thirty-seven months in prison and $370,000 in restitution to Microsoft after he imported more than one thousand counterfeit Microsoft Office CD-ROMS and sold them on the Internet. As an investigation by ICE and HSI revealed, Harper contacted reputable dealers on eBay and hired them to sell his counterfeit software by listing the product as "new" and authentic. After the sellers paid him and gave him the customers' addresses, he shipped the counterfeit software to them, reportedly selling nearly one thousand counterfeit software packages this way.

6.   In another ICE and HSI–led investigation, Naveed Sheikh of Baltimore pleaded guilty on November 19, 2012, to illegally reproducing and distributing more than one thousand copyrighted commercial software programs valued at more than $4 million, which he sold through multiple websites. Sheikh even told purchasers that the programs were not legal, because they were copies of the original software programs or they featured "cracked" codes to modify software to disable the security protections. So this software could not be registered with the companies that developed it. But buyers could obtain the programs by downloading them from the Internet, or Sheikh would send them a CD. For payment, he collected funds through credit card charges and electric funds transfers, using a credit card processing account for a defunct business his family previously owned, and he did not report any of this income on his tax returns. To obtain the software copies, he recruited and paid a number of co-conspirators to obtain infringing copies of the software for

him, some from overseas and from multiple sources, including Microsoft, Adobe, and Quicken. While the server hosting his website was in Scranton, Pennsylvania, he used remote computers in Bel Air, Maryland, and multiple Internet domains.

For a time, the government engaged in plea negotiations with Sheikh during the fall of 2010, but he suddenly left for Pakistan. However, his departure enabled the Federal investigators to further build the case against him from one hundred to one thousand infringed-upon titles. When he returned on January 31, 2012, he was arrested at Dulles airport, and he even had electronic media on him, evidence that he and his co-conspirators were responsible for selling the infringing software (http://www.forbes.com/sites/billsinger/2012/11/20/fugitive-software-pirate-nabbed-at-dulles-with-incriminating-evidence). Not too bright, since this arrest led to his June 28 indictment and November 19 guilty plea, whereby he agreed to forfeit $4 million—the same value as the software he illegally sold. Yet, while Sheikh then faced sentencing on February 19, 2013, for up to five years in prison and a $250,000 fine, he managed to delay that until June 6, 2013, when he was sentenced to eighty-seven months—over seven years in prison, plus three years of supervised release, along with forfeiting the $4 million (http://www.fbi.gov/baltimore/press-releases/2013/baltimore-man-sentenced-to-more-than-seven-years-in-prison-for-infringing-the-copyrights-of-more-than-1-000-commercial-software-programs).

These cases illustrate the risk of engaging in IP piracy for those who end up in the crosshairs of the investigators from ICE, HSI, or other law enforcement agencies. While a great many pirates get away with it, especially book pirates who haven't yet been the focus of any investigations, these cases show that those targeted and indicted commonly have their websites and illegal sources of income shut down. Additionally, most of them plead guilty and are sentenced to some jail time—typically between two to five years, along with restitution, and often two to three years of supervision after they leave prison, though more serious offenders like Sheikh get even more prison time. Although some targets, like Sheikh, are able to prolong the process, it is at a great cost, not only because they can no longer pursue their lucrative illegal business, but because they commonly have high legal costs to keep them out of prison, and then can receive even stiffer sentences. Ultimately, most bow to the inevitable, given the power of the government investigators and prosecutors, so they plead guilty and serve their sentence.

While the book pirates as yet appear to have been ignored by government prosecutors, it may be only a matter of time before they are targeted, once writers and publishers play a more active role in providing leads and witness testimony, much like Adobe investigators contributed leads to government investigators in the Baxter case. Then, with the help of a growing number of government investigators from different departments, the writers and publishers will have strong allies to pursue these cases. The hope is that this contributes to discouraging other prospective book pirates from the increasingly dangerous Internet seas.

PART V

How to Fight the Pirates

CHAPTER 28

Some Strategies to Combat the Internet Book Pirates

THE BATTLE AGAINST THE INTERNET book pirates is really a battle both publishers and professional book writers have to win to survive and thrive. While many piracy advocates defend their activities, these are all false arguments. Some common arguments are that the pirates provide books to those who can't afford the higher prices; that people who download books for free wouldn't buy them anyway; that the many downloads help new authors get better known; that they are only taking sales away from big corporations with plenty of money; or that information on the Internet wants to be free. In rebuttal, people can borrow books from friends or the library if they can't afford them. People would be more likely to pay for books if not offered the chance to get them for free or for much less. The downloads don't help publicize authors who hope to plan their own publicity with the help of publicists and their publishing company. And any reduced sale of legitimate books takes money directly from the pockets of professional writers struggling to earn a living. Moreover, it is one thing for the writer or publisher to offer by choice some information for free on the Internet but require payment for other copyrighted information. But pirates steal that opportunity for choice or earning a fair income from an intellectual property that a writer and others on their publishing team have spent hundreds of hours, if not more, to produce. So by any measure—piracy is *theft*!

In turn, if writers and publishers don't do something soon, their very survival is at risk—and in the long run, that will be bad for both consumers who want to read books and for society, too. Think of it this way. Hunters and poachers may go after easy but endangered game, because they can make a good living selling the hide, meat, or horns of the animal. So they keep hunting, and an underground market for what they are selling is thriving. But as they continue the hunt, there are fewer and fewer animals because they have been killed off. After awhile, they could go extinct, wiping out the very industry that the hunters and poachers were serving.

So it is with pirates and writers and publishers. As sales and income go down, more and more professional writers may decide they can't afford to write books, while more and more small to large mainstream publishers may decide they can't afford to compete either. This results in more publishers consolidating with other publishers, leaving the industry, or producing fewer books with high-profile writers who have the necessary income to successfully challenge the pirates and win. Then, perhaps more and more non-professional writers—those who are writing for fun, for their friends and families, or to promote their business or themselves—will self-publish their books, and not care about the risk of piracy, because they will typically sell the self-publishing norm of fewer than 150 books. They aren't in it for the money because they have another career or independent source of income.

Thus, the victims of book piracy need to act quickly, using various strategies to defeat the pirates. A number of blogs and online articles now offer suggestions on what to do. For example, on the WikiHow site, an article on "How to Combat Book Piracy" recommends these key steps:

- Make a record of the links where your files occur, so you have a copy to advise the site of the infringement, go back and check if it has been removed or not, and have a record for a future lawsuit for damages.

- Search the site for all versions of your work, since if one book was pirated, there is a good chance others were uploaded as well. Check on variations in the listing of the title or spelling of your name, since sometimes book pirates shorten the title or misspell your name to trick the search engines.

- Look for any link on the same page as your file that indicates the name, usually the screen name, of the person who uploaded the file. While some people may have naively uploaded the file, not realizing they have passed along stolen material, those who have uploaded dozens or more files are dedicated pirates. In either case, you can start with a cease and desist letter or takedown notice to remove the file, as well as collect the information for a possible lawsuit.

- After you request a takedown, check to see if the file has been removed. Additionally, check on the site's search engine to see that the book hasn't been uploaded by someone else or by the same person under a new screen name. If your book is not gone in a week, be ready to take further action (http://www.wikihow. com/Combat-Book-Piracy).

Some other strategies suggested by Stephanie Lawton include:

- Write your own blog post where you embed the same terms pirates use in posting or searching for an illegal copy of your book, such as your name, title, and publisher. Then, potential pirates may come across your site and think twice about obtaining an illegal copy.

- Contact Google and Word Press's parent company, since both will remove illegal content and links to illegal content from their sites (http://stephanielawton.com/2012/06/24/for-writers-steps-to-deal-with-book-piracy).

Here are several more suggestions shared by Jason Boog on "How to Fight Book Pirates" (http://www.mediabistro.com/appnewser/how-to-save-your-ebook-from-pirates_b24489):

- Start a daily Google Alert for your name and the name of your book, since if your book is indexed on a pirate website, the alert will pick up most mentions of your book or your name.

- Besides saving a list of all the sites where you discover pirated copies, so you can later check if the site has removed your material after you have given notice, send a list of all the infringing sites to your publisher. Many publishers seek to defeat the pirates, too, and will help you in the battle.

- Send a DMCA takedown notice, which is a Digital Millennium Copyright Act form letter. (While you can find a copy of this online, you can also send a notice that includes the basic information that you are the copyright holder, along with your name, address, phone, email address, and a description of the nature and location of the content that infringes on your copyright.)

Still another suggestion made by one of the commentators on the article is to join an email list dedicated to the fight against pirates and pool your information sources with others, so you can all inundate the Internet host sites with complaints and takedown notices. (http://www.mediabistro.com/appnewser/how-to-save-your-ebook-from-pirates_b24489)

And here are a few last suggestions from Pavarti K. Tyler in a post, "Protect Yourself from Book Pirates." As Tyler points out, a good strategy is to join with other authors who are committed to fighting pirates, such as on Facebook. Another is to become familiar with 17USC 512(c)(3)A, which indicates what should be in a notice of infringement. In addition, you might note the rest of this code at 17USC512, which states that the service provider isn't liable if unaware of the infringement and acts diligently to warn the infringer, or takes down or removes access to the infringing material after receiving your notice. Also note that 17USC504 outlines the remedies for infringements, which include damages and profits (http://www.novelpublicity.com/2012/08/protect-yourself-from-book-pirates-theyre-more-common-than-you-think-and-theyre-out-to-steal-your-work/).

In short, a battle against book pirates is finally gathering steam, and writers are increasingly becoming aware of what they can do themselves. While writers may not have the resources individually to launch lawsuits to engage the pirates in hand-to-hand legal combat, at least they can start the process with cease and desist and takedown notices, as well as join with other writers and complain to the relevant authorities—from Google to Word Press to government officials—who might be able to take action. Additionally, by documenting what the pirates have done, and what they haven't done when asked to cease and desist or take down the infringing book files, writers may be in a position to join a lawsuit undertaken by a group of authors or as a class action. They may also be able to join in the recent efforts by publishers to confront and stop the pirates. Plus, penalties for victimized writers can be in the offing as a result of the prosecution of pirates as criminals by various government agencies, if you have documented evidence of the stolen books online.

CHAPTER 29

What You Can Do if a Victim of Piracy

WHAT CAN YOU DO IF you are a victim of piracy? How can you find out who the pirates are and stop your material from being pirated? How can you get compensation for your pirated material, particularly if the piracy has led to a large amount of lost income?

There are various steps you can take. You can even hire services to help you find pirated material, and professional takedown services to get your material removed. While the focus here is on pirated books, these methods can help you find other pirated material as well. Following are some key tips:

1. As a first step, learn who has pirated your books. There are several ways to do this:

    • Put your name in the Google search engine to see what turns up, which is how I found the first site with eighteen of my books on the fourth page of my search, which produced about one hundred thousand results. Put quotation marks around your name to direct the search on your whole name. To focus it even more, put in your name and various modifiers, such as "books," and try out alternative spellings and combinations of your name, such as your first, middle, and last name and only your first and last name. Then, look through the list of mentions for any sites that are distributing or selling your books where you haven't given permission. Exclude any legitimate booksellers, such as Barnes and Noble, from the list of likely pirates.

- Put the name of individual books in the Google search engine to learn where that book is listed. If this is a short title or one with a phrase that might be used in other contexts, such as "Conflict Resolution" or "Resolving Conflict," put in your full name or last name after that title. Again, search through the listings to look for possible piracy sites, and exclude any legitimate booksellers.

- Check if your book is listed on any of the popular piracy sites, such as those listed in the resource section, if the site permits a search by your name or the title of your book. If your book is listed, note who uploaded it to be sure it wasn't you or your publisher, since some sites with pirated copy also have legitimately uploaded copy for sale. If the uploader wasn't you, your publisher, or a legitimate bookseller, then this could well be a pirated book.

- Even though you, your publisher, or a legitimate bookseller didn't upload the book, there is still a possibility that the book is selling there due to a placement by a third-party distributor to whom you or your publisher did give permission, and they are collecting funds for the sale that will then be shared with your publisher or you. If this could be the case, check with any distributors, such as Smashwords or CreateSpace, to learn about their sales affiliates and exclude these sites in your search for Internet pirates.

- If you are not the publisher, check with your publisher to determine if they have a sales arrangement with this site or a third-party distributor, or if it is a pirated book. Also, for future reference, find out where your publisher or third-party distributors have listed the book, so you will know not to consider a book sold there as pirated.

- If you have a publisher, ask them if they want to conduct the search for pirated books themselves or work with you to locate these sites.

2. Create a list of the companies or organizations that are freely distributing or are selling your books. Note their website address and contact information, if available.

   - If the contact information isn't provided on their site, you might be able to get it by looking at the website WhoIs Record. To find it, put in the name of a WhoIs search service, such as www.whois.domaintools.com or www.internic.net/whois.html, and then the name of the website without the "http://" or www.

   - For example, when I did this for BookOs.org, I found the name of the Registrant organization (Fundation), the country (Panama), and phone number for them. While you may find the company owner has a third-party administrator handling the site, at least this information is a start.

3. If the website is freely distributing or selling your book without permission, note the number of times it is listed, since on some sites, there may be multiple uploads. If available, note the number of times the book has been read and/or downloaded for each uploaded copy. Also note what the website is charging for reading and/or downloading your book. Sometimes there will be an individual charge, or sometimes users can read and/or download up to a certain number of books for free, after which there is a charge, often stated as a monthly or yearly subscription or donation (e.g., ten downloads for free; up to twenty-five for $9.99; even more for $25 a month).

4. Print out the homepage of the website, the page or pages with your pirated books, and the site's "about us," "contact" information, and "payments" pages. Alternatively, take a screenshot of each page (using the Prt Scr key on your computer; then copy and paste the screenshot into a Word document, which will turn

the image into a JPEG). Or do both. Then, save a copy of the posting so you can subsequently prove infringement if there is litigation or law enforcement wants to pursue a copyright infringement case against this website.

5.   Check if the website has a piracy policy on its website about complying with the DMCA (Digital Millennium Copyright Act) or a form for submitting a notice of copyright infringement, and you can use that. Such a piracy policy or form can be a good sign that the company, which has legitimate books on its site, is trying to avoid piracy when someone else uploads pirated material; or it may be the company's way of evading a claim of infringement, when it is a repository for a vast number of pirated works. Sometimes you can only know whether this is a pirate site or not by the cumulative reports of piracy victims.

6.   Send the owner of the website and the hosting company a takedown notice, or have your publisher or takedown service do this for you.

  •   If you engage in the takedown process yourself, you will commonly receive a return reply that the owner has taken down your material or prevented access to it, as when I got a notice back from support@booksos.org stating simply "removed," or from info@booksonline.com saying "done." However, this statement of removal doesn't mean your books have actually been removed or access has been denied, since after I got the "removed" noticed from Booksos, an associate went there and downloaded one of my books. So go back and check, and if the site hasn't removed your material, advise them again. Also, keep a record of this correspondence and any noncompliance, which can be useful in the event of a subsequent lawsuit or if a law enforcement agency takes action against that site. In the Booksonline case, when I checked the site five days later, the site itself was gone, suggesting that it might have been subjected to a series of piracy complaints. It's likely that the owner closed the site, since if it was closed by law enforcement, it would probably have a warning that the site was closed for a copyright law violation. There is a description of what to include in a takedown notice and a sample letter in the Appendix.

○ If your book is not self-published, ask if your publisher will send out the takedown notice for you. Also ask if your publisher wants to take other steps to pursue any damages for infringement, such as filing a lawsuit or reporting the situation to law enforcement authorities. If so, work out arrangements on how to go forward together, such as sharing the costs for any litigation or hiring a takedown service. If not, ask the publisher for permission to take these steps yourself, and often the publisher will agree. You can then proceed as the copyright holder of the work, since normally the rights are only assigned to the publisher; if you do proceed on your own, you will receive any damages owed to you. For example, when I asked AMACOM whether they might want to move forward with me on any claims for the many of my books they published on the Booksos site, the president and publisher said the company would send out a takedown notice, noted that "it's unfortunate there are sites like this," and gave me permission to pursue any piracy cases on my own.

○ If neither you nor your publisher wants to send out these takedown letters, which could be very time consuming if you have multiple books on multiple sites, you can hire a takedown service, such as DMCA.Com (www.dmca.com) or the Guardlex Takedown Service (www.guardlex.com). The way it works is that you provide the company with your name, company name, email address, URL of your stolen copy, and any URL where it might have been copied from, along with a detailed description of the infringement that took place. Then, the company will send out a notice to the infringer to take down the work from their site. However, with multiple infringements on different sites, this service could become expensive—for example,

DMCA.Com charges $199 for one site, and the cost is a little more for a site based internationally. Guardlex charges $64.55 for sending out takedown notices and providing you with reports on up to ten infringing sites.

7. Report the site and its infringement to websites that share information on piracy problems with other writers (such as Writers Beware (http://www.sfwa.org/other-resources/for-authors/writer-beware) or any writers groups you belong to, such as the American Society of Journalists and Authors (ASJA).

8. Report the site to the major law enforcement agencies that pursue copyright infringement cases, such as the Internet Fraud Complaint Center (http://www.ic3.gov/default.aspx), the National White Collar Crime Center (http://www.nw3c.org), or your local FBI field office (http://www.fbi.gov/contact-us/field). Other agencies include the Immigration Customs and Enforcement Agency (http://www.ice.gov) and the Homeland Security Investigations Tipline (http://www.ice.gov/tipline). The more tips the law enforcement agencies get from individuals and companies about infringement, the more likely they will be to take some action against it. Additional details are in the Resources and References section.

9. Notify the major search engines, such as Google and Yahoo, that the website has pirated copy. Then, especially if they get a great number of such advisories, the search engines will either lower that site in their rankings or remove it entirely, thereby reducing the potential for losses from users who might read or download your material on that site.

10. If you feel your damages are sufficiently extensive, contact an intellectual property lawyer about pursuing litigation. In many cases, as occurred in the John Wiley case, a lawyer may be able to obtain a settlement by simply writing a letter with a settlement offer and negotiating with that offender rather than having to file suit. Or the lawyer might engage in a negotiation after filing a suit listing that defendant or multiple John Does, without

further pursuing the suit in court. For example, in the John Wiley case, the average settlement was $750 per defendant, and in other cases, such as when the RIAA sued twenty thousand defendants, the average settlement was $3,000 to $7,000. To find a lawyer, look for lawyers handling intellectual property cases in your area. Use a search engine and input "intellectual property lawyers" or "intellectual property law firms" and the name of your city, or go to a "find a lawyer" site, such as www.findlaw. com or www.martindale.com, and put in your preferred type of lawyer and your city, such as I did in looking for a lawyer in San Francisco (http://lawyers.findlaw.com/lawyer/firm/intellectual-property-law/san-francisco/california).

11. You can also take some steps to prevent piracy before it happens, although there are no guarantees, such as putting up an FBI Anti-Piracy Warning Seal on your website. Doing so is like putting up a warning sign in your neighborhood to alert would-be burglars and home invasion robbers that your home is protected by video cams, an alarm system that goes to your local police station, or a neighborhood watch group. But while a warning might deter many burglars and robbers, others may still seek to get into your house and do so successfully. Likewise, your efforts to warn book pirates might discourage many pirates. And at least you can use your anti-piracy efforts to support your case if you hire a private lawyer, or if the government agencies go after the pirates as criminals in your case. If you do want to put up the FBI Anti-Piracy Warning Seal, you can download it from an FBI download site to warn potential pirates that your book is subject to protection under the US Criminal Code provisions, which makes the unauthorized reproduction or distribution of a copyrighted work illegal (http://www.fbi.gov/about-us/investi-gate/white_collar/ipr/download-the-fbis-anti-piracy-warning-seal). In addition, for further protection, you can register your copyright with the US government Copyright Office (http://www.copyright.gov), which you can do online through the eCO online system (http://www.copyright.gov/eco)

Then, good luck. Your efforts should at least get your pirated books taken down from these sites. And if you go the legal or law enforcement route, you might get damages, too, and/or the satisfaction of seeing the pirate site taken down and the pirates arrested, convicted, and sent to prison.

What's Next?

As THE FOREGOING CHAPTERS HAVE illustrated, book piracy is a billion-dollar industry affecting millions of books and millions of writers and publishers. There are hundreds if not thousands of websites with pirated material, and complicating the problem is that many sites include both pirated and legitimately uploaded books, with many of the infringing books uploaded by users of the site. Often these pirated books are available for free or for a subscription price for downloading multiple books, with any payments to the site owner, not the writer or publisher, who are potentially losing thousands of dollars on individual titles.

The piracy problem has been further exacerbated by the widespread popularity of ebooks, which are available in electronic files or as PDFs that can easily be downloaded, so a single uploaded copy can result in hundreds or thousands or even more downloaded books. Meanwhile, writers and publishers have little control over the process, since it can be hard to know where one's books are spreading. And many writers, suffering from reduced incomes due to piracy, may decide to stop writing, while their publishers may stop offering them book contracts due to reduced sales.

While there have been some efforts to go after the Internet pirates through private litigation—and over a dozen federal law enforcement agencies, as well as some state and international organizations, have made arrests resulting in some pirates going to prison—for the most part, book piracy has been ignored. Rather, almost all of these cases have involved music, film, and software piracy, spearheaded by industry groups like the Motion Picture Association of America and the Recording Industry Association of America, and big software companies like Adobe and Microsoft. But apart from some recent litigation from Wiley to target and work out settlements with the uploaders and downloaders of a few *Dummies* series books and a new Simon & Schuster database to collect information on pirated books, writers and publishers have remained largely on the sidelines, and law enforcement has not pursued book piracy cases.

Perhaps a reason for the limited involvement of the publishing industry is that millions of writers have self-published books or books with small and medium-sized publishers who don't have the necessary resources to fight back. Also, writers and publishers are likely unaware of the many law enforcement agencies that are now targeting the Internet pirates, since most of the arrests, prosecutions, and prison sentences receive little publicity, aside from a big case like the Megaupload seizure and Kim Dotcom arrest. Thus, for the most part, if the writers and publishers take any action, it is to send out a takedown notice and hope for the best. However, their books may appear on so many sites or are repeatedly uploaded to an infringing site, so this whack-a-mole strategy may seem like a losing effort.

Thus, given the vast scope of the book piracy problem, the limited efforts to combat it so far, and the emergence of many law enforcement agencies making intellectual property piracy a priority, there is a need for book writers and publishers to actively fight back against the pirates. To this end, the following actions are proposed:

1. Writers and publishers need to more actively identify instances of book piracy and notify the site owners, website service providers, and search engines of the infringement in order to get their pirated material removed and the sites identified, so appropriate actions can be taken against them. Such actions might range from reducing their site rankings and removing their sites from search engines to targeting them for litigation or criminal charges.

2. Writers and publishers need to become more organized in combating the pirates, much like the film and recording industries joining together through the MPAA and RIAA to pursue civil

litigation and assist the FBI and other law enforcement agencies in pursuing piracy as a crime. Entering information about pirated books into the Simon & Schuster database might certainly help. But this piracy fight should not be led by just one company. Instead, there is a need for an organization that represents the industry as a whole to take up the fight. Such an organization might already exist, such as the American Booksellers Association, or a new organization might be formed, consisting of writers, booksellers, and all types of publishers, from the small independents to large mainstream publishers.

3.   Writers and publishers need to actively contact law enforcement agencies—individually and through organized groups—to encourage them to target book pirates, as well as other IP pirates. Then, these agencies will be more apt to add book piracy cases to others IP cases they are pursuing.

4.   Writers and publishers might individually and as a group work with intellectual property attorneys to target the worst piracy offenders and seek compensation. This strategy might include seeking settlements from not only the owners of infringing websites, but also the users who upload and download content, with the size of the settlement depending on the extent of the piracy. Additionally, the worst offenders and those who won't settle might be brought to trial for compensation as an example to discourage other pirates.

5.   There is a need for an ombudsman to coordinate book piracy criminal cases, since there are now over a dozen law enforcement agencies pursuing piracy cases, sometimes individually and sometimes working together. The result is that a great many writers and publishers not only don't know about these different agencies, but they can be easily confused about which agencies to contact and what to do. Thus, an ombudsman in the form of a central clearing house or coordinator for book piracy cases is needed to be a one-stop shop for any writers and publishers with piracy claims. Such an ombudsman could operate as a division of one of the many law enforcement agencies that already exist,

or a new agency could be created to take on this role. To this end, new legislation is needed to create this ombudsman position, and the newly formed Stop Book Piracy Organization (https://www.facebook.com/Stopbookpiracy) will make it a mission to get such legislation passed by appealing to the House, Senate, and White House.

This book is designed to promote awareness and contribute to the anti–book piracy effort.

Appendix

Appendix

Sending a Takedown Notice

To get your copy removed, or at least get evidence that you sought to remove it but it wasn't removed, send out a takedown notice. If your material is removed, that will reduce the damages, although the service or website owner can still be liable for other damages, while the infringed-upon material was posted, distributed, and sold. And even if your material is not removed or replaced, at least you can show you tried, which can be further evidence that the service provider or website owner was not acting in good faith. This can contribute to damages you might get and any punishment for copyright infringement.

The steps to take in filing a takedown notice include:

1. Determine if the work is infringing, which may include checking with your publisher and any third-party distributors to make sure they didn't upload the material.

2. Take screenshots or print out the infringing site, which will be helpful if there should be a later dispute about the infringement.

3. Identify the URL or URLs where your copyrighted material is posted, so you can include that in your takedown letter.

4. Obtain a DMCA notice template or use the letter below as a guide, and include the required information.

5. Locate the host of the site where the infringed-upon work is located, using a service such as Internic (http://www.internic. net), WhoIsHostingThis (http://www.whoishostingthis.com), or Domain Tools (http://www.domaintools.com).

6. Check the site where your copyrighted work is hosted and look for any contact information for the infringer or the host.

7. If you still are unable to get contact information for the website owner or service provider, check if the service provider hosting the site has registered with the US Copyright Office and provided the needed information there. Alternatively, send the notice to the website host's abuse team.

8. After sending the notice, check that the work has been removed. Although it might be removed within a day, wait up to seventy-two hours. While some infringers and website hosts will send confirmations by email, many won't, so you may need to monitor the removal process yourself.

9. If the work is not removed or access is not disabled, send a notice to each of the major search engines, since they will be likely to lower the site's rankings or remove it entirely from the search engine.

Here, more specifically, is what to do in sending out a takedown notice and what to expect as a response of infringers and website-hosting services.

Ideally, send your takedown notice to the owner of the website service that is illegally posting and distributing or selling your material, and to the website hosting that service. If the owner combines legitimate and pirated material, usually uploaded from users on the site, the owner will commonly have posted contact information, and many will have a notice about their compliance with the Digital Millennium Copyright Act. Some of these site owners will even have a form you can use to report illegal copy on the site. In such a case, the owner will generally act quickly to take your material down to comply with this act and avoid jeopardizing their ownership of the website.

Or even if the site primarily or only features pirated material, the owner may provide a contact email or form to send a removal request, and then you may get a reply, as I did, that the offending material was "removed" or the removal action was "done." Even so, check back to see if this removal actually occurred, since it may not have—or in some cases, the site may be gone, if the owner fears or is subject to litigation or criminal action.

Also, send your notice to the web-hosting company that is housing the infringing material. According to IP Watchdog owner, patent attorney Gene Quinn, these website service providers will almost always take action. That's because the Digital Millennium Copyright Act "provides protection from copyright infringement lawsuits for service providers." But this immunity from lawsuits only occurs if they take "reasonable and swift action to remedy an infringement once they are notified." Accordingly, since the service providers don't want to lose their immunity, "if you notify them of an ongoing infringement they will almost always order the website owner to take down the infringing material, or they will" (www.ipwatchdog.com/2009/07/06/sample-dmca-takedown-letter/id=4501).

To find out the information on the web-hosting company, you can learn through a WhoIs lookup provided by various services, including InterNic (http://www.internic.net/whois.html) and DomainTools (whois.domaintools.com). This search will tell you the name of the registrant, the administrator, and the tech organization, which may be the same, if the owner hosts its own service. If this is a private listing, the look-up will also provide you with an email address to contact the registrant, administrator, or technical organization through privatewhois. net. Additionally, you can use Domain Tools to learn the domain's current name server, which indicates the domain host, or do a reverse WhoIs, where you can discover other domains owned by the same organization (http://reversewhois.domaintools.com). Plus, you can use a Registrant Alert to get notified whenever a person or company registers a new domain, has one transferred to them, or transfers a domain out of their control, which could be useful information when a pirate changes names or controls multiple websites (http://www.domaintools. com/monitor/registrant-alert). The advantage of determining the name server is that it indicates who is hosting the domain so you can then email that host directly.

For example, when I searched for one of my domains hosted on AccountSupport.com, I obtained the email addresses for the administrative, technical contact, and registration provider, who I could notify if one of their hosted domains had infringing copyrighted material. Plus you can get a more comprehensive domain report for a small fee ($49) in a PDF document, which includes one year of history, the name of the server, registrar, and IP address changes, the most recent website screenshot, the owner's (registrant's) name and email address, the IP location, and website traffic statistics.

Once you have this information on where to send your takedown notice, you can send out a notice which, according to the DMCA law, must contain these elements, as noted on Brainz (http://brainz.org/dmca-takedown-101), IPWatchdog (www.ipwatchdog.com/2009/07/06/sample-dmca-takedown-letter/id=4501), and other sites:

1. A physical or electronic signature of the owner or a person authorized to act on behalf of the owner of an exclusive right that is allegedly infringed.

2. Identification of the copyrighted work claimed to have been infringed, or, if a single notification is used to cover multiple copyrighted works at a single online site, the notification should list all or a representative list of the works at that site.

3. Identification of the alleged infringing material that is to be removed or to which access is to be disabled, and reasonably sufficient information to permit the service provider to locate the material.

4. Information that is reasonably sufficient to permit the service provider to contact the complaining party, such as an address, telephone number, and, if available, an email address at which the complaining party may be contacted.

5. A statement that the complaining party has a good faith belief that use of the material in the manner complained of is not authorized by the copyright owner, its agent, or the law.

6. A statement that the information in the notification is accurate, and under penalty of perjury, that the complaining party is authorized to act on behalf of the owner of the copyright that is allegedly infringed.

You can write the letter in your own words, as long as it contains this essential information. For example, your letter might be something like this:

Dear **********

My name is _____ and I am the _____ (title) of _____ (company name). A website that your company hosts (according to WhoIs) is infringing on the copyright of my book (s) entitled: _____. This book (these books) was placed onto your servers without permission. The unauthorized and infringing copy(s) can be found at (website URL or URLs). Also, any other books or materials under my name should be removed.

I am sending you this letter as an official notification under Section 512(c) of the Digital Millennium Copyright Act (DMCA), and I am requesting that you remove this aforementioned infringing material from your servers. I also request that you immediately notify the owner of the website and advise them of their duty to remove this material immediately, and to cease any further posting of it on your server in the future.

I also want to advise you that as a service provider you are required by law to remove or disable access to the infringing materials upon receiving this notice. Under the DMCA, as a service provider, you are immune to a copyright lawsuit if you act with diligence to investigate and rectify any ongoing infringement, and if you do not, you will lose this immunity. Therefore, to remain immune from a copyright infringement action, you must investigate and then remove or otherwise disable access to the infringing material on your service, if the direct infringer using your hosting service does not immediately comply.

I am sending you this notice in good faith with the reasonable belief that the rights I and my company own are being infringed. Under the penalty of perjury, I certify that the information contained in this notice is true and accurate and that I am the owner/have the authority to act on behalf of the owner of the copyrights cited above.

If you wish to discuss this with me, you can contact me directly at the number or email address below.

Sincerely,

Your Name

Address

City, State, Zip Code

Phone

Email

You can also send a similar notification to the owner of the infringing website, although my email to several infringers was much shorter, and did evoke a response within a day that the infringement would cease. However, in one case the work wasn't removed and in the other case, the site was closed down. Here's a copy of my email to the site owners.

"This is to advise you that you do not have my permission or my publisher's permission to upload any of my books and offer them for free. Please be advised that I am making a copy of your pages, and this is to request that you immediately remove any of my books from your site. You are interfering with my ability to make a living as a writer, as well as with the other writers whose books you have copied on your site and are offering for free. I am also bringing this to the attention of members of ASJA and other writers groups, as well as my attorney who will be in touch with you regarding the penalties for copyright infringement and other applicable offenses."

Assuming you own the copyright, the usual result is one of the following: Your copyrighted material will be removed, the infringer will agree to remove the material but will not, or your request will be ignored. However, the site owner or service provider who receives a DMCA notice does have the option of filing a counter notice stating that the material was removed or disabled due to a mistake or misidentification, and that the service provider intends to restore the work that was taken down within ten to fourteen days. According to Brainz (http://brainz.org/dmca-takedown-101), such a counter notice is required to have these key elements:

1. A physical or electronic signature of the subscriber.

2. Identification of the material that has been removed or to which access has been disabled and the location at which the material appeared before it was removed or access was disabled.

3. A statement under penalty of perjury that the subscriber has a good faith belief that the material was removed or disabled as a result of mistake or misidentification of the material to be removed or disabled.

4. The subscriber's name, address, and telephone number, and a statement that the subscriber consents to the jurisdiction of Federal District Court for the judicial district in which the address is located, or if the subscriber's address is outside of the United States, for any judicial district in which the service provider may be found, and that the subscriber will accept service of process from the person who provided notification.

In the event you do get such a counter notice, to further pursue the infringement, you can turn to the courts to resolve the matter and obtain an injunction to keep the work offline. However, while you should be aware of this possibility of a counterclaim, if you own the copyright, the infringer and hosting service will not commonly respond with such a notice, because they have infringed on your work and will not attempt to deny it.

This takedown approach may seem like a daunting process, but once you have created one of these takedown notices, it is a routine process to send them to other infringers and website hosts. Or consider hiring an assistant, such as a student or intern, to send out these notices for you—certainly much less expensive than hiring a takedown service, when you have multiple books or there are multiple sites that are infringing on your copyright.

Sites with Pirated Books

The following sites have been identified as hosting pirated books, either because they only or mainly have such books, or include them along with legitimately posted books. Should you know of additional piracy sites, let us know, so we can include them in a future edition or in a piracy alert. The sites where I have found my pirated books are starred, along with the number of books in parentheses. Only active websites as of this writing are included, though some websites could be shut down by the time you contact them. If so, let us know, so we can remove them in the future. Contact information is included where available.

4shared
www.4shared.com
pr@4shared.com
781-583-1451

Baen Free Library
www.baen.com/library
info@baen.com

BitSnoop
www.bitsnoop.com
info@bitsnoop.com

Bookyards
www.bookyards.com
Contact through website form. Contact information not available.

Box
www.box.com
Contact through website form. Contact information not available.
877-729-4269

Chomikuj.pl
www.chomikuj.pl
Must log in to obtain contact information.

Crocko
www.crocko.com
Contact through website form. Contact information not available.

Deposit Files
www.depositfiles.com
support@depositfiles.com

Docstoc* (2)
www.docstoc.com
support@docstoc.com

EBooks Download Free
www.ebooksdownloadfree.com
ebooksdownloadfree@gmail.com

Filecloud.Io
www.filecloud.io
support@filecloud.io

FileFactory
www.filefactory.com
Contact information not available.

FilePost
www.filepost.com
Contact through website form. Contact information not available.

Fileserve
www.fileserve.com
dmca@fileserv.com
Contact through website form. Contact information not available.

Free Book Spot* (5)
www.freebookspot.es
Contact through website form. Contact information not available.

Free-eBooks
www.free-ebooks.net
Contact through website form. Contact information not available.

FreeComputerBooks
www.freecomputerbooks.com
Contact information not available.

FreeTechBooks
www.freetechbooks.com
Contact through website form. Contact information not available.

Get Free eBooks
www.getfreeebooks.com
Contact through website form. Contact information not available.

Interfilm
www.interfilm.ru
Contact through website form. Contact information not available.

iOffer
www.ioffer.com
Contact through website form. Contact information not available.

KnowFree
www.knowfree.tradepub.com
Contact through website form. Contact information not available.

Letitbit
www.letitbit.com
Contact through website form. Contact information not available.

ManyBooks
www.manybooks.net
Contact through website form. Contact information not available.

MediaFire
www.mediafire.com
prteam@mediafire.com
Contact through website form.
877-688-0068

Mobile9
www.mobile9.com
Contact through website form. Contact information not available.

Mobilism
www.mobilism.org
admin@mobilism.org

Nakido* (1)
www.nakido.com
Contact through website form. Contact information not available.

Netload
www.netload.in
support@netload.in
+49 (0)180-5881140-061

OBooko
www.obooko.com
info@obooko.com
Contact through website form.

Online Programming Books
www.onlineprogrammingbooks.com
Contact through website form. Contact information not available.

PutLocker
www.putlocker.com
general@putlocker.com
+44-0121-288-3422

RapidShare
www.RapidShare.com
support@RapidShare.com
+41-41-748-78-80

Scribd* (24)
www.scribd.com
support@scribd.com

Share-Online
www.share-online.biz
Contact through website form. Contact information not available.

SnipFiles
www.snipfiles.com
Contact through website form. Contact information not available.

Torrentz
www.torrentz.eu
admin@torrentz.eu

Truly-free
www.truly-free.org
Contact information not available.

Tuebl
www.tuebl.com
info@tuebl.com
888-294-1031

Uploaded
www.uploaded.net
advertising@uploaded.net
800-935-0734

Uploading
www.uploading.com
support@uploading.com

Wattpad
www.wattpad.com
Contact through website form. Contact information not available.

Ziddu
www.ziddu.com
Contact through website form. Contact information not available.

Resources And References

Music & Film Industries

Motion Picture Association of America (MPAA)
www.mpaa.org
ContactUs@mpaa.org
818-995-6600 (Los Angeles)
914-333-8892 (New York)
202-293-1966 (Washington, D.C.)
708-660-0481 (Chicago)
972-756-9078 (Dallas)

Recording Industry Association of America (RIAA)
www.riaa.com
202-775-0101

Writers Organizations and Piracy Reporting Sites

The American Society of Journalists and Authors (ASJA)
www.asja.org
212-997-0947

Science Fiction & Fantasy Writers of America (SFWA)
Writers Beware
www.sfwa.org/other-resources/for-authors/writer-beware/
webeditor@sfwa.org

Preditors & Editors
David Kuzminski
http://pred-ed.com
prededitors@att.net

Simon & Schuster
www.simonandschuster.biz/online_piracy_report

Ebook Conferences

Digital Book World Conference
www.digitalbookworld.com
http://digitalbookworldconference.com

Online Monitoring Services

Attributor
www.attributor.com
pr@digimarc.com
888-300-9114
650-340-9601

Copyright Alert System (CAS)
www.copyrightinformation.org
press@copyrightinformation.org
Contact through website form.

MarkMonitor
www.markmonitor.com
admin@markmonitor.com
415-278-8400

Takedown Notice Information and Services

Brainz
www.brainz.org
http://brainz.org/dmca-takedown-101

DMCA
www.dmca.com
protectionpro@dmca.com
778-747-0442

DMCA Solutions
www.dmcasolutions.com
info@dmcasolutions.com
202-350-0200

The Guardlex Takedown Service
www.guardlex.com
866-605-7087
Contact through website form. Contact information not available.

IP Watchdog
www.ipwatchdog.com/2009/07/06/sample-dmca-takedown-letter/
id=4501

Website and Domain Information Services

Internic
www.internic.com
Contact information not available.

IPTrackeronline
www.iptrackeronline.com

Whoer
www.whoer.net
Contact through website form. Contact information not available.

WhoIs
Domain Tools
www.domaintools.com
bizdev@domaintools.com
206-838-9035

WhoIs Hosting This?
www.whoishostingthis.com
Contact through website form. Contact information not available.

Government and Law Enforcement Organizations

Bureau of Justice Assistance (BJA)
www.bja.gov
202-616-6500

Intellectual Property Theft Enforcement Program (IPEP)
www.bja.gov/ProgramDetails.aspx?Program_ID=64
202-616-6500

Consumer Product Safety Commission (CPSC)
www.cpsc.gov
301-504-7923

Defense Logistics Agency Office of Inspector General
www.dla.mil
703-767-5440

Federal Bureau of Investigation (FBI)
www.fbi.gov

FBI Anti-Piracy Warning Seal
www.fbi.gov/about-us/investigate/white_collar/ipr/anti-piracy
310-477-6565 (Los Angeles)
916-481-9110 (Sacramento)
858-320-1800 (San Diego)
415-553-7400 (San Francisco)

Food and Drug Administration (FDA)
www.fda.gov
888-463-6332
Contact: George Strait, Office of Regulatory Affairs Communications
george.strait@fda.hhs.gov
510-337-6847

General Services Administration (GSA) Office of the Inspector General
www.gsaig.gov
OIG_PublicAffairs@gsaig.gov
202-501-0450

Internet Crime Complaint Center (IC3)
www.ic3.gov

National Association of Attorneys General (NAAG)
www.naag.org
202-326-6000

National Sheriffs' Association
www.sheriffs.org
800-424-7827

National Intellectual Property Rights Coordination Center (IPR Center)
www.iprcenter.gov

National White Collar Crime Center (NW3C)
www.nw3c.org

Regional Organized Crime Information Center (ROCIC)
(For Southern US)
www.rocic.com
Contact: Joseph Costa, Board Chairman Chief
469-658-3000

US Army Criminal Investigation Command's Major Procurement
Fraud Unit (MPFU)
www.iprcenter.gov/partners/u.s.-army-criminal-investigation-com-
mand
IPRCenter@dhs.gov
866-IPR-2060

US Customs and Border Protection (CBP)
www.cbp.gov
877-CBP-5511

US Department of Justice – Divisions and Programs
www.justice.gov

Criminal Division's Computer Crime and Intellectual Property Section
(CCIPS)
www.justice.gov/criminal/cybercrime/

Department of Commerce International Criminal Investigative Service
www.justice.gov/usao/dc/divisions/criminal_national_security.html

Intellectual Property Section
www.justice.gov/civil/commercial/intellectual/c-ip.html

Intellectual Property Task Force
www.justice.gov/dag/iptaskforce/

Operation Fastlink
www.justice.gov/opa/pr/2004/April/04_crm_263.htm

US Marshals Service
www.justice.gov/marshals
Contact Information:
AskDOJ@usdoj.gov
202-353-1555

US Immigration and Customs Enforcement (ICE)
www.ice.gov

Homeland Security Investigations (HSI)
www.ice.gov/about/offices/homeland-security-investigations

Operation In Our Sites
www.ice.gov/doclib/news/library/factsheets/pdf/operation-in-our-sites.pdf
202-732-4242

US Postal Inspection Service (USPIS)
www.postalinspectors.uspis.gov
877-876-2455

International Government and Law Enforcement Organizations

Government of Mexico Tax Administration Service
www.ciat.org/index.php/en/products-and-services/ciatdata/countries/mexico.html

Global Intellectual Property Academy (GIPA)
www.uspto.gov/ip/training
usptoinfo@uspto.gov
571-272-8400

Inter-American Center of Tax Administrations
www.ciat.org
507-265-2766

International Association of Chiefs of Police
www.theiacp.org
703-836-6767
Contact through website form.

INTERPOL
www.interpol.int
Contact through website form.

Royal Canadian Mounted Police
www.rcmp-grc.gc.ca
613-993-7267
Contact through website form.

World Intellectual Property Organization (WIPO)
www.wipo.int
+41-22-338-8730
Contact through website form.

Copyright Registration, Information, and Legislation

Digital Millennium Copyright Act (DMCA)
www.copyright.gov/onlinesp/
202-707-3000
Contact through website form.

US Government Publishing Office
www.gpo.gov
17USC 512(c)(3)A
www.gpo.gov/fdsys/pkg/USCODE-2011-title17/pdf/USCODE-
2011-title17-chap5-sec512.pdf
ContactCenter@gpo.gov
866-512-1800

US Government Copyright Office
www.copyright.gov

eCO Registration System
www.copyright.gov/eco
202-707-5959

The Intellectual Property Protection Act
www.publicknowledge.org/issues/hr2391

Public Knowledge
www.publicknowledge.org
pk@publicknowledge.org
202-861-0020

Research Groups

Working Group on the Economics of Crimes (CRI)
http://www.nber.org/workinggroups/cri/cri.html

National Bureau of Economic Research
www.nber.org
info@nber.org
617-868-3900

Havocscope
www.havocscope.com
contact@havocscope.com

Lawyers

Finding Lawyers in Your Area

FindLaw
www.findlaw.com

Martindale
www.martindale.com

Practicing IP Attorneys Cited in Book

Dunnegan & Scileppi
www.dunnegan.com
Contact: William Dunnegan
wd@dunnegan.com
212-332-8303

IPWatchdog
Contact: Gene Quinn
www.ipwatchdog.com

Dunlap, Bennett & Ludwig
www.dbllawyers.com/
800-747-9354
mail@dbllawyers.com
877-223-7212

Notes

1   Wayne Scholes, "Piracy's Ripple Effect on the Global Economy," Diplomatic Courier, Jan 13, 2014. http://www.diplomaticcourier.com/news/sponsored/2011-piracy-s-ripple-effect-on-the-global-economy

2   Scholes, Ibid.

3   Scholes, Ibid.

4   Katy Bachman, "Study: Internet Piracy Is 'Tenacious and Persistent,' *Adweek*, September 17, 2013. http://www.adweek.com/news/technology/study-internet-piracy-tenacious-and-persistent-152488; Richard Verrier, "Online Piracy of Entertainment Content Keeps Soaring", *Los Angeles Times*, September 17, 2013. http://articles.latimes.com/2013/sep/17/business/la-fi-ct-piracy-bandwith-20130917

5   Tom Risen, "Online Piracy Grows, Reflecting Consumer Trends," U.S. News, September 18, 2013. http://www.usnews.com/news/articles/2013/09/18/online-piracy-grows-reflecting-consumer-trends

6   Bachman, Ibid.

7   Koren Heilbig, "11 Numbers that Show How Prolific Illegal Downloading Is Right Now," Global Post, April 20, 2014. http://www.globalpost.com/dispatch/news/business/technology/140411/11-number-show-how-prolific-illegal-downloading-right-now

8   Risen, Ibid.

9   Shota, "Book Piracy: 63% of Kindle Bestsellers Are Pirated," PiracyTakeDown, May 13, 2014. http://piracytakedown.com/blog/book-piracy-63-percent-kindle-bestsellers-pirated

10   Koren Heilbig, "11 Numbers that Show How Prolific Illegal Downloading Is Right Now," Global Post, April 20, 2014. http://www.globalpost.com/dispatch/news/business/technology/140411/11-number-show-how-prolific-illegal-downloading-right-now

11   Heilbig, Ibid.

12   Paul St. John Mackintosh, "Worried about Ebook Theft? Here's the Whole Story –
in Pictures," TeleRead: News and Views on E-Books, Libraries, Publishing and Related
Topics, July 3, 2014. http://www.teleread.com/piracy/worried-ebook-theft-heres-whole-
story-pictures

13   Ibid.
http://www.hollywoodreporter.com/thr-esq/president-obama-nominates-new-
piracy-729028

14   Matthew Belloni, "White House: Obama Won't Support Piracy Bill that 'Undermines'
Online Freedom," Hollywood Reporter, January 14, 2012. http://www.hollywoodreporter.
com/thr-esq/white-house-obama-piracy-bill-281880, Jennifer Martinez and Mike
Zapler, "On SOPA, Obama Walks a Thin Line," Politico, January 14, 2012. http://www.
politico.com/news/stories/0112/71445.html/

15   Ted Johnson, "President Obama Nominates Danny Marti as New 'Piracy Czar,"
Variety, August 28, 2014. http://variety.com/2014/biz/news/danny-marti-piracy-czar-
president-obama-1201293284

16   Heilbig.

17   Peter Mountford, "Steal My Book!," The Atlantic, November 2012. http://www.
theatlantic.com/magazine/print/2012/11/steal-my-book/309105

18   Moses Talemwa, "Schools Accused of Abetting Book Piracy," Observer, November
10, 2014. http://www.observer.ug/index.php?view=article&catid=95%3Aeducation&id=
34848%3A-scholls-accused-of-abetting-book-piracy

19   Mohamed Abdullahi Abubakar, "Somalia: Book Piracy Kills Author Creativity,"
News Blaze, October 13, 2014. http://newsblaze.com/story/20141013162908dhal.nb/
topstory.html

20   Beaven Tapureta, "Zimbabwe: The Paradox of BookPiracy," The Herald, June 2014.
http://allafrica.com/stories/201406110897

21   Vincent Gono, "Piracy Hits Local Book Industry," The Sunday News, August 10,
2014. http://www.sundaynews.co.zq/piracy-hits-local-book-industry

22   Ibid.

23   Remi Feyisipo, "Book Piracy Threatens Nigeria's Intellectual Industry Growth,"
Business Day, November 25, 2014. http://businessdayonline.com/2014/11/book-piracy-
threatens-nigerias-intellectual-industry-growth/#.VK9cYivF98E

24   "Commission Arrests Man for Book Piracy in Niger," Leadership, October 16, 2014.
http://leadership.ng/news/387221/commission-arrests-man-book-piracy-niger

25 "Piracy, Taxes Will Cripple the Book Industry," *Daily Nation*, November 10, 2014. http://www.nation.co.ke/lifestyle/artculture/Piracy-and-taxes-will-cripple-the-book-industry/-/1954194/2483430/-/p98262z/-/index.html

26 "Online Piracy Costs Polish Economy PLN 700 MLN – Study," Telecom Paper, April 18, 2014. http://www.telecompaper.com/news/online-piracy-costs-polish-economy-pln-700-mln-study--1008964

27 "Online Film Piracy Costs Industry $3.3bn, *ScreenDaily,* June 12, 2013. http://www.screendaily.com/news/online-film-piracy-costs-industry-33bn/5057266.article

28 Alan You, "Hong Kong Comic Book Industry Struggles Against Rising Tide of Digital Piracy," *South China Morning Post*, August 8, 2014. http://www.scmp.com/lifestyle/arts-culture/article/1568416/local-comic-book-industry-struggles-against-rising-tide

29 Manuel Vigo, "Amid an Epidemic of Book Piracy, Authors Say, 'At Least They're Reading,' *The Rockefeller Foundation's Informal City Dialogues,* August 28, 2013. http://nextcity.org/informalcity/entry/amid-an-epidemic-of-book-piracy-authors-shrug-and-say-at-least-theyre-readi

30 Corry Elyda, "College Students Rely on Pirated Books for Studying," *The Jakarta Post*, September 22, 2014. http://www.thejakartapost.com/news/2014/09/22/college-students-rely-pirated-books-studying.html

31 Mark Sweney, "Music, TV and film piracy rises among UK internet users," *Guardian*, May 28, 2013. http://www.havocscope.com/digital-piracy-united-kingdom/

32 "Pirated Books Seized in Chile," http://www.havocscope.com/pirated-books-seized-in-chile

33 "Australia Extends Global Internet Piracy Lead," Delimiter Jan. 10, 2013. http://delimiter.com.au/2013/10/01/australia-extends-global-internet-piracy-lead/

34 "Illegal Downloading: Should You Think Twice Before Using Torrenting Websites?" News.Com.Au, August 2, 2014. http://www.news.com.au/technology/online/illegal-downloading-should-you-think-twice-before-using-torrenting-websites/story-fnjwneld-1227011134471

35 "Piracy: Australians Lead the World for Illegal Downloads of *Game of Thrones*," *Mumbrella*, April 8, 2014. http://mumbrella.com.au/australia-leads-way-illegal-downloads-game-thrones-219249

36 Paul Smith, "Online Piracy Fuelled by 'Australia Tax' Price Gouging," *Financial Review*, July 29, 2014. http://www.afr.com/p/technology/online_piracy_fuelled_by_australia_sTHHmyBeds918mmdk4zoDM

37   Michael Kozlowski, "The Philippines Starts to Combat Book Piracy," *Good EReader,* November 23, 2014. http://goodereader.com/blog/digital-publishing/the-philippines-starts-to-combat-book-piracy

38   "UAE Steps Up Efforts to Address Book Piracy in the Schools," *Teach UAE Magazine,* November 8, 2014. http://teachuae.com/uae-steps-efforts-address-book-piracy-school

39   Supratim Adhikari, "Cabinet to Deliberate on Online Piracy Crackdown," *The Australian,* December 9, 2014. http://www.businessspectator.com.au/news/2014/12/9/technology/cabinet-deliberate-online-piracy-crackdown

40   Paul Smith, "Online Piracy Fuelled by 'Australia Tax' Price Gouging," *Financial Review,* July 29, 2014. http://www.afr.com/p/technology/online_piracy_fuelled_by_australia_sTHHmyBeds918mmdk4zoDM

41   Supratim Adhikari, "Cabinet to Deliberate on Online Piracy Crackdown," *The Australian,* December 9, 2014. http://www.businessspectator.com.au/news/2014/12/9/technology/cabinet-deliberate-online-piracy-crackdown

42   Josh Taylor, "Mandatory Data Retention to Be Used to Fight Piracy," *ZD Net,* October 30, 2014. http://www.zdnet.com/article/mandatory-data-retention-to-be-used-to-fight-piracy/

43   Deborah Gough, "Most Australians Have Never Pirated TV Shows or Movies, Choice Survey Finds," *Sunday Morning Herald,* December 9, 2014. http://www.smh.com.au/national/most-australians-have-never-pirated-tv-shows-or-movies-choice-survey-finds-20141208-12319x.html

44   "New Laws Would Ban Piracy Websites in Australia," News.Com.Au, December 9, 2014. http://www.news.com.au/technology/online/new-laws-would-ban-piracy-websites-in-australia/story-fnjwmwrh-1227149556089

45   Matthew Knott, "Anti-Piracy Push Will Lead to Higher Music, Movie Prices," *The Sydney Morning Herald,* September 15, 2014. http://www.smh.com.au/federal-politics/political-news/antipiracy-push-will-lead-to-higher-music-movie-prices-allan-fels-henry-ergas-20140915-10h47m.html

46   Matthew Knott, "Anti-Piracy Push Will Lead to Higher Music, Movie Prices," *The Sydney Morning Herald,* September 15, 2014. http://www.smh.com.au/federal-politics/political-news/antipiracy-push-will-lead-to-higher-music-movie-prices-allan-fels-henry-ergas-20140915-10h47m.html

47   Alan Kirkland, "The Lunacy of Trying to Stop Piracy at Any Cost," *The Drum,* September 9, 2014. http://www.abc.net.au/news/2014-09-09/kirkland-the-lunacy-of-trying-to-stop-piracy-at-any-cost/5731414

48   Pierre Chauvin, "Anti-Piracy Firm Targeting Canadians Who Download Illegally," *The Globe and Mail,* May 12, 2013. http://www.theglobeandmail.com/technology/tech-news/anti-piracy-firm-targeting-canadians-who-download-illegally/article11877622/

49   "New Unit to Tackle Online Piracy and Counterfeit Crime," *Gov.UK,* June 28, 2013. https://www.gov.uk/government/news/new-unit-to-tackle-online-piracy-and-counterfeit-crime

50   Chris Green, "New Internet Piracy Warning Letters Rules Dismissed as 'Toothless.'" *The Independent,* July 23, 2014. http://www.independent.co.uk/life-style/gadgets-and-tech/news/new-internet-piracy-warning-letters-rules-dismissed-as-toothless-9623907.html

51   Chris Green, "New Internet Piracy Warning Letters Rules Dismissed as 'Toothless.'" *The Independent,* July 23, 2014. http://www.independent.co.uk/life-style/gadgets-and-tech/news/new-internet-piracy-warning-letters-rules-dismissed-as-toothless-9623907.html

52   "Piracy Crackdown Imminent – How Will It Affect You?" *The Week,* May 9, 2014. http://www.theweek.co.uk/technology/58464/piracy-crackdown-imminent-how-will-it-affect-you

53   "Commission Arrests Man for Book Piracy in Niger," *Leadership,* October 16, 2014. http://leadership.ng/news/387221/commission-arrests-man-book-piracy-niger

54   Andy, "Downloaded Dallas Buyers Club? The Piracy Lawsuits Are Coming," *TorrentFreak,* February 7, 2014. https://torrentfreak.com/downloaded-dallas-buyers-club-the-piracy-lawsuits-are-coming-140207/

55   Jessica Oh, "Hundreds of Coloradans Sued by 'Dallas Buyers Club' Maker," *9News,* December 26, 2014. http://www.9news.com/story/news/local/2014/12/26/dallas-buyers-club-lawesuit-colorado-pirating/20923933/

56   Gregg Kilday, "Sony Pictures Hires Cybersecurity Firm to Fight Hack, Investigates Piracy," *Hollywood Reporter,* November 30, 2014. http://www.hollywoodreporter.com/news/sony-pictures-hires-cybersecurity-firm-752869

57   Andrew Wallenstein, "Sony's New Movies Leak Online Following Hack Attack," *Variety,* November 29, 2014. http://variety.com/2014/digital/news/new-sony-films-pirated-in-wake-of-hack-attack-1201367036/

58   Wallenstein, Ibid.

59   Brooks Barnes and Nicole Perlroth, "Sony Films Are Pirated, and Hackers Leak Studio Salaries." *The New York Times,* December 2, 2014. http://www.nytimes.com/2014/12/03/business/media/sony-is-again-target-of-hackers.html

60   Ibid.

61   Ibid.

62   Brooks Barnes and Nicole Perlroth, "Sony Films Are Pirated, and Hackers Leak Studio Salaries," *The New York Times*, December 2, 2014. http://www.nytimes.com/2014/12/03/business/media/sony-is-again-target-of-hackers.html

63   Sean Gallagher, "Hackers Promise 'Christmas Present' Sony Pictures Won't Like," *Ars Technica*, December 14, 2014. http://arstechnica.com/security/2014/12/hackers-promise-christmas-present-sony-pictures-wont-like/

64   Gallagher, Ibid.

65   Gallagher, Ibid.

66   Brent Lang and Cynthia Littleton, "Sony Tells Theater Owners They Can Pull 'The Interview," *Variety*, December 16, 2014. http://variety.com/2014/film/news/sony-threats-leave-employees-movie-theater-owners-shaken-1201380983/

67   Jacob Kastrenakes, "Sony Hackers Threaten Terror Attacks Against People Who See *The Interview* in theaters, The Verge, December 16, 2014. http://www.theverge.com/2014/12/16/7402649/sony-hackers-threaten-terror-attacks-on-people-seeing-the-interview

68   Christopher Rosen, "Sony Cancels Plans to Release 'The Interview' on Christmas Day," *The Huffington Post*, December 17, 2014. http://www.huffingtonpost.com/2014/12/17/sony-cancels-the-interview_n_6343926.html

69   Michael Cieply and Brooks Barnes, "Sony Hack Fallout Includes Unraveling of Relationships in Hollywood," *The New York Times*, December 18, 2014. http://www.nytimes.com/2014/12/19/business/media/sony-attack-is-unraveling-relationships-in-hollywood.html

70   Cieply and Barnes, Ibid.

71   Cieply and Barnes, Ibid.

72   Anthony McCartney and Bernard Condon, "Sony Facing 2 Suits by Ex-Workers Over Data Breach," *The Seattle Times*, December 16, 2014. http://seattletimes.com/html/businesstechnology/2025247294_apxtecsonyhacklawsuit.html

73   Sheila Marikar, "I Work at Sony Pictures: This Is What It Was Like After We Got Hacked," *Fortune*, December 20, 2014. http://fortune.com/2014/12/20/sony-pictures-entertainment-essay/

74   Claudia Kienzle, "Taking Steps to Fight Piracy in Online Video," *Streaming Media. com*, June/July 2013. http://www.streamingmedia.com/Articles/Editorial/Featured-Articles/Taking-Steps-to-Fight-Piracy-in-Online-Video-90584.aspx

75   Kienzle, Ibid.

76   Kienzle, Ibid.

77   Kienzle, Ibid.

78   Kienzle, Ibid.

79   Kienzle, Ibid.

80   Colin Mann, "California Brothers on Piracy Charges," *Advanced Television*, January 10, 2015. http://advanced-television.com/2013/06/17/california-brothers-on-piracy-charges/

81   Ted Johnson, "Three Brothers Face Criminal Charges for Operating Piracy Website," *Variety*, June 14, 2013. http://variety.com/2013/biz/news/iphonetvshows-net-shut-down-by-california-authorities-1200497115/

82   Mann, Ibid.

83   Ernesto, "Judge Understands BitTorrent, Kills Mass Piracy Lawsuits," *Torrent Freak*, January 30, 2014. https://torrentfreak.com/judge-understands-bittorrent-kills-mass-piracy-lawsuits-140130/

84   Ernesto, Ibid.

85   Dana Liebelson, "Why It's Getting Harder to Sue Illegal Movie Downloaders," *Mother Jones*, February 17, 2014. http://www.motherjones.com/politics/2014/02/bittorrent-illegal-downloads-ip-address-lawsuit

86   Liebelson, Ibid.

87   Liebelson, Ibid.

88   Lucia Moses, "New Report Says How Much Advertising Is Going to Piracy Sites," *AdWeek*, February 18, 2014. http://www.adweek.com/news/advertising-branding/new-report-says-how-much-advertising-going-piracy-sites-155770

89   "ANA, 4A Release Statement of Best Practices Addressing Online Piracy and Counterfeiting," http://www.ana.net/content/show/id/23408

90   Moses, Ibid.

91 Taylor Cast, "Popcorn Time Lets You Watch Any Movie for Free (P.S. It's Illegal)," *The Huffington Post,* March 12, 2014. http://www.huffingtonpost.com/2014/03/12/popcorn-time-movies_n_4943351.html

92 Cast, Ibid.

93 Todd Spangler, "Movie Studies Sue Defunct Piracy Site Megaupload, Seeking Millions in Damages," *Variety,* April 7, 2014. http://variety.com/2014/biz/news/movie-studios-sue-defunct-piracy-site-megaupload-seeking-millions-in-damages-1201153704/

94 Eriq Gardner, "Lionsgate Sues Over 'Expendables 3' Leak," *Hollywood Reporter,* August 1, 2014. http://www.hollywoodreporter.com/thr-esq/lionsgate-sues-expendables-3-leak-722806

95 Gardner, Ibid.

96 Robin Parrish, "Lionsgate Takes on 'Expendables 3' Pirates with Major Lawsuit," *Tech Times,* August 2, 2014. http://www.techtimes.com/articles/11958/20140802/lionsgate-takes-expendables-3-pirates-major-lawsuit.htm

97 Kienzle, Ibid.

98 Kienzle, Ibid.

99 Andrew Couts, "What's On, Matey? Online Piracy Helps Netflix Decide Which Shows to Buy," *Digital Trends,* September 16, 2013. http://www.digitaltrends.com/home-theater/netflix-torrent-shows/

100 Couts, Ibid.

101 Kienzle, Ibid.

102 Karen Dionne, "E-Piracy: The High Cost of Stolen Books" *Daily Finance,* January 8, 2011. http://www.dailyfinance.com/2011/01/08/e-piracy-the-high-cost-of-stolen-books

103 A. Giovanni, "Online Book Piracy," *Convolutionary,* March 14, 2013. convolutionary.rssing.com/chan-1133174/all_p172.html

104 "Global Publishers Win Ruling to Stop RapidShare from Profiting from Pirated Works," Wiley. http://www.wiley.com/WileyCDA/PressRelease/pressReleaseId-69777.html

105 Maria Danzilo, interview for the Documentary, *The Battle Against Internet Book Piracy: The Publishers,* directed, written, and produced by Gini Graham Scott for Changemakers Productions, released January 14, 2014.

106 "Global Publishers Win Ruling to Stop RapidShare from Profiting from Pirated Works," Wiley, http://www.wiley.com/WileyCDA/PressRelease/pressReleaseId-69777.html

107 Ibid.

108 Jeff John Roberts, "Updated: Book Publishers Force Down Piracy Sites" *Gagacom*, February 12, 2012. https://gigaom.com/2012/02/15/419-book-publishers-take-down-piracy-sites; http://paidcontent.org/2012/02/15/419-book-publishers-takedown-piracy-sites

109 Andrew Losowsky, "Library.Nu, Book Downloading Site, Targeted in Injunctions Requested by 17 Publishers, *Huffington Post*, February 15, 2012. http://www.huffingtonpost.com/2012/02/15/librarynu-book-downloading-injunction_n_1280383.html

110 Losowsky, Ibid.

111 Losowsky, Ibid.

112 Chris Meadows, "John Wiley & Sons Wins Default Judgment in Peer-to-Peer Lawsuit," *Teleread*, July 5, 2012. http://www.teleread.com/copy-right/john-wiley-sons-wins-default-judgment-in-peer-to-peer-lawsuit

113 Bill Dunnegan, "Publishers Mount Strategies to Target E-Book Pirates," *The Passive Voice*, March 14, 2012. www.thepassivevoice.com/03/2012/publishers-mount-strategies-to-target-e-book-pirates

114 Chris Meadows, "John Wiley & Sons Wins Default Judgment in Peer-to-Peer Lawsuit," *Teleread*, July 5, 2012. http://www.teleread.com/copy-right/john-wiley-sons-wins-default-judgment-in-peer-to-peer-lawsuit

115 Enid Burns, "Book Publisher Wiley Files Suit Against Piracy Offenders," RedOrbit.com, April 20, 2012. http://www.redorbit.com/news/technology/1112518018/book-publisher-wiley-files-suit-gainst-piracy-offenders

116 Michael Kozlowski, "John Wiley Files Lawsuit against eBook Pirates" Goodereader, April 20, 2012. http://goodereader.com/blog/e-book-news/john-wiley-files-lawsuit-against-ebook-pirates

117 "First Lawsuit Won by Book Publishers Against Downloaders," P2Pon.Com. (Site no longer listed: http://www.p2pon.com/2013/01/12/first-lawsuit-won-by-book-publishers-against-downloaders)

118 John Paul Titlow, "Why Winning a $7000 Piracy Lawsuit Could Be the Worst News Ever for Book Publishers," Readwrite.com, January 10, 2013. http://readwrite.

com/2013/01/10/why-winning-a-7-000-piracy-lawsuit-could-be-the-worst-news-ever-for-book-publishers

119   Sheri Qualters, "Publishers Developing Strategies to Target E-Book Pirates," *The National Law Journal,* March 12, 2012. http://www.ipinbrief.com/wp-content/uploads/2010/03/National-Law-Journal-e-book-article.pdf

120   Attributor, "Fighting Digital Piracy Increases EBook Sales," Digital Book World Convention Presentation, January 14, 2013. (No longer online: http://www.attributor.com/data/php/press_releases/20130114-fighting-digital-piracy-increases-ebook-sales.php)

121   DBW, "Simon & Schuster Brings Attributor Anti-Piracy Data to Authors," March 21, 2013. http://www.digitalbookworld.com/2013/simon-schuster-brings-attributor-anti-piracy-data-to-authors

122   In Archives: http://www.mediabistro.com/galleycat/category/piracy

123   Rick Townley, "Frustrated Publishers Find There Are No Easy Solutions to Book Piracy," *The Washington Times*, June 19, 2913. http://communities.washingtontimes.com/neighborhood/its-about-time/2013/jun/19/frustrated-publishers-find-solutions-book-piracy-e

124   John Aziz, "Britain Has Basically Decriminalized Internet Piracy. The U.S. Should, Too," *The Week,* July 23, 2014. http://theweek.com/articles/445071/britain-basically-decriminalized-internet-piracy-should

125   Bachman, Ibid.

126   Townley, Ibid.

127   Townley, Ibid.

128   Charlie Osborne, "E-Book Piracy? Tsk, students," *ZDNet*, October 17, 2013. http://www.zdnet.com/article/e-book-piracy-tsk-students

129   Charlie Osborne, "E-Book Piracy? Tsk, students," *ZDNet*, October 17, 2013. http://www.zdnet.com/article/e-book-piracy-tsk-students

130   Karen Springen, "What YA Publishers and Authors Can Do to Fight E-Book Piracy," *Publishers Weekly*, July 18, 2014. http://www.publishersweekly.com/pw/by-topic/childrens/childrens-industry-news/article/63357-the-piracy-problem.html

131   Springen, Ibid.

132   Karen Springen, "What YA Publishers and Authors Can Do to Fight E-Book Piracy," *Publishers Weekly*, July 18, 2014. http://www.publishersweekly.com/pw/by-topic/childrens/childrens-industry-news/article/63357-the-piracy-problem.html

133   Katy Bachman, "Study: Internet Piracy is 'Tenacious and Persistent', *Adweek,* September 17, 2013. http://www.adweek.com/news/technology/study-internet-piracy-tenacious-and-persistent-152488

134   In Archives: http://www.mediabistro.com/galleycat/category/piracy

135   DMCA Force, "Google's Trusted Pirate Program," DMCA Force, November 25, 2014. https://www.dmcaforce.com/googles-trusted-pirate-program

136   Fred von Lohmann, "Google's DMCA Notice-And-Takedown Tools," Google, May 2014. http://www.uspto.gov/ip/global/copyrights/Google.pdf

137   "Transparency Report," Google, February 17, 2014.

138   Ibid.

139   Springen, Ibid.

140   Luke, "On the Piracy of Books," *Sonlight,* August 19, 2013. http://www.sonlight.com/blog/2013/08/on-the-piracy-of-books.html

141   David Pogue, "The E-Book Piracy Debate, Revisited," *The New York Times*, May 9, 2013. http://pogue.blogs.nytimes.com//2013/05/09/the-e-book-piracy-debate-revisited

142   Pogue, Ibid.

143   Claire Ruhlin, "New E-Book DRM to Change Wording to Combat Piracy," *Paste*, June 18, 2013. http://www.pastemagazine.com/articles/2013/06/new-e-book-drm-will-alter-wording-to-combat-piracy.html

144   Karen Springen, "What YA Publishers and Authors Can Do to Fight E-Book Piracy," *Publishers Weekly*, July 18, 2014. http://www.publishersweekly.com/pw/by-topic/childrens/childrens-industry-news/article/63357-the-piracy-problem.html

145   Tom Pritchard, "Harper Collins Is Implementing Digital Watermarks to Curb E-Book Piracy," *ShinyShiny*, September 16, 2014. http://www.shinyshiny.tv/2014/09/harper-collins-implementing-digital-watermarks-curb-e-book-piracy.html

146   James Glynn, "Russian App Wants E-Book Piracy to End, Happily Ever After," *NPR*, November 20, 2013. http://www.npr.org/blogs/alltechconsidered/2013/11/19/246177912/russian-app-wants-e-book-piracy-to-end-happily-ever-after

147   Sophie Curtis, "Could Subscription Services Help Curb Book Piracy," *The Telegraph*, December 8, 2013. http://www.telegraph.co.uk/technology/news/10499712/Could-subscription-services-help-curb-book-piracy.html

148   Glynn, Ibid.

149 Sophie Curtis, "Could Subscription Services Help Curb Book Piracy," *The Telegraph*, December 8, 2013. http://www.telegraph.co.uk/technology/news/10499712/Could-subscription-services-help-curb-book-piracy.html

150 Curtis, Ibid.

151 Calvin Reid, "Scribd Responds to Writer Beware on Pirated Content," *PW Publishers Weekly*, January 9, 2014. http://www.publishersweekly.com/pw/by-topic/digital/content-and-e-books/article/60589-scribd-responds-to-writer-beware-on-pirated-content.html

152 Reid, Ibid.

153 Reid, Ibid.

154 Matt Forney, "The Pointlessness of Fighting E-Book Piracy," *Matt Forney*, February 28, 2104. http://mattforney.com/2014/02/28/the-pointlessness-of-fighting-e-book-piracy

155 Forney, Ibid.

156 Naturi Thomas-Millard, "Digital Piracy Is the Best Thing to Ever Happen to Us, Said No Writer, Ever. 6 Reasons It's a Bigger Threat than You Think," *Lit Reactor*, April 29 2014. http://litreactor.com/columns/digital-piracy-is-the-best-thing-to-ever-happen-to-us-said-no-writer-ever-6-reasons-its-a-bi

157 Thomas-Millard, Ibid.

158 Thomas-Millard, Ibid.

159 Thomas Umstattd, "Authors: Piracy Is Not Your Enemy," *Author Media*, April 3, 2014. http://www.authormedia.com/authors-piracy-is-not-your-enemy

160 Umstattd, Ibid.

161 David Gaughran, "How to Increase Piracy," *Let's Get Digital*, May 12, 2014. https://davidgaughran.wordpress.com/2014/05/12/how-to-increase-piracy

162 Gaughran, Ibid.

163 Pratik Kanjilal, "Aye Captain, Nay Captain: In Book Publishing, Piracy Is Still Rampant," *The Indian Express*, October 5, 2014. http://indianexpress.com/profile/columnist/pratik-kanjilal

164 Lucy Powrie, "On Book Piracy," *Queen of Contemporary*, June 22, 2014. http://queenofcontemporary.com/2014/06/book-piracy.html

165 Springen, Ibid.

166 John Aziz, "Britain Has Basically Decriminalized Internet Piracy. The U.S. Should, Too," *The Week*, July 23, 2104. http://theweek.com/articles/445071/britain-basically-decriminalized-internet-piracy-should

167 Andy, "Internet Pirates Always a Step Ahead, Aussies Say, "*Torrent Freak,* November 12, 2014. https://torrentfreak.com/internet-pirates-always-a-step-ahead-aussies-say-141112

168 Ernesto, "U.S. Government Fears End of Megaupload Case," *Torrent Freak,* May 5, 2013. https://torrentfreak.com/united-states-fears-end-of-megaupload-case-130505

169 Andy, "Megaupload Cases Put on Hold, But Asset Freezing Still an Option," *Torrent Freak,* June 11, 2014. https://torrentfreak.com/megaupload-cases-put-on-hold-but-asset-freezing-still-an-option-140611

170 Rob Waugh, "MegaUpload's Kim Dotcom Avoids Jail in Trial for Internet Piracy," *Metro*, December 1, 2014. http://metro.co.uk/2014/12/01/megauploads-kim-dotcom-avoids-jail-in-trial-for-internet-piracy-4968888

171 Waugh, Ibid.

172 Timothy J. Seppala, "The Pirate Bay Shutdown: The Whole Story (So Far), *Engadget*, December 16, 2014. http://www.engadget.com/2014/12/16/pirate-bay-shutdown-explainer

173 Seppala, Ibid.

174 Seppala, Ibid.

175 Charlie Osborne, "Isohunt Resurrects Torrent Search Site The Pirate Bay," *ZDNet*, December 15, 2014. http://www.zdnet.com/article/isohunt-steps-in-to-resurrect-pirate-bay

176 David Murphy, "The Pirate Bay's Site Goes Back Online (with a Giant, Waving Flag for Now)," *PC*, December 21, 2014. http://www.pcmag.com/article2/0,2817,2474022,00.asp

177 Seppala, Ibid.

178 Dante D'Orazio, "Justice Department Files Its First Criminal Charges Against Mobile App Pirates," *The Verge*, January 25, 2014. http://www.theverge.com/2014/1/25/5345182/justice-department-files-charges-against-android-app-pirates

179 D'Orazio, Ibid.

180   Andrew Grossman, "Federal Prosecutors Pursue Digital Piracy Cases," *The Wall Street Journal*, February 10, 2014. http://www.wsj.com/articles/SB100014240527023038 74504579375191975209328

181   "Florida Man Pleads Guilty to Computer Intrusion and Wiretapping Scheme Targeting Celebrities," FBI, March 26, 2012. http://www.fbi.gov/losangeles/press-releases/2012/florida-man-pleads-guilty-to-computer-intrusion-and-wiretapping-scheme-targeting-celebrities

182   "Florida Man Convicted in Wiretapping Scheme Targeting Celebrities Sentenced to 10 Years in Federal Prison for Stealing Personal Data," FBI, December 17, 2012. http://www.fbi.gov/losangeles/press-releases/2012/florida-man-convicted-in-wiretapping-scheme-targeting-celebrities-sentenced-to-10-years-in-federal-prison-for-stealing-personal-data

183   "Former Silicon Valley Engineer Sentenced to Prison After Conviction for Stealing Marvell Trade Secrets," FBI, February 23, 2013. http://www.fbi.gov/sanfrancisco/press-releases/2013/former-silicon-valley-engineer-sentenced-to-prison-after-conviction-for-stealing-marvell-trade-secrets

184   "The National White Collar Crime Center and Symantec Empower Cybercrime Victims through Voice Website." http://www.nw3c.org/News/press-releases/article/2014/04/04/the-national-white-collar-crime-center-and-symantec-empower-cybercrime-victims-through-voice-website

185   "2013 Internet Crime Report," FBI Internet Crime Complaint Center. https://www.victimvoice.org/fileadmin/media/resources/2013_IC3_Report.pdf

Index

Books from Allworth Press

Allworth Press is an imprint of Skyhorse Publishing, Inc. Selected titles are listed below.

Scammed
by Gini Graham Scott, PhD (6 x 9, 256 pages, paperback, $14.99)

The Writer's Legal Guide, Fourth Edition
by Kay Murray and Tad Crawford (6 x 9, 352 pages, paperback, $19.95)

Business and Legal Forms for Authors and Self-Publishers, Fourth Edition
by Tad Crawford with Stevie Fitzgerald and Michael Gross (8 ½ x 11, 176 pages, paperback, $24.99)

The Pocket Legal Companion to Copyright
by Lee Wilson (5 x 7 ½, 336 pages, paperback, $16.95)

The Pocket Legal Companion to Trademark
by Lee Wilson (5 x 7 ½, 320 pages, paperback, $16.95)

The Pocket Legal Companion to Patents
by Carl Battle (5 x 7 ½, 384 pages, paperback, $16.95)

Legal Forms for Everyone
by Carl Battle (8 ½ x 11, 240 pages, paperback, $24.95)

The Author's Toolkit, Fourth Edition
by Mary Embree (5 ½ x 8 ¼, 194 pages, paperback, $16.99)

Starting Your Career as a Freelance Writer
by Moira Anderson Allen (6 x 9, 304 pages, paperback, $24.95)

To see our complete catalog or to order online, please visit *www.allworth.com*.